T0194215

Unpaved Road

An Iranian Girl's Real Life Story Of Struggle, Deception, And Breaking the Rules.

NIKI BAHARA

iUniverse, Inc.
Bloomington

Unpaved Road
An Iranian Girl's Real Life Story Of Struggle,
Deception, And Breaking the Rules.

iUniverse books may be ordered through booksellers or by contacting:

iUniverse
1663 Liberty Drive
Bloomington, IN 47403
www.iuniverse.com
1-800-Authors (1-800-288-4677)

ISBN: 978-1-4502-9181-1 (sc)
ISBN: 978-1-4502-9182-8 (ebk)

Printed in the United States of America

iUniverse rev. date: 5/12/2011

Front Cover Designer: Mana Alison

Dedication:

I dedicate this book to my beautiful adorable daughter, who is pride, joy and the meaning of my life.

ACKNOWLEDGEMENTS

I could never have written this book without the love and support of my family. My husband was not only my cheerleader—he was my second pair of eyes, helping me to edit this story and make it the work it is today. I'm continually inspired by my daughter's creativity and ideas, and they certainly weren't lacking during the development of this book. My brother's advice was invaluable, and I cannot express my gratitude enough.

I have many friends that aided me on my writer's journey, and I am forever indebted to them for their help. Jamal read my manuscript before anyone else and encouraged me to publish it. Fidel was brave enough to give me both positive and negative feedback after reading my first draft. Brandon, Byron, Jasmine, Zheila and Jennifer offered generous advice that motivated me to keep going.

I want to thank my mother, sister, and brothers—simply for being in my life. They are the reason I am the woman I am today.

I must also thank my publisher, iUniverse, and its professional editors and staff. Working with them was a breeze; I could not have asked for better people to collaborate with.

Table of Contents

Appendix   269

My Path in Life

M y life story is a succession of unusual and exciting events that have occurred since the Islamic Revolution in 1979. This revolution transformed the 2500 years of kingdom rule in my ancient country, the old Persia, and later Iran, from a monarchy to the Islamic Republic of Iran. (Appendix A)

In 1980, one year after the revolution, the unfortunate mutation of my country and unexpected circumstances compelled me to escape to Iraq. The hazardous track and the incidents of the journey exposed me to unpredictable jeopardy and an unforgettable experience.

In 2007, I returned to Iran for the first time after twenty-seven years of living abroad. This trip brought back many memories, and I began to reminisce about my life in Iran. The unique events on my path in life—love, deception, excitement, and horror—during a period of political and cultural changes have brought me to the present day.

I am an Iranian woman, and this is my true story. However, to protect and respect the privacy of individuals involved, the names of some people and places have been changed.

Chapter 1

⌒✦⌒

Welcome Home

It was July 2007. The airplane got closer to its final destination, Tehran airport.

I was totally worn out after such a long flight, and despite spending most of the time asleep, I was still exhausted and could feel the jet lag.

Noticing that I had awakened, the passenger sitting next to me smiled and said, "You are up just in time!"

"Have we arrived?" I asked.

"Oh, yes, we are flying over Tehran," she replied nonchalantly in a weary voice. "I am sick of being tossed back and forth, up and down. Bastards, they have made us all stragglers …."

She was an old lady, who, I thought, had been longing for the chance to chat with someone. Despite the lines and creases all over her small face, the signs of a beautiful, younger woman lingered.

"Do you travel often?" I interrupted her.

She grinned and responded, "I don't know if you can call it traveling! I'm of an age now where these long flights are kind of a drag. My children live in different corners of the world. If we had a stable homeland, our children would not have needed to leave the country in pursuit of a better life."

I took a closer look at her. She seemed really sad and worn out. "I understand. Let's hope to God everything will change for the better," I replied in an attempt to comfort her.

Staring at me, she complained in a sad tone, "Dear, time is running out for me and I'm getting closer to my grave. I won't live long enough to see any changes."

I could not find anything more to say. Her distress was understandable. I thought of my mother and the trips she used to take. She not only made trips to the United States to visit me, but she also traveled to other parts of the world where my siblings and their families lived. That was the only way she could see her children. However, as she was getting older, her visits became less frequent. She no longer had enough strength for such trips.

As the older woman put on her scarf, she turned to me again and said, "It seems like covering up women's hair is all they care about. A while back, before they took over, we believed in Islam even without covering up our hair. We prayed and had faith in God and Islam; everything was in its place." After taking a deep, long breath, she continued, "Thanks to them, we lost our faith and respect for Islam."

I kept to myself and rolled the window shade up, noticing that the old woman was right; it did seem as if we were flying over Tehran. I noticed all the beautiful flickering lights of the city and thought: *This is the moment I have been waiting for, for almost thirty years. What am I feeling now?*

Surprisingly, I really did not feel anything. My answer to my question was, *Nothing!* I struggled with myself to find an answer, *why don't I feel anything?*

In 1979, about twenty-seven years earlier when I was still living in Iran, Ayatollah Khomeini returned to the country after nearly fifteen years of exile. A reporter asked him the very same question that I had just asked myself to which he had responded, "Nothing." His response caused everyone great disappointment and disbelief.

I chuckled and consoled myself, *If Ayatollah Khomeini, leader of the revolution, whose arrival was eagerly awaited by the entire nation, had no feeling upon his return from exile, why should I? Perhaps, I should be the leader of the next revolution! At least the ayatollah and I have this matter in common!*

*   *   *

"Fasten your seat belts and prepare for landing," the flight attendant announced over the intercom. Suddenly, there was no time for further self-reflection or doubt. It was the middle of the night, and everyone was preparing to leave the plane. I turned to my neighbor to say good-bye and then followed the line of passengers toward the exit.

Following the crowd, I entered the transit hall. There was not much difference between this airport and all the others that I had seen before. To my surprise, I still had no feelings and my mind was numb. I joined the line to go through the passport control station. This particular spot had been in my mind for many years.

Even though decades had passed, entering the country was a great risk for some.

The government had in the recent years made returning home easier for Iranian refugees by promising no risk of retaliation. As a result, many Iranians applied for passports and returned home. Unfortunately, even with all the promises made by the government, things could take a turn for the worse at the last minute for the person who was returning home.

The line became shorter and shorter. Soon it was my turn to approach the passport control window. I expected myself to be nervous and frightened. I thought my heart would beat so fast that I would hear the sound of it, but it did not. I was calm and cool. My hands did not shake. No beads of sweat ran down my brow either. How could it be possible? Years of suffocating my painful desire for returning home due to uncertainty and fear were nowhere in sight.

Now, was I brave and should I be proud of myself? Or was that unnatural numbness an indication of my submission? I asked myself. After all, I was there with no turning point. The smart move was to just trust destiny. I calmly moved toward the window when the young officer gestured sharply with his hand for me to come forward.

"Hello," I said to the officer.

"Hello," he responded indifferently as he reached for my passport.

I handed him the passport and waited for his reaction. He turned over the pages, looked at the picture, and then cast a glance at me. "How long have you been out of the country?" he asked in a raspy voice.

"Twenty-seven years," I responded softly with a smile.

"Twenty-seven years? Long time!" he said as he stamped the passport.

"Yes, a long time!" I confirmed.

Smiling, he said, "Welcome home," and handed me the passport.

I took the passport and paused for a moment before thanking him in a tentative voice, which could have revealed my surprise. I assured myself that I had understood him correctly before I walked away. I could not believe how simple the process had been.

All these years, I had created an image in my mind of what it would be like at this exact point in time and place. I expected to be questioned thoroughly and perhaps even be asked to go to a different room for further interrogation. I thought I might be searched by the authorities as I had been warned that could happen. I had heard many stories and different scenarios about the return of Iranians who had sought refuge in other countries. Upon returning to Iran, they had been arrested and taken to prison without a trace. In milder cases, their passports were taken by the authorities so that they could not leave the country. *Apparently, all these episodes do not happen anymore,* I thought optimistically. *So I will have my own story to tell when I return to the United States.*

Some footsteps away from the passport control window, I realized I was really here, I was finally home! My own people were all over the place. Everyone spoke Farsi. My steps became faster and faster. Quickly, I walked to the baggage claim and waited impatiently for the baggage ring to start rolling and my suitcases to appear. Finally, the band started moving and I spotted my luggage. A tall, middle-aged man helped me pull them up. I placed the baggage on a cart and pushed it toward customs. The line was long, but moved quickly. Most of the passengers passed through with no problem. After a few moments, it was my turn. An older officer asked if I had anything to declare to which I replied that I did not. He just smiled and once again I heard the two delightful words, "Welcome home." It was like music to my ears. I returned the smile and thanked him. Having made it through the two encounters with authorities with no confrontation, I was free to go.

I pushed my cart through what seemed like an endless tunnel as I rushed toward the exit. Shoving and pushing through the crowd, I was anxious to get to my family. I looked around for them. I was not sure if they would recognize me after all this time.

Suddenly, I felt a tap on my shoulder. I looked back and saw a handsome, young man who asked, "Niki?" I recognized my nephew from his pictures I had seen. Even though this was our first encounter, I hugged him as if I had known him all my life. One by one, I was surrounded by my family who I had not seen for so many years. At that moment, all my feelings erupted, and I barely held back my tears of joy.

On that summer night in 2007, the warm wind touched my body, and the air of the land had a wonderful scent. It was like a dream. I was in my homeland surrounded by my loved ones. It felt unbelievable, unreal!

I had been quite unhappy over the years when I forced myself to accept the fact that I would never again see Iran. But on that night, I felt my nieces' arms around my shoulders as my nephew pushed my luggage cart. When I left Iran, they had not even been born. Still, I was no stranger to them. On the contrary, their warm welcome and expression of happiness gave me a sense of having been missed.

My mother tearfully handed me a bouquet of beautiful roses. I had seen her a few times when she had come to visit me. However, she seemed weaker and meager, not the same healthy and active person I saw on our last visit.

My brother Shahrooz had also changed noticeably. He was not the same tall, young man I remembered, but still had the same nice smile that made his eyes brighter. His gray full beard and mustache made him look much older. Mahtab, his wife, was still a tall and beautiful woman even in her complete hijab. Ironically, I remembered her as she was before the revolution—a young, modern, and elegant girl with long, brown hair. But now, it was strange to see her wrapped in the black Islamic hijab. Shahrooz's beard and Mahtab's proper black hijab indicated that they had become faithful Muslims.

The family had come to the airport in three cars. My teenaged nieces guided me to one of the cars. They sat next to me and kept holding my hands. As we entered the freeway, I momentarily thought I was back in Los Angeles. The signs were green and entrances and exits were built like the clogged arteries we called freeways in the United States.

I had expected a drastic transformation of the face of the country. But still, foolishly, I had wished for no changes. I wished I could go back in time to once again experience the city and the life I had left behind about three decades ago. Nevertheless, I had to prepare myself to face more changes in the coming days.

*   *   *

It was 2:00 AM when we reached the apartment where my mother had been living since she had sold our house years earlier. It was a nice, small apartment on the second floor of a five-floor tower in a good neighborhood of Tehran.

My mother made tea; we all sat down and talked. It did not take long before the gap of time and place between us evaporated. It felt as if those years of my absence had never existed. Finally, I felt a sense of belonging that was an enormously pleasant feeling. I belonged to this family.

What a pleasure and blessing it is to live amongst my own folk and have a place to call my homeland, I thought. *I no longer need to try to fit in. No longer am I different. I no longer am embarrassed for misunderstanding or being misunderstood.*

I did not feel tired after the flight. I could have sat there the whole night just to be with them, but it was very late, around 4:00 AM. The following day was a work day and the children had school. So, they left and promised to come back later that afternoon. My mother and I continued to talk for a while before I forced myself to go to bed and try to sleep. I had many places and many people in mind to visit during my short stay

*   *   *

I was too excited to feel tired. The sun was already up. My mother had slept next to me. I got up and moved at a snail's pace, trying not to wake her. I opened the door to the terrace to see a view of the city.

"Where are you going? Aren't you tired?" I heard my mother groaning while rubbing her eyes.

"No *Mamman*. Go back to sleep, I'm fine," I responded. I stepped out onto the balcony. Looking around, I saw buildings before my eyes, most of them high rises. I looked down at the street. Traffic was already heavy. I was eager to go outside, walk on the streets, and familiarize myself with every corner of my town.

My mother got up to set the table for breakfast. Hungry for the traditional Iranian bread, I went back inside and said, "Mamman, I want fresh *sangak*. I'll go buy one."

"Where're you going to buy the bread?" she asked with a smile. "You don't know this area."

"I won't get lost! I'll find the place and my way back home. Don't worry." I kissed her cheek and reassured her.

"My child! You've always been stubborn. Okay, go," she said with a grin.

I put on a T-shirt and a pair of jeans, but before I made it to the door, my mother stopped me by asking, "Where are you going dressed like that?"

"What do you mean?" I asked, and before she answered, I laughed and blurted, "I completely forgot. You're right; I have to put a *ropoosh* on."

I put the light overcoat on and covered my hair with a scarf. This was my first realization of a changed homeland. At the time I left the country, hijab for the women had not been mandatory.

Now that I followed the dress code, I was ready to leave and rode the elevator down to the reception area. I greeted the clean-shaven old man sitting behind the reception desk by saying, "*salaam*" He stood up and politely responded to me with a friendly smile. I asked him where I could find a sangak bakery. He escorted me outside the building and patiently gave me clear directions to the bakery.

I looked around the busy street and started walking the several blocks to the bakery. All my senses were active. I didn't miss even the smallest detail of everything around me. Shops, banks, pharmacies, restaurants, and even the road signs looked as I had remembered them. I was so happy that I could have walked around the entire day, refreshing my memories from the time I had lived in this beautiful city.

It was still early in the morning and few people were on the streets. I greeted an old woman wearing a traditional chador that was a long head covering, and a young girl in ropoosh and scarf. Both hesitated a moment, looked at me doubtfully, before they replied.

At that time, I could have hugged and kissed everyone I came across on my walk. They all were my folk, and I had missed them for years.

Following the receptionist's directions, I found my way to the bakery. The scent of fresh bread made me hungry. I got two sangak loaves and paid 1000 rial. Years ago when I left the country, one could buy two sangaks for 10 rials. What a big difference! Was the Rial so badly devaluated?

*   *   *

After several days in my homeland, I gradually realized that I was experiencing a new people and a new Iran. Sadly, I found myself a stranger in my own country. In every aspect, Tehran was not the city that I had departed from years ago. The traffic, and the way people drove around town, was traumatizing. Traffic rules were ignored by all. There was no respect for drivers or pedestrians. Yet the very same people would show the utmost hospitality and respect to others in their homes. They would insist the guests enter the house ahead of them. However, when they were behind the wheel, their only concern was to weave between the lanes of cars like snakes to be the first to catch a green light.

I thought, for a moment, that perhaps this was a way to get even with the government, since traffic rules were the only laws, which if broken, did not lead to jail time or torture.

*   *   *

For the first few days, I walked around to become familiar with my new people and new city once again. The face of the city appeared very different. Young girls, who were dressed in dark and gloomy colored hijab, chitchatted very quietly.

This was in stark contrast to when I was a young girl in Tehran hanging out with my friends.

There was no sense of happiness and colorful aura around town. It seemed that days of joy were gone and laughter was not allowed to fill the air. *When had happiness become a sin?* The boys were not as restricted by the government and the new society; yet, it seemed as if they were missing out on a great part of their young lives.

Pictures, posters, and various slogans of Ayatollah Khomeini, the founder and the first supreme leader of Islamic Republic of Iran, and his successor as supreme leader, Ayatollah Khamenii, were everywhere; there was no way to miss the images.

Humiliating signs, such as: "Women without the Proper Hijab Are Not Permitted to Enter", were posted at the entrance of almost every public facility. It was bothersome to see all those slogans everywhere telling women how they should dress, act, and behave. One of the slogans clearly stated: "Wearing Hijab Makes a Woman Pure and Decent." This particular insulting sign made me furious. It was hard to imagine how the women of my country were forced to face these types of demeaning offensive statements every single day without being able to reject or protest the message.

*   *   *

I was eager to see my old colleagues, so I called the last company that I had worked for prior to leaving Iran, and gave their names to the operator. Despite so many years passed, I still hoped to find some of them.

After moments of searching, the operator found the name Pari and connected me to her extension. Amazingly, she recognized my voice right away. After talking for a short while, I learned that three other colleagues still worked there. I was so excited to see them that I decided to go there the same day.

*   *   *

I entered the receptionist area and asked for Pari. Security called her extension and let me go to the financial department. As I entered the elevator, I recalled the crowded mornings and afternoons as people tried to squeeze into the packed elevator.

When the elevator reached the floor, I entered my old worksite. Immediately, I noticed everything was different. The cheerful and hectic atmosphere that I remembered was no longer present. Few people roamed the halls. The women were covered head to toe in extremely dull clothes. I was dressed in a cream-colored ropoosh and brown scarf, but I felt I was overdressed or even naked compare to them. The vibrant dresses, pleasurable perfumes, and fashionable high-heel shoes that had contributed to the working atmosphere were all gone.

The men wore unappealing stubbly beards. The place lacked the fresh scent of men wearing cologne and savvy business attire. Most importantly, the cheerful and contented looks were no longer to be found.

I asked myself the painful question, *What happened to my people?*

*　　　*　　　*

Pari had not changed as much as I had expected. The black scarf, which covered her hair, had made her small, sweet face look innocent. Amir and Reza, my two former male colleagues, joined us in Pari's office. The visible creases on their face were the only proof of the lapse in time. We reminisced about the past for a while; suddenly it was noon and time for lunch. Pari suggested we eat in the company's canteen. With pleasure, I accepted. Unexpectedly, Amir and Reza stood up to return to their offices.

"Aren't you going to join us?" I asked.

"Come on, Niki! Those days are gone. We men are no longer allowed to sit at the same table as *na-mah-ram*[1] women in public; we don't even share the same canteen," Reza replied with a smirk on his face before sarcastically adding, "Those times of mischief have ended."

"Too bad, I miss those days," I replied with a smile.

Pari and I headed to the canteen, picked up our food, and sat at a table in a corner to talk. I asked Pari to tell me what was going on in her life. She briefly told me that she was now married and had a sixteen-year-old son. She then went on to complain. "Good for you that you left years ago. If I could, I would have left too. Life here is not easy. But ... it's our life. Not much good to say about it. Many of us have given up on any positive changes. Do you remember all the fun we had at work? It is not the same anymore." She stopped here and changed the subject. She was curious to know about me. "Now you tell me. Why did you disappear suddenly?" she asked.

I told her briefly about my life over the past years. Then I asked her about Susan, a former coworker. Pari confessed regretfully, "The last time I spoke with her, she was not in a good state of mind. I haven't heard anything from her recently. To be honest, I don't even have her number anymore and feel so guilty about it." Then she consoled herself by adding, "You know, nowadays everyone has their own miseries; there is no time left to think about others."

"What was wrong with her? Why didn't she feel well the last time you talked to her?" I asked.

"Oh, I forgot that you were not here when she was kicked out," Pari replied.

"Kicked out? Why?" I asked

Pari brought her face closer to mine and whispered, "Do you know that the

---

1　**Na-mah-ram, a** term refers to the men and the women who are not related to each other by blood or marriage. Per Islamic rule, men and women are NOT allowed to speak with each other or be seen together if they are NOT married or blood related, such as siblings.

parliament was bombed two years after the revolution? The prime minister and some other dignitaries were killed in that bombing."

"Yes, I know," I responded.

"That day when we heard the news, Susan rubbed her hands together with great joy and murmured, 'Oh ... yeah.' Someone, who is still anonymous to us, reported the incident." Pari paused for a moment before continuing, "In no time, security men came to the department as if they were going after a murderer. They dragged her out while swearing, and threw her out of the office. She could not even pack up her stuff."

"Poor Susan! Can you imagine what would have happened to her if she had showed more delight by laughing or saying something in joy? They would have beheaded her!" I scoffed.

"These jerks can do whatever they like, believe me! They have created such a terrifying environment that no one dares to speak up or protest against them," Pari said in disgust.

*   *   *

After a while, Pari returned to her office. I remained seated, thinking about Susan and regretted that I had lost contact with her years ago. I wished I could find her somehow and remembered how active she was during the revolution. She secretly copied the revolutionary flyers and distributed them inside the company. She was my adviser and an honest friend, whom I could trust with my secrets during that period of my life when I needed a friend to rely on.

Obviously, what Pari shared with me about her own life and Susan's was simply a drop of misery of the people in a tormented ocean.

*   *   *

My next agenda was to find my other friends. Sayeh was the first one I contacted. Like the others, I had lost contact with her long ago even though she had been my closest friend.

She was still the same cool and funny girl that I remembered. Any noticeable aging signs were not apparent on the fair skin of her cute, round face. Her blue, sparkly eyes and long, blonde hair gave her a unique beauty.

In four years of college time, we seldom missed a day being together. We had been like members of each other's family. Sayeh's German mother had died in an automobile accident, and Sayeh lived with her father and grandmother at that time. I lived in the same neighborhood with my younger brother Ramin and my mother.

Being with Sayeh after so many years was emotional. It evoked a sense of pleasure and an unknown strange feeling. During the first few hours, we talked about the old days. At one point, it seemed as though we were challenging each other to remember names and events so that we could hang on to those good moments a bit longer.

When we turned from discussing the past to the present, a strange feeling replaced the pleasant one. There was nothing more to be said since all our memories were from the past. We had lost almost three decades to share our lives. It was obvious that we no longer shared a close bond and sincere friendship.

Still, Sayeh told me that for some years after the revolution, she had isolated herself from the outside world, hoping for some changes in the society. The bumpy years after the revolution, followed by a period of the disastrous war, had led her to a state of psychological instability.

Nonetheless, she had to acknowledge the fact that there would be no changes in the horizon, so she decided to end the isolation and became a part of the adverse, new society. She got out of the house, started working, and got married. Now, she had a high position in a private company, a nice husband, and a teenage daughter.

This is where our closeness ended. She had no more to say—not then or later on. We were no longer the confidantes we had once been. We used to share our innermost secrets, but now neither of us would go further to exercise the trust we had shared.

During the hardships of my life and far from homeland, Sayeh's face always came to my mind when I longed for a close, trusted friend to comfort me. Now she sat next to me, but the sense of closeness did not exist anymore. I tried to tell her the story of my life and the emotional times when I needed her to listen and comfort me, as she used to do, but I could not. I merely came up with no more than a condensed, general portion of my life story to share with her. The time and distance, had left its trace.

*　　*　　*

With Sayeh's help, I contacted some other friends and then later met them. It felt wonderful to go back in time to the days of our youth—even though it was momentary. Laughter and joy filled the air. We had so many memories together that we nearly forgot about the present.

We were all contemporaries, but Zari had visibly aged the most. I heard from Sayeh that Zari had led a very underprivileged life. The Zari I remembered was a tall and rather chubby, cute girl, shy and quiet. Now she had transformed into a talkative and irate person. I felt that somehow her soul had been crushed. After I heard her story, I understood how and where she had lost her soul and her youth.

Zari told me a brief version of her eight years in jail, the mental torture, and her lost years.

In 1980, during the first years of the establishment of the Islamic Republic of Iran, she and her fiancé participated in a demonstration against the newly formed Islamic government. *Pasdaran*—the Islamic Revolutionary Guards—and other governmental forces crashed the demonstration and attacked the participants, who were mostly teens and students. Some of the demonstrators were killed, and some were arrested. Zari and her fiancé were among those who were arrested. She was found guilty as an "Enemy of the Islamic Revolution" and was sentenced to thirty years in jail. Her fiancé was charged with the same crime; in addition he found also guilty of being *mof-sede-fel-arz*—The Filthiest Human on the Earth—and sentenced to death. He was hanged shortly after.

While Zari was in prison, she struggled with depression and was admitted to the prison's psychiatric hospital. Her illness deteriorated over time.

Ayatollah Montazeri[2] appointed a committee to investigate the condition and status of political detainees. As a result, after eight years in prison, Zari and some other prisoners were released by the recommendation of that committee.

Coping with the daily life after imprisonment was not easy for her. Given the fact that she was not mentally stable, she could no longer function normally. Her background was a roadblock to her future. It was almost impossible for her to obtain a job and return to a normal life.

I asked her if she had been physically tortured and what her daily life in the jail was like. In response, she only said, "It was just a jail." I realized she did not want to talk about it. Either she could not bear to recall those terrible years, or she was not allowed to reveal anything about the life in the prison.

*   *   *

I easily bonded with my family once again. However, I felt like an outsider to the city and its people. Politics, current economic situations, and daily social issues were topics of discussions and conversation everywhere. Regardless which region of the country people were from or what religion they practiced, everyone seemed to be discontented and critical of the government and its barbaric manner. However, since the regime created such a fearful and intimidating image of itself, it was quite terrifying to openly criticize the establishment. It required a huge sacrifice and courage to oppose the government and the other unofficial Islamic organizations affiliated with the establishment.

*   *   *

During my five weeks' stay in Iran, I met people from many different backgrounds and social levels. I was invited to many homes as a guest. My impression was that the vast majority of Iranians led two different lives—one inside their homes and one in public to fit into the new norm of a restricted society.

People easily disobeyed Islamic laws inside their homes. Women attended private parties or gatherings in their best, fashionable outfits and elegant hair

---

2   **Ayatollah Montazeri** was very well respected religious leader and appointed by Ayatollah Khomeini as his successor. Later on he was under house arrest because of his criticism of the regime. He died in December 2009.

styles and make-up. They were in the company of men in modish and chic suits and ties, which the government had declared inappropriate.

Alcoholic beverages were available in many houses even though possessing or drinking alcohol is forbidden by Islamic law. A person found with alcohol faced a harsh penalty that ranged from prison time to a whipping or a fine amounting to a huge sum of cash. At times, all three penalties were handed down.

In social gatherings, men and women would drink, dance, and have fun. I wondered if they were not afraid of prison and lashes. Everyone knew that at any time Islamic guards could crash the party and turn a cheerful time into a living hell.

Interestingly, the day after a party and outside their home or at work, the same individuals appeared and acted completely differently. One could see the women in Islamic attire with no make-up, and the unshaven men in their shabby clothes and shoes. In fact, it was a kind of double morality which the system encouraged or forced the people to implement.

In contrast, I met those who adopted the Islamic way of living. My aunt and her family are respectable, honest people, and as far as I knew, they have never been religious. During this trip, one of my male cousins and I visited them in their house. To my surprise, my aunt covered her hair for him. Her act made me curious, and I asked her why she did so. She simply replied, "I don't really know the reason. I just did it. I think I'm somehow addicted to my head scarf. It has now become a routine, a part of my life as a woman."

Another example is my friend Mina. As I knew her she did not practice any religious rites, such as prayer—*namaaz*—that Shi'a Muslims are obligated to do three times a day.

On one occasion, we, all old friends, were gathered at Mina's to have lunch and some nice time together. At noon after the lunch was served and Mina came with some good dessert, she excused herself to leave us for namaaz. It was not my place to judge her faith in case she had become a believer, but the curiosity took over and made me ask her how and when she decided to become a faithful Muslim.

She smiled and said, "I really don't know. I think these propagations of Islam that you hear everywhere and all the time have influenced me."

"It's a good influence if it makes you happy," I replied

Sayeh joined our conversation and commented, "It has not affected me at all. Mina, do you really believe what these mullahs say?"

"No, I don't believe them! I don't care about these *akhonds*. To me, namaaz is like talking to God, and it gives me peace, it is kind of meditation," Mina stated.

Suddenly, Zari jumped into the discussion and furiously objected to what Mina had said: "What are you talking about? If you like to talk to God, just do it. You don't need to listen to these charlatans. Just look outside the window to see what these con-artists, who claim to be God's men, have done to the people."

Zari seemed really mad, and everyone tried to calm her down. Mina said nothing.

"Okay Zari jan, don't be so upset. Mina did say that she didn't believe in them," I pointed out as I tried to calm her down.

In a gloomy tone, Zari expressed her regret, "I'm sorry, Mina. I didn't mean to jump on you like this. You know me, I'm crazy! I was a Muslim before these bastards took everything away from me, including my belief. Damn them!"

Mina hugged her and said, "I'm not upset about you. Don't worry."

We changed the subject and Mina left for namaaz.

*   *   *

There were other people that I wished to see. This included the Sohrabi family, whom I always liked and greatly respected. Mr. Sohrabi had a passion for poetry and literature and held a high governmental position during the shah's regime. Mrs. Sohrabi was a quiet, tiny woman who always had a nice smile. The couple's two sons and one daughter had all become physicians. The younger brother, Fery, was a dermatologist and surgeon. He was an attractive man, and I had a secret crush on him when I was a teenager. At the time, he was in his early thirties and I was just a kid in his eyes.

During the years I was away from the country, many unfortunate and nasty events occurred to people—including my relatives. I had lost my stepbrothers, sisters, and some other close relatives. Young cousins of mine were killed in the war with Iraq; others were killed by the Islamic regime, which they had opposed. However, a sad, heartbreaking, and cruel incident had occurred in the Sohrabi family that was beyond my comprehension at the time, which made those losses less painful.

The incident had occurred a few years after the revolution. My mother described the day of the awful incident.

"Once on the day of *Eid-e- norouz*—Iranian New Year—the Sohrabi family got together to celebrate, and they waited for Fery to join them. He never showed up. They kept calling his house, but there was no answer. They were really worried. His brother, Vahab, and Mrs. Sohrabi went to his house to look for him.

"When they got there, they found the door to his house wide open. They entered and saw the place was messy. They called his name, but there was no answer. Mrs. Sohrabi went to Fery's bedroom while Vahab searched the other parts of the house. As she entered the bedroom, she found her son covered in blood. She screamed and fainted.

"Vahab ran into the bedroom and found Fery naked and tied to a chair. He approached his brother's bloody, lifeless body that had numerous stabs wounds. Vahab removed the handkerchief tied around Fery's mouth and noticed something."

My mother stopped here. She seemed not to be sure how to continue to the end of that brutal story.

"Go on Mamman, tell me what was in his mouth," I asked impatiently.

She said, "It's hard to say. It's just painful!" Once again, she paused for some moments before she finally continued in a shaking voice. "It was his penis. Those bastards had cut off his penis and stuffed it into his mouth."

Tears rolled down my face. I was speechless. It seemed as if my mother had just finished describing a scene from a horror movie. It couldn't be real.

I kept asking: "Who were those bastards? Why did they do that? Were they ever caught?"

"It is obvious who did it. They were the very same bastards who killed many others. Don't you know about the Ghatlhaie Zangirehee—the chained murders? This disgusting, wicked, criminal act is on the hands of the same devils." (Appendix B)

"But, why Fery? Why did they kill him?" I asked.

"He, as you know, was a dermatologist. He used also to perform surgical vasectomies. We never got to know if the reason was the vasectomy surgeries he used to do, or it was other political issues involved," my mother responded.

"What do you mean? Was there no arrest, no police report, nothing?" I burst out.

"You must be living on another planet," she mocked me before answering, "Of course, the police came. They showed up and pretended to investigate the case. As expected, the case was eventually closed without any arrests.

"How are the Sohrabis coping with it now? I asked.

"Ever since then, Mrs. Sohrabi has been in a depression and still is in a state of shock. Now she has Alzheimer's disease too. To this day, the only thing she can remember and talk about is how she saw her son in that room."

"Mr. Sohrabi died soon after the incident; the pain was too much for him to tolerate," my mother added.

"What are Vahab and his sister Shohreh doing?" I asked.

"Shohreh became ill and was always terrified that something else was going to happen to her family. She couldn't continue living in Iran so she immigrated to Europe with her family. They have never returned. Vahab and his wife still live here. He has his own office and lives day to day as others do," she said.

*   *   *

After learning the disastrous fate of that family, my older brother Shahram, my mother, and I went to visit them.

With a smile on her face, Mrs. Sohrabi opened the door to us. She looked so much smaller and her face appeared wizened. She welcomed us warmly. I hugged her as Shahram reminded her who I was: "Mrs. Sohrabi, this is Niki. Do you remember her?"

"Yes, yes, I do remember her," she said hastily, but the look on her face did not agree with her words.

She led us inside the house through the big yard. The large, tall, apple tree still occupied most of the yard. The small pond in the middle of the grassy area was empty. Once inside the living room, I found everything, including the furniture, to be exactly as I remembered it from decades ago. I remembered my family and the Sohrabis sitting on these couches while talking and having a good time.

Mrs. Sohrabi invited us to sit down and left to inform Vahab, who lived on the second floor, of our arrival. Shortly, she returned with Vahab and his wife. Vahab had changed dramatically. He appeared wilted and looked like an old man. His voice was calm and dim. The energetic and humorous person I knew no longer existed.

I looked around the room and noticed a picture on the wall of Fery and his father, Mr. Sohrabi. It was the only change to the decor of the room. The atmosphere was tense and gloomy. Nobody talked much. I stood up and walked over to the picture.

It felt as if it was yesterday that Mr. Sohrabi sat beside me and recited his poems to me. It was just yesterday when Fery joined us and cheerfully told the joke of the day to make everyone laugh. As I stared at the picture, my eyes filled with tears. An absolute silence filled the room.

After I returned to the couch, Mrs. Sohrabi started telling us about the horrific scene of Fery's murder and how her husband died shortly after to join his son. When she quit speaking, she stared at the floor. The atmosphere was unbearable. Shahram's eyes were filled with tears.

Vahab unsuccessfully tried to change the mood. His wife offered fruits and tea. Mrs. Sohrabi repeated the same story over and over again, using the same exact words. I realized the old, dreadful sore on the family's heart had ruined their lives forever.

As we left the Sohrabis, my mother told me, "You should have seen his funeral; hundreds of people participated." She sighed before continuing, "May God damn those who committed this crime and those who protected the criminals."

Chapter 2

Childhood Memories

I made a trip to my childhood town. For many years, the idea of doing so was only a dream. However, the "Welcome to Carvand" sign on the road signified that I was not dreaming. It was real.

I did not have to walk long through the city before I was disappointed. There was no similarity between this cluttered place and the small, serene town I was born in. With the large number of people, shops, and cars, the town had become messy and hazy.

The town's bazaar, which once included my father's grocery store and many businesses and shops of our large family, was no longer recognizable to me.

By walking around the busy market and asking people, I was finally led to my cousin's store—a cousin I had never seen before. I introduced myself to him as his cousin. Arash, as he introduced himself, was surprised to meet a cousin he never knew he had. I asked him to direct me to my late father's store.

The store looked much smaller than it did in my childhood memories. I talked to the owner, who was also a remote relative of mine. As a young boy, he had worked for my father. I took some pictures of the store and the completely changed surroundings.

Arash spent the day with me and drove me around sightseeing. I asked him to take me to my childhood house. Since I did not know the street address, I tried to describe the place. After passing through some crowded streets and not finding it, Arash took me to his Aunt Mahin, who was our neighbor years ago. Her sister, who lived in America, owned my childhood house now, and she had the key to the house.

Mahin was my cousin. A middle-aged, talkative, happy woman, she was exactly as I remembered her. She updated me about most of the relatives who still lived in town and the many others who had passed away. I enjoyed hearing the sound of my lost dialect and forgotten words. Mahin gave Arash the key to the house and we headed out.

*   *   *

Arash stopped the car in front of a house at a very busy street. He pointed to an iron door on the house and said, "Here it is, Miss Niki, your house."

Not recognizing the house, I asked him, "This house? Are you sure?"

"Yes, this is it. Here is the address Aunt Mahin gave me," he said.

"But the house door was inside the alley and completely different from this," I said hesitantly.

"Miss Niki, you're talking about forty years ago. Nothing would be exactly the same now," he reminded me.

"Of course, it would not," I agreed. "Let's go inside."

We got out of the car and looked around. The stream at the side of the sidewalk in front of the house flowed slowly. No women sat at its side to wash dishes as they did years ago. No kids played around it. The stream looked narrow and not as large as in my childhood memories. The only memory that was close to reality was the bridge over the stream in front of the alley, although it too seemed much smaller now.

I walked to the alley. It was the same alley, although the door had been removed. My uncle's house, now unoccupied, was still at the end of the alley. "You're right, Arash, this is the house."

All the buildings in the neighborhood had been renovated. I glanced around and tried to recall how it had looked when I lived there.

"What are you looking for?" Arash asked.

"Nothing, I am just trying to remember who used to live where."

Pointing to the large school on the other side of the street, I said, "This was Dr. Habibi's house. It was such a big house with gorgeous landscaping. Too bad it's torn down. Diana, their daughter, was my friend. Do they still live in this town?"

"No, not anymore, one year after the revolution, a group of people occupied their home and threw them out of the town. Nobody has heard from them since," he replied with a grimace.

"Why? Had they done something wrong?" I asked

Arash answered my question and briefly told me the story:

"No, they had not done a thing. Their only sin was their religion."

"As religious leaders, the clergies declared that believers of the *Baha'i faith* were considered impure and infidel (Appendix C). Thus, it was a blessing to Muslims to confiscate their belongings and their homes. The mullahs also declared that *Baha'i believers* did not have the right to live next to Muslims. So, some fanatics took over their home and forced them to leave the town. They were fortunate to have escaped alive."

"Later on, some people occupied the house until the government evicted them and built this school."

My heart ached. I wondered if these types of fanatics really lived amongst us. I realized, yes, they did, and apparently they waited for the right moment.

I remembered the days when I played with Diana. Her parents were warm and kind. Interestingly, I never saw anyone visiting them. I was Diana's only friend. Not many Muslims would allow their child to have Baha'i friends. Dr. Habibi had a good reputation as a doctor and a human being. But, due to his religious beliefs, in the eyes of fanatics, associating with him and his family was considered a great sin.

My cousin's voice brought me back to reality, "You haven't heard the most ridiculous part. You know these days, namaaz is mandatory in the schools for the students and the staff. After the government took over the house and the school was built, the mullahs declared that since this property was confiscated and its owner was thrown out by force, namaaz at this place was *batel*—invalid, not acceptable by God."

"These fools … they think they can trick God too?" I bitterly asked. "As if any kind of brutality in the name of God is justified? These idiots believe that the confiscation of Bahia's property was justified as long as namaaz was not performed in the place? How can anyone buy this kind of crap?"

*   *   *

Arash unlocked the gray, metal door, which had replaced the old wooden one with a clanging doorknob. "Here you go. Don't expect to find the house looking nice," he said while he held the door open for me.

"I know. I've already seen changes everywhere; I don't think anything can surprise me anymore," I said. Then I stopped at the entrance and turned to him, "Do you mind leaving me alone here for a while?"

"Not at all, I'll wait for you in the coffeehouse on the corner. Take your time," he responded.

He left, and I paused for a moment before taking a deep breath and entering the house. The atmosphere of the house had been covered by the dust of abandonment. It felt as though I was visiting a dear pal on her last legs. My childhood house was dying; I could not let it take all my precious memories to its grave.

Room by room, I glanced around each corner of the house. Regardless of the emptiness and melancholy of the house, my memories burned brightly and an animated feeling surrounded me. Familiar voices echoed in my ears.

Suddenly, I could sense life had come back to this soulless house. It was a weird, yet wonderful sensation. My eyes filled with tears.

I sat down on the third step of the stairway. It was the same block of cement that I had sat on when we returned home after my father's funeral. I had sat there, watching the sad faces of the crowd mingle throughout the house and wished everyone would leave. There were many other times that I had taken a seat on that same stair, coping with sad times or being light of heart on joyful occasions.

Images and familiar voices of my past life came to mind. I could hear my mother's voice telling me, "You know, the moment you were born, everyone in the room screamed; I was scared to death."

My mother had sat next to me on this step on a summer evening. She had just finished soaking the yard to cool it down and make it pleasant for us to sit outside to escape the high temperature of the room. She pointed to the big, long room behind us and said, "The day you were born was a cold winter day and we had the first heavy snow for the season. You were born right here at home, in the *pang dari—five door room*. Rasha was the midwife. You entered the world still inside the amniotic sac, and your shape was like that of a melon.

"Your aunts and some other women were in the room with me. The melon shape horrified them. They screamed *'astagh feroallah'* to ask God for his forgiveness for this creature. Then, Rasha laughed and told them not to be frightened; the creature was a human baby. She cut the sac and removed you from of it. The unexpected screams turned to laughter. Everyone in the house jammed behind the door, wondering what was happening inside the room. Oh, it was so funny," my mother had added and laughed cheerfully.

*   *   *

The young, cute face of Souri, my older sister, came to my mind as I gazed out at the empty blue pond. On that sunny, cold winter day, Souri had worn her long, braided hair down. Her hands had turned red because of the icy cold water of the pond. She sat by the pond rinsing dishes. I was jumping rope in the other corner of the yard.

"Niki, come here," she said loudly.

"Why?" I stopped jumping.

"Come here, I want tell you something," she said.

"Tell me, I can hear you from here," I said.

"No, come here, I can't shout," she insisted.

I gave up and went to her and sat by her at the edge of the pond.

"Niki, you won't say anything to Mamman about what you heard today, right? If you tell her, I will kill you." She was warning me not to reveal what I overheard when she and her friends were talking about the boys earlier.

I liked snooping on her as she and her friends playfully talked about the love letters they had received. I usually did that to blackmail her, hoping that she would do something for me in return. Despite being a teenager, Souri acted motherly toward me and Ramin, my younger brother. I liked to get the motherly treatment from her as long as it was of benefit to me.

*   *   *

From across the passageway between the yard and the house's door, my father's gentle voice echoed in my ears, "Shahram, I'm hungry," he called to my mother as he arrived home in the evening. In those days, for some reason, some men called their wives by the name of their oldest child or just *khaanom*, which meant lady.

A tall and good-looking man, my father was not used to expressing his love, but I felt his affection by the way he talked to me. I was his *baba joon*—daddy's dear. He never came home empty-handed. He always had something for me in his pocket.

Every evening, when he got home, he called to me to get the goodies. "How are you, baba joon? You haven't bothered your mamman today, have you?"

Since my answer was always no, he responded by patting my hair and saying, "What a good girl!" Those effortless phrases expressed his love, which I loved to hear.

*   *   *

Now I walked up the stairs, passing the narrow patio to enter the pang dari. This large room was used as a living room, dining room, and bedroom. Two sides of the lengthy room extended to two smaller rooms. One was our parents' bedroom and the other was used as a storage room. The two small rooms were separated from the pang dari by tall wooden doors.

Standing in the middle of the pang dari, no effort was needed on my part to remember the old, lively times of the now dusty room. The reflection of sunlight through the five round and small glass windows with pictorial illustration of colorful peacocks engraved, above each door, sparked off my reminiscences.

I could hear my young mother yelling at Souri and Shahrooz, my second oldest brother, to wake them up for the morning namaaz that had to be done before sunrise. "Get up! Get up. It is time for namaaz. The sun is coming up soon. Don't be lazy!"

We sat on the floor, around the *sofreh*—the table cloth—and waited for Father to join us for breakfast. Ramin ran to him and pulled him along by his hand. Father responded to our morning greeting of salaam and sat on the floor with us. Ramin sat on his lap while father made a sandwich of cheese and butter for him. I sat by him, wishing he would do the same for me, but he patted my hair, smiled, and asked, "How's my big girl, baba joon?" This was enough to make me feel proud of being bigger than Ramin and that I could make my own sandwich. Mother poured tea for everyone except me and Ramin. She believed we were too young to drink tea. Instead she poured warm water in a cup and mixed it with some sugar for us.

*   *   *

As I continued to wander around the house, I stopped at the kitchen door, which was located at the corner of the yard.

The oven, or *tanoor*,[3] that was built into the wall for baking bread was still there. Once a month, a baker came to our house to help my mother bake bread.

---

3   **Tanoor**, an oven made of clay, built like a hole inside the kitchen, used for baking bread on the heated sand.

Turning on the tanoor and making it hot enough took quite a long time. Baking usually was an all-day task. The smell of freshly baked bread filled the air. I loved to sit with my mother and the baker to watch them, but I was not allowed to get too close to the fire. Now I stood in the same spot as I had as a child to watch them make bread.

My mother was different from the other women in our neighborhood who gathered in front of their houses every afternoon and chatted while cracking and eating seeds. I never saw my mother in their company. She was busy at home most of the time. To occupy herself, she had different hobbies and a lot of work to do. She cracked huge quantities of almonds to separate the shells from the seeds. My father then sold the seeds in his store. Cracking almonds took weeks.

My mother constantly used the dark storage room attached to the kitchen for things out of the ordinary, which included breeding caterpillars. Then she used the silky cover—the cocoon in which the caterpillar enclosed itself during its transition to butterflies—for producing silk. For me, the best part about the caterpillars was the transition from larva to butterfly. I was not supposed to open the storage door during the process, but I was too impatient to wait. I secretly went into the storage room to catch the butterflies before they flew away. At other times, my mother used the room for hanging up sweet grapes to dry and processing them into raisins.

*   *   *

I continued my stroll to the small, empty pond in the middle of the yard. Once, it had been a sparkling blue pond full with clean water and vibrant, colorful fishes swimming around. It was surrounded by a small garden full of beautiful, colorful flowers. It, too, brought forth memories.

A nice, old woman named *JanJan* came once a week. She set up her cleaning supplies at the pond, next to a large laundry tub, and washed our dirty clothes. My mother and Souri usually helped her hang the rinsed items on ropes to dry.

Sitting at the edge of the empty pond, I looked across it toward the basement. The basement was seven stairs down from the yard level. I still was not courageous enough to go down into that dark basement because a snake had built a shelter in a wall. The snake's nest had a small opening to the yard. The snake was a "homey" as everyone used to say. It was a common belief that a domestic snake would never harm any member of the household as long as it felt safe. Moreover, tradition held that if a person killed or made a snake go away, the household members would become vagrants.

My mother kept many animals inside that basement. For me, it was fun to have hens, cocks, and even turkeys at home. I could boss around the other kids, who would come to us to play with them. My mother used to go to the basement every day to feed the animals and collect the eggs. She was not afraid of anything.

No one in our house dared to go into the basement. She even put a big bowl in front of the snake's nest and regularly filled it with water for the snake. However, the snake was known to make its way to the pond in the middle of the night to drink water.

The snake was a member of our household and we lived together. I had a particularly vivid memory of the snake.

Early on a summer morning, we were awakened by my mother's reedy and short howl. She had found a long skin of the snake across Ramin's bed. Mother held two-year-old Ramin to her bosom and looked for the snake, but it was already gone. Everyone was scared. My mother calmly said, "Don't be scared, it is a homey. It is a good thing that it molt its skin in this place. This is a really good omen."

Once again, another incident with the snake occurred in the middle of the night.

Noises of the chickens from the basement woke everyone in the house up.

With a light in hand, my mother went down to the basement. She found some pets running around and others dead. The only thing she could do at the time was to lead those that had survived out of the basement and up to the yard.

In the morning, she returned to the basement to pick up the slain pets. The bodies of the dead pets were so dried out that it looked as though they had been dead for a long time. It seemed that the snake had ingested the blood and other liquid of the pets' bodies.

No one knew what happened to the snake after we left the house and the town. Some believed that the snake left the house before we did, which caused our family to move from the house forever. Others speculated that after we left the house the abandoned snake was lonely and left the house as well.

*   *   *

I could have stayed in that house for many more hours and relived the first eight years of my life. I remembered relatives, neighbors, and others who had played various roles in my early years and those who left me with pleasurable memories of my childhood for life.

"Come on Niki, let's go. Do you know how many cups of tea I had in that teahouse?" Arash's voice brought me back from the past to the present.

"I'm sorry, Arash. I lost track of the time. Okay, let's go to the teahouse for another cup of tea, my treat," I said humorously. As I got up to leave the house, I knew this was the last time I would ever see this house.

*   *   *

As my cousin drove through the hectic streets of Carvand, I felt slightly uneasy over the changes. *Had I really expected time would have halted in that particular small part of the world?*

The city I remembered was much smaller and less populated. Our family was well known in the town. It seemed as though our relatives comprised the majority of the population of the city. I remembered that my hometown had only three main streets and hardly any traffic. The city, my city, had only one mosque, one female public bathhouse, and one male public bathhouse. It had one power station, one small health care center, and one pharmacy. A textile and weaving factory was the only industry in the town.

Private gardens with tall, dried brick walls and wooden gates had been scattered all over the city. The sole leisure and fun for the citizens of the city was to spend a day with family and friends in the public park. Next to the park, there was a small newspaper stand where I used to buy *Keyhan Bacheha*—a weekly magazine for children.

Bakeries and some grocery stores were located on both sides of the main streets. The few tea houses had mainly been occupied by men. The cemetery was a few kilometers away from the city.

The water place was my favorite place. I would stop for water whenever I passed it on my way to my father's store. It was a cool place with a water pipe for thirsty pedestrians to stop for some cold, fresh water, mainly in the summer. The water place was built a few stone stairs below ground level with a narrow and stony bench across its wall. The shaft of daylight was its only light source.

The school was close to my house. I envied kids whose houses were far from the school, so they had more time to walk together, play, and chitchat.

The mosque was located on the street that led to the bazaar. From its *minaret*[4], the *moazzen*[5] reads *azan*[6]. With both hands on the sides of his mouth, the moazzen's pleasant voice calls the faithful Muslims to prayer.

A short distance from the mosque was the public bath facility.

The man in charge of the men's bathhouse, wearing a waistcloth, used to sit sluggishly at the front of the bath's gate.

The women's bathhouse was adjacent to the men's bathhouse. Wearing the chador, women entered and left the bathhouse in a steady stream all day. They carried a bundle with a change of clothes under their arms, which made it more difficult to keep the chador in place.

The bazaar, where my father's grocery was located, was my favorite place, and I loved to go there with my father. When I was there, I rambled about visiting my favorite shops. Most of the owners knew me since I was talkative and cheerful. They always had something for me, whether it was a piece of candy, chocolates,

4   **Minaret** is a tall slender tower of a mosque.
5   **Moazzen** is a vocalist who chants a particular verse from the Quran (azan), calling the Muslims to daily namaaz.
6   **Azan** is a verse of the Quran, which a moazzen chants.

or other sweets and stuffs.

My uncle owned a pastry shop. He had a long, white beard, and I called him *amoo reeshee* (bearded uncle). I used to sit on his lap and play with his soft beard, which I loved to touch. I often visited his store first. He usually saved the tin-plated bins that had once been full of sweets for me. I loved those empty bins. I couldn't really play with them, but I just liked to have them.

Another relative owned an electric and lighting shop. He put aside the crystal chandelier prisms that had been left or separated from the chandeliers. I loved to hold the crystal prisms up against the sunlight to see the variety of beautiful colors reflected by the light spectrum. With a feeling of self-importance, I would take this home and show them off to my friends down the street. During those days, we did not have toys. The smallest thing could entertain us. My only toy was a doll that my mother had made out of fabric.

*   *   *

My mother was a young, cheerful woman. My father was a tall, handsome man, who was thirty years older than my mother. At the age of sixteen, my mother had been forced to marry my father, who had recently lost his wife.

Marrying an old man had never been my mother's dream. She rejected the idea and begged her parents not to impose this marriage on her. However, realizing that they did not respect her will, she hid herself inside a large suitcase in the closet on the wedding day. Turmoil broke out. Everyone looked for the runaway bride. Finally, they found her and dragged her in tears to the ceremony. Her destiny was determined by a choice that was not her own.

My father was well-respected by the family members and the people of the town. He was looked upon as an advisor. He was a serious man, yet kind. He had five children from his previous marriage. They were all older than his new wife, my mother. Even though he had married a teenage girl, he encouraged other parents not to wed their daughters in their teenage years. He advised them to let their daughters get an education.

The first modern school in our town was founded by my father with the help of two of his acquaintances in the late nineteenth century. There, the students were able to get a real scientific education. Prior to this school, there had been some traditional religious schools called *maktab khaneh*. These schools were running by mullahs with a curriculum of religion and the Islamic holy book, the Quran. The modern school stirred rage amongst the mullahs. They became extremely furious and accused my father and his friends of being pagans.

*   *   *

My father's contradictory deeds always confused me. Years later, when I was old enough to question this, I asked my mother about him. In my view, my mother was a victim. I needed to hear her opinion about my father.

"Mamman, you always say that *Baba* was a very open-minded person who paid much attention to the education of women and was against marrying off girls at a young age. Then how could he marry a sixteen-year-old girl? This does not make any sense to me."

My mother replied briefly, "Life was very different in those days. Your father lived under different circumstances at the time."

"Which circumstances? Why did your sister marry a young man then?" I asked.

"Everyone has a destiny. You can't go against your fate," she said innocently.

"I don't buy it at all, and I can't find any justification for Baba's double standard deed," I argued.

"Girls had to marry very young at that time. Your baba married off all his daughters at an early age as well before marrying me. If he had not done so, rumors would spread about those poor girls. The people of the town would tell tales that something must be wrong with those girls who still were unmarried. You can't imagine how nasty some people could be. Those types of rumors could have a devastating impact on their lives," she said.

I discerned that she was trying to give me a good excuse for my father. Then sarcastically, she continued, "You know, once your father married me at my young age, he forbade others to do the same!"

I chuckled, then asked, "Okay, Mamman, so you think there was nothing wrong with Baba marrying you; then you should blame your parents!"

"No, I told you it was my destiny. It was nobody's fault," she said in defense of her parents.

"I can't believe you, Mamman. How can you defend them? I blame them more than I blame Baba. They forced you into this marriage. You told me that you were crying and begging them not to, but they did anyway. It was not your destiny, they made it your destiny," I argued.

"Whatever happened, happened. You can't change the past now. Besides, they were my parents and meant well. Now I thank God that I had a good life, and I have five successful and honest children. What else should I have expected from my life?" she asked.

Giving up on the argument, I said, "If you liked your life with Baba, then I'm happy about it. But I think you are too nice."

"Your baba was a nice and gentle man. I never had any problem with him, but his family used to bother me a lot just because I was so young. Thank God that your baba was a wise man and paid no attention to their gossip. He was a good man. Are you satisfied now?" she said.

"No, I am not. If you had married a younger man, I still would have a baba," I replied humorously.

She smiled and said, "Not necessarily, many fathers die young."

"Then you should have remarried so I would have a stepfather," I added laughingly.

"Having one baba was enough for you, and one husband was more than enough for me," she said with a laugh to end the conversation.

However, I never got a straight answer to my question, but I realized that even though the marriage took place under compelling circumstances, my mother was happy with my father.

*   *   *

My oldest brother, Shahram, is a good-natured, optimistic, and humble person. He left Carvand for Tehran to attend university when I was very young. My brother Shahrooz is two years younger than Shahram. I remember hearing him arguing with Souri, my older sister, and also with my father much of the time. Shahrooz was different from the other boys in our family. While he was not rebellious, he was stubborn. After high school graduation at eighteen, and with help from Shahram, he left the country for higher education in England.

Souri is my older sister. She actively took part in doing housework most of the time when she was not at school. She was good to me, and I looked up to her.

Ramin is my youngest brother. I remember the day he was born in the panj dari, the same room of the house as I was born in. My mother was attended to by the same midwife, Rasha. My father worried and paced back and forth in the yard. My mother's scream scared me too. Souri consoled me by telling me that my mother was very happy to give us a brother or a sister. Therefore, she was bawling out of happiness. My father lifted me up, sat on the step, and kept me on his lap for a while. I was no longer scared.

*   *   *

In 1962, at the age of six, I wore the gray-colored school uniform; and for the first time, I put on the chador my mother had sewed for me. With much excitement, I started going to school. During the school year, as life passed by at its normal pace, my father became ill. Souri had just finished high school and my older brother Shahram had graduated from college. My brother Sharooz was still studying in England.

As the days passed, my father's health worsened. The illness soon made him weak and fragile. The doctors diagnosed lung cancer and explained that he was not going to get any better. My stepbrother dadash Nasser, who lived in Teheran, had asked my father to go there where the hospitals and care facilities were equipped with more advanced medical resources.

*   *   *

The day before my father's departure to Tehran was a sizzling summer day. Like other summer days, my mother had spread out a colorful Persian rug along the terrace and placed the shiny samovar against the wall in one corner. She sat next to my father, who was laid back on the handmade cushions. Ramin rode his red tricycle around the yard. Souri arranged the tea cups and sugar bowl on a tray. I sat next to my father and caressed his bruised thumb that he had hurt the night before trying to break a chunk of sugar loaf into small pieces with a tong.

We waited for Shahram to arrive. He would accompany my father to Tehran the day after. We also expected some relatives and friends to come by to bid farewell to my father. A photographer, who had come to take some family pictures, sat at the edge of the terrace drinking tea.

My mother constantly paced back and forth as she anxiously waited for Shahram. When he arrived, she cried the moment she opened the door to him. I left my father's side and ran to Shahram. I was confused why my mother would cry. I was happy to see Shahram, and other times she was very happy and cheerful to see Shahram. So why not this time?

The photographer took family pictures before the visitors arrived. Everyone sat around the terrace on the carpet. My mother poured tea, and Souri carried around the tea tray to offer tea and fruits to the guests. No one said much, and I noticed the tearful eyes. It felt strange.

I walked over to my father and sat beside him. What I felt at the time was much different than the reality that took place around me. I knew that something was going to happen, I could truly feel it. However, death was beyond my imagination. The thought of my father's temporary absence made me not want to leave his side. His cheeks had shriveled and dark circles were visible under his eyes. It was obvious to everyone else that this vile cancer had taken over his entire body, but I was too young to understand it. He smiled at the visitors, reassuring them the trip would be short and that he would return soon. In the meantime, the photographer took the last few pictures of him with his family.

*   *   *

The next morning, dadash Nasser's driver arrived at Carvand. My father, along with my mother and Shahram, with a small suitcase in hand, was ready to leave. When they were in the car and about to head toward the airport, I begged my mother to take me along. I liked riding in a car. The last time I had been in a car was to visit my grandparents in Isfahan—a cultural city located central part of Iran. Riding in the car had made me dizzy, but it was fun.

My mother wanted me to stay with Souri and Ramin, but I was too stubborn to give up begging. Finally, my father asked my mother to let me go with them. I proudly sat between Shahram and my mother in backseat as my envious friends watched me. The car was surrounded by many people who had come to see my father off.

*   *   *

The airport departure hall was undersized. Small hallways led straight to the airplane since gates did not exist at that time. My mother and I followed my father and Shahram through the hallway. It was the first time that I had seen an airplane. I could recall many times when I had heard the roar of an airplane in the endless sky and looked up. From that perspective, they seemed so puny. Now, standing next to one, I realized how huge a plane actually was.

My father kissed my cheeks and caressed my hair before saying good-bye to my mother. Then along with Shahram and a few other passengers, he boarded the plane. I remember his heartrending smile as he turned back and waved to us before entering the plane. He was seated next to the window; we could see his face until the plane took off.

Dadash Nasser's driver drove us home. My mother was sad and said nothing while I chitchatted. I was excited about the next day when we would go to Tehran to stay with daei Kareem—uncle Kareem.

*   *   *

The next morning, dadash Nasser's driver picked my mother, Souri, Ramin, and me up for the drive to Tehran. After many hours, we arrived at daei Kareem's house. My cousin Saghee was about my age. My other cousin was much older than me and was about Souri's age. Poor Ramin did not have anyone to play with, and I felt sorry for him.

During the two months that my father was hospitalized, we stayed with daei Kareem. Souri and my mother visited my father daily. Most of the time, my mother stayed over the night with him at the hospital. Sometimes Souri and my mother took me to the hospital to visit. I was not happy about going there. The last thing I wanted to see was the tiny man lying helplessly on his hospital bed. He was very different from my tall, brawny father.

Uncomfortable seeing my father like this, I stood a distance from his bed. My father asked me to come closer to him. As I took small steps to get near him, he reached out and touched my hand while inviting me to sit at his bedside. I despised the place and envied Ramin because he seldom was brought to the hospital. I wished for the father I knew to get on the airplane to return home.

One day, Souri and my mother returned home earlier than usual from the hospital. Both were sobbing. Monir, daei Kareem's wife, immediately went to them and joined in on the weeping. They held each other as they shed their tears. I grabbed Ramin's hand and tried to pick him up, but he was too heavy. My cousin Saghee stood next to me, and we both stared at the sad and mournful adults. I knew that their tears had something to do with my father, but I did not want to know the reason. I took Ramin's hand and asked Saghee to play. We went to the yard and used chalk to draw our favorite game, hopscotch, on the ground.

With the sounds of Souri and my mother crying, I wasn't able to concentrate on the game. Saghee kept winning over and over, and Ramin did not know how to play hopscotch. Finally, I took hold of Ramin's hand and returned to the room. My mother had calmed down a bit, but Souri was still crying.

Later, my mother said that dadash Nasser's driver would take us home; and Shahram had arranged for my father's return by air. I was excited. It was just what I had been waiting and wishing for. Soon, all of us would be back home.

*   *   *

The next day, dadash Nasser's driver came by to pick us up. I really wanted Saghee to come with us, but her mother would not let her. During the drive home, Souri and my mother wept constantly. Ramin was so tired that he took his pacifier, placed it in his mouth, and rested his head on my mother's lap until his eyes closed. I was not tired, but I did wish my mother and Souri would stop crying. The driver remained quiet throughout the trip. In a loud voice, I yelled, "Why are you guys crying so much? Baba is coming home by airplane. Shahram said so." The driver turned and stared at me for a moment. My mother stroked my hair and Souri cried even more.

We finally arrived home. There was chaos in our house, and everything seemed to be covered in black. The sound of crying and expressions of grief filled the house. At the end of the night, Shahram arrived without my father. I don't recall who mentioned it, but I heard that the funeral was the day after. That night, I slept next to Ramin since my mother and sister were still shedding tears.

The next morning, commotion arose again. My Aunt Nahid hugged me and Ramin and whispered, "Poor kids. You've become yatim (orphan)."

I did not understand what she meant. I was starving, but my mother had not turned on the samovar. Nor had she laid out the breakfast sofreh. I went to the kitchen and grabbed some bread.

One by one, people left the house. Aunt Nahid took Ramin in her arms. I heard my mother's sad voice calling me. I ran to her and grabbed her hand. She said we were going to walk to the mosque. I was not curious to know why.

*   *   *

Outside the house, on the street, a large crowd wearing black was everywhere. We heard the sound of men chanting, *"Allah-O-Akbar"*—God is the Great. The chant became louder and louder as those who blocked the entrance of the mosque tried to step aside to let the men carrying the coffin on their shoulders exit.

I was stuck between women's chadors and could feel touches of fabrics on my face. I wished someone would pick me up so I could see what was going on around me. Once again, I envied Ramin. He could see everything from his vantage point in Aunt Nahid's arms.

As the men carried the casket, another group of men followed and chanted. Some buses waiting along the sides of the street were already filled with women and children. My mother pulled me toward one of them and took me inside. All the seats were taken. A lady gave up her seat for my mother as I stood next to her watching the crowd and the casket. Other buses and marching people followed our bus. A crying Souri and her friend sat a couple of seats behind my mother's seat.

By pressing my hands on my face and tightening my eyes, I could force myself to cry. But this time, no tears came out. I acted as though I was crying to get some attention. It worked. My mother pulled me closer to her and let me sit on her lap. Some women then shook their heads and cried harder.

I had absolutely no feelings at the time. The night before, I had dreamed that someone knocked at the door. When I opened the door, an old man with a long, white beard gave me a letter and said, "This is a letter from your baba." Then he disappeared. As my dream continued, I was surrounded by a crowd of weeping women, who had been hiding under their chador. I pushed myself out of the crowd to read the letter my father had written, which said, "I am not dead and will be back to you by airplane."

When I woke up that morning, I told my mother about the letter. She patted my head and said, "That was just a dream. Baba is not coming back anymore." I didn't believe her, but I said nothing. I thought to myself, *when Baba comes back, she will see that it was not just a dream.*

The bus had to move very slowly, but the men carrying the coffin on their shoulders in front of the bus walked faster. They were followed by men who continued to chant, "Allah-O-Akbar." It was hot inside the bus even though all the windows were open. I wanted to get out of the bus to join some kids in the middle of the crowd on the street, but my mother asked me to stay with her.

It took a long time before we arrived at the cemetery—at least it seemed long to me. As soon as we got out of the bus, I left my mother and joined the kids. Staying there to witness the grief was boring for us. Instead, we played. Chasing each other, we came across a mortuary. Because the door to the mortuary was made of wooden planks, we were able to sneak a look through a crack. Two men busily washed the corpse of an old man. Trying not to make a sound, I stealthily pushed the door open, but the brightness of a narrow beam of sunlight caught the men's attention. Their loud yell scared us. We slammed the door shut and ran away.

I returned to my mother just after the burial and ceremony were over. Everyone was ready to get back home.

*   *   *

When we finally returned home, many people dressed in black were still inside. Our home was gloomy and sad. I grumbled to myself, *why are these people still here? Why don't they go back to their own houses?*

I needed the house to be our house again. I wanted it to be like it was before, when there were not so many people present. I wanted my mother making food in the kitchen, Souri washing dishes, and Baba returning home hungry.

I saw Ramin in a neighbor's arms and Souri sitting at the corner of panj dari surrounded by her friends. My mother was not serving the guests. The guests were serving my mother. Some were in the kitchen; others served tea. The children played. They asked me to join them, but I wished them to leave too. I wandered around and looked for Shahram, but I couldn't find him. A few men stood around the pond and smoked. Everyone talked quietly.

There was no one I wanted to talk to. Roaming back into the house, I found my father's dentures on the mantel and felt heaviness in my heart. I turned around slowly and walked to the stairs to sit on my favorite seat, seeking some comfort.

I was so perplexed that I doubted myself. *Why didn't Baba take his dentures with him? He can't eat without them. What if my dream was just a dream as Mamman said?*

I didn't want an answer to my question; I just sat there. Everyone who passed by me patted my head. I rudely tried to ignore everyone and focused my thoughts on my dream of the night before. *Maybe Mamman was right. But if Mamman was right then Baba is dead. Is it possible that God had heard what I said the day Baba asked me to get him his slippers?*

I thought back to the day when I was playing and Baba asked me to bring his slippers for him. I threw the slippers in front of his feet and ran back to play. He called me over and with those same slippers spanked me on the butt and said, "No one should ever throw anything in front of others."

It didn't hurt me at all, but my pride was hurt because he had never acted like that toward me before. On that moment, I wished him to die. *What if God had heard me? I said it very quietly, how could God have heard me?*

Terrified, I looked around to make sure no one knew what I had done. I was at a loss as what to do. *Should I tell Mamman that she was right and Baba was really dead? Should I tell her that I had prayed for Baba to die? But if I did tell her, she would never love me again. She would tell the whole world about it.*

Those thoughts and feelings occupied my mind for quite a while. When I realized that I could not come up with a solution, I decided not to tell a soul and not to think about it anymore. However, the gloomy feeling left inside my soul from that day on still haunts me.

*   *   *

Shahrooz, who still was in England, was not aware of my father's illness and his death. Everyone tried to keep it a secret so he would not be sad while he was far from home. It is part of the Iranian culture to keep bad news from a person who is away from home to spare that person distress and apprehension.

Later, I was told my father persistently asked for Shahrooz on his last days in this world. Since Shahrooz was not in Iran, one of my cousins suggested going to see my father, pretending to be Shahrooz in order to comfort my father.

My cousin did just that. Apparently, my father was not in a stable condition to recognize anyone, so he hugged and kissed my cousin dearly, unaware of the ruse.

Time passed and Shahrooz still was not informed about our father's death. Once he stopped receiving any response to his letters from our father, he became concerned. He wondered what was going on. Finally, his friends told him the truth.

Chapter 3

~m~

City Life

Now a young widow in a small, closed society such as Carvand, my mother found that a serene, contented life in this small town was a challenge—if not impossible. The reality of annoying buzzing rumors was not unfamiliar to my mother. She knew that sooner or later the nosy relatives and neighbors would interfere in her daily life and cause her misery. Thus she wisely made the decision to move the family to the large city of Tehran.

Once the ceremony and gatherings of my father's memorial were over, my mother and Souri packed everything in preparation for our migration to Tehran. Ignoring desperate efforts of relatives to change her mind, my mother strongly stood by her decision to relocate.

With three children, my mother set off for a new life in a big city. We arrived at daei Kareem's house and stayed there for a while. At that time, Shahram was twenty-four and had just graduated from the university. As the eldest son of our family, the moment we unexpectedly set foot in Tehran, he felt a huge sense of responsibility on his shoulders. In no time, he quickly started searching for a place for us to live and rented a nice apartment in a decent area of Tehran for us. With the move to a new place, a new chapter of our lives began.

*   *   *

There was not much comparison between the lifestyle in Tehran and in Carvand; nonetheless, we had no choice but to adapt to the changes.

Tehran was an immense and populated city. The women did not have the same restrictions as they had in the small religious towns such as Carvand.

While Souri stopped wearing the chador, my mother kept to her habit and never took the chador off in public.

Like other big cities, the citizens of Tehran were too busy with their hectic daily lives to find time to poke their noses into another's business. Thus, unlike Carvand, there were no prying relatives and neighbors. This was the most positive factor to my mother's advantage.

Souri, now eighteen years old and a high school graduate, started working in a company as typist, although Shahram was not happy about it. He was in favor of higher education for her and had tried to convince her to attend college, but she did not want to be another burden on his shoulders.

Unexpectedly, Shahram now had a family of four to support. The inheritances we had received from our father would not cover the expenses of such an expensive city like Tehran.

The first few weeks of a new school and dealing with city kids were awkward. My dialect was funny to them, so I stopped talking. My appearance was different, so I was embarrassed. I felt like a stranger. The once cheerful and energetic child no longer existed. She had been transformed to a shy, quiet child, who prayed to God every night that her life would return to the way it used to be.

*   *   *

I was seven years old. My miserable life seemed to last forever until a not so intelligent and childish reaction of a teacher forced me out of my shell.

On that day, the teacher asked for a volunteer to read a section of the reading book for the class. As usual, being the one who loved to be center of attention, I raised my hand and volunteered to read. The moment after the first word loudly came out from my mouth, I became dumb. I looked around; outlandish eyes looked back at me. These were not the familiar faces that I had grown up with.

The teacher impatiently waited for me to continue reading. This young, beautiful, and stylish teacher wearing a short skirt and high-heeled shoes was not a bit like any teacher in Carvand. I panicked; the next word hardly made its way out of my mouth. Everyone waited for me; I forced myself to continue reading. The tone of shyness and nervousness was so obvious that the teacher stopped me. "That's enough!" she said harshly and asked another student to continue.

Since I had always been the teacher's pet at my old school, the harsh tone of this teacher crushed my ego. Suddenly, I totally forgot about my shyness and the panic of a few moments earlier. "Why can't I finish reading? I want to read," I said in the same harsh tone as the teacher's, which shocked her.

She looked sharply at me as she said, "You read quietly, nobody hears you."

"I can read louder," I challenged, which made her furious.

"Now I don't want you to read," the teacher said in an angry tone.

"I can read loudly, I don't see any reason not to let me continue reading," I stated.

Enraged over this response, she aggressively took my hand and pulled me along to the door and said. "I'll show you who needs to give you a reason, you cheeky girl." She kicked me out of the class and then threw my books as well.

I still admire my mother for never leaving matters, fair or unfair, unresolved when it came to her children. This time was no exception. She went to the school to hear the teacher's version of the story. The teacher would not let me go to her class unless I apologized for my behavior.

So stubborn as I was, I preferred not to go back to school and apologize since she had thrown me out of the class. My mother spoke to the teacher again and convinced her that I did not mean to be rude. She explained that since everything was new to me, I just did not know how to handle the situation.

The next day, my mother gave me a rose and asked me to give it to the teacher just because she was a teacher. Mamman assured me that it was a sign of respect for the teacher. I did not need to apologize.

I took the rose to school, but did not hand it to her. I simply put it on her desk before she got to the class. When she saw the flower, she did not need to ask who left it there. Amazingly, that incident brought me back to my old self, lively, talkative, and bold.

*   *   *

Over time, Shahram took full responsibility of our household. He soon became more like a father figure than an older brother to me. He made sure we had a good and prosperous life. As a successful engineer, his career progressed gradually as he moved up the path to more advance and higher ranking positions.

I was fourteen years old when Shahram married Tara—a petite, beautiful girl. Shortly after their marriage, Shahram's company sent the couple to the United State for a couple of years. Shahram would learn new skills and knowledge that would benefit his company.

After working as a typist for two years, with help from Shahram, Souri moved to England for higher education. She stayed with Shahrooz for a short period of time before marrying Hamid, whom she had met in college.

I was a teenager and Ramin was going school. My mother became involved in many different hobbies. Still a young, attractive woman, she was determined not to remarry even though she had some good opportunities to do so. She believed that our good, peaceful family life was precious. She was not about to let a stranger change it.

During the summers, my mother took me and Ramin to Isfahan to stay with our grandmother usually for the entire summer. Most of my cousins from my mother's side of the family lived in Isfahan, so Ramin and I were never bored during our long, summer visit. We also usually made short visits to relatives in Carvand while we were in Isfahan.

*   *   *

After nearly four years, Shahram and Tara returned to Iran with their two-year-old sweet, little girl, Neda. A year earlier, Souri and Hamid had returned from England. We all lived just blocks away from each other. After some trips to Iran, Shahrooz finally decided to return home.

The entire family was reunited once again. The baby of the family, Ramin, had launched into his teens.

I was in my last year of high school. For the most part, those years were the most pleasurable and harmonic period of my life.

Chapter 4

Lost Love

I graduated from high school in 1975 and was admitted to college the same year.

My early teenage years when I had crushes on young, handsome teachers or neighbors' boys were over. Now I was a beautiful and playful eighteen-year-old woman who attracted attention on the campus. I enjoyed being popular and fascinating the hearts of boys, but I was not attracted to them. From my viewpoint, they were just boys and too young for me. The man I was waiting for came into my life on a cold and beautiful white winter day during my second year of college.

On that day, my closest friend Sayeh and I had finished the last lecture session of the day. We joined a group of girls whom we often met with on campus. On that day, fresh snowflakes were falling to the ground, which already was covered by white snow. We playfully threw snow at each other. Laughing and covered by the clean and fresh snow, we ran one after the other to the cafeteria for our daily routine of having a cup of tea together before going home.

The cafeteria was warm and crowded. We sat around a long table while two of the girls got tea for all of us. During all of the chatting and laughing, I saw a new face in the middle of the crowd. He was tall and handsome with light brown hair that had softly touched his forehead and eyebrows. Leaning against the wall, he seemed to be deep in thought and paid no attention to the surroundings. He was different from the other boys on the campus and seemed more mature.

I wanted to catch his attention. As I joked around and giggled with the other girls, I kept an eye on him. Soon he noticed me and our eyes locked for a moment before I deliberately turned my face from him and back to the girls. Shortly afterward, I looked back to make sure that he was still watching me, but he was gone.

The next day, Sayeh and I went to the cafeteria later than usual. It was not as crowded as the day before, and we chose to sit at a table in a corner to study for an exam. Deep into studying, I heard a whisper in my ear from behind my neck, "This is a cafeteria not a library."

Startled, I turned my head. The stranger in the cafeteria from the prior day chuckled and politely asked, "Oh, I'm sorry. Did I scare you?"

"Yes, you sure did," I said with a smile.

"I didn't mean that. Sorry! To make it up to you, let me get you a cup of tea," he said, still chuckling.

"You don't need to. I survived," I said.

"But I have to have an excuse for sitting at your table," he said as he headed to the service order area.

Sayeh and I looked at each other and giggled quietly. "Who was he?" Sayeh asked.

"I don't know. He must be a new student," I answered.

"He's old to be new," she stated.

"But he's handsome. Isn't he?" I asked.

"Not bad. Don't talk much with him, okay? We have to study," she said, concerned about the upcoming test.

"Okay. You're always worried. We have the whole night to study," I reminded her.

We were still arguing about the studying time when he came back with a tray carrying three cups of tea. He put the tray on the table and sat on the chair at my side.

"Thank you," I said.

"Don't mention it," he said as held out his hand, "My name is Dariush."

He looked more handsome to me now. Sitting so close to him, I clearly saw his bright, light brown eyes and heard his sleepy and rather mystical low voice. His shabby appearance and even the way he spoke certainly made him very different from the other tidy, ordinary guys on the campus. He was different and I liked that.

Since Sayeh was worried about the next day's test and reminded me over and over again that we should go home to study, my first conversation with Dariush was short. However, I learned a lot in that short time. He had taken a break for a couple of years to solve some personal problems. Now, he was back to finish college and graduate at the end of the college year.

* * *

The next morning, when Sayeh and I arrived on campus, I found Dariush in front of the entrance waiting for me. It was a cold day, and he paced back and forth on the icy snow. He came toward us and complained as though he knew us forever. "It's not nice to make people wait in the cold and freeze."

I was pleased to see that he was waiting for me. Laughing, I said, "Nobody asked you to wait."

"Is this true? Then I must have dreamt it," he replied as he joined us to walk into the building.

"Yes, you must have dreamt it. We are freezing too, but we're not complaining," I said.

"Then let's go to get some hot tea," he suggested.

"Not now, we have an exam to take, but after that would be okay," I suggested.

"Okay, I'll be waiting in the cafeteria." he said.

*   *   *

That winter day I experienced the magnificent feeling of love for the first time. I was nineteen years old, full of emotions, and thirsty for the love I finally had found. From that day on, Dariush filled my life. Since my family, like most other Iranian families, had restrictions for their daughters' relations with boys, I had to keep my secret from my family.

Our relation was very pure and innocent. We really loved each other. Every opportunity we got, we went for a ride in his violet Ford. In a small alley with tall trees on both sides, we had found a spherical shaped house that was under construction. Because of the cold winter, it was abandoned. We often drove there and parked in front of that house, which we called "Our House." We talked and dreamed about a life together in that beautiful spherical house.

At the beginning of our relationship, Dariush told me about his past. He had been married for three years before getting divorced two years earlier. He said that he was just twenty-three years old when he got married. Now he was twenty-eight years old, divorced, and the father of a four-year-old daughter. He had gone through a long period of struggle, sadness, and depression. However, all that tragedy was behind him now, we were happy together.

His marital background did not bother me; I still was madly in love with him. But I was aware of the difficulty I would face with my family. I knew that they would not let me marry a divorced man with a child. However, I pushed the negative thinking and the problem aside. What I needed was just to be with him.

Months passed; Dariush wanted me to bring up our relationship to my family. I was not sure whether it was good idea or the right timing. I was scared at how they would react when they learned of his previous marriage. However, I had no choice. Sooner or later, I had to tell them the truth.

So I made up my mind to take a chance and tell Shahram. Once I was alone with him, I just started talking, "His name is Dariush. He's twenty-eight. And this is his last year of college."

"Aha!" Shahram said very calmly as he looked into my eyes and waited for the rest.

"We've been dating for about three months now," I continued.

"And?" he said, waiting for me to say more.

I paused for a moment. So far it was safe, but I was not sure how to continue. I had a feeling that Shahram, somehow, suspected that there had to be more.

Shahram had a calm and peaceful personality. I had never seen him angry or mean. He was nice to everyone. Was it possible that I would see his anger this time? I did not want him to be disappointed in me. However, I knew in my heart that I was going to upset him by telling him the rest of the story.

With kind eyes, he looked at me and waited.

"He's a very nice guy and comes from a good family. He wants our families to meet and get to know each other," I said.

"Okay, but it's too soon now. Let us get to know him before meeting his family. First of all, tell me why he has not graduated yet? You said he is twenty-eight."

"He had a break for three years, now he's back to finish school," I answered. My trembling voice was strange to my own ears.

"Why did he take a break?" Shahram wanted to know.

"He was going through a divorce." There, I finally said it. Without a break, I told him the whole history of Dariush and desperately tried to simplify his life situation. "His daughter lives with her mother. He has no problem with them. *Shahram jan*—dear Shahram—you don't know how nice he is. I wish you would see him."

As I talked nonstop, Shahram listened in silence. He rubbed his forehead as he used to do while thinking. It was difficult to read his thoughts. Finally I stopped talking and waited for him to say something. I did not have to wait long since he had already made his mind.

"My dear, he is not suitable for you," Shahram said softly.

"Why not?" I asked.

"I thought you were smarter than this. Do you know what it means to have a child and be divorced?"

"But it's been a while now, and his child does not live with him," I countered.

Shahram replied, "It doesn't matter. You deserve a good life. Just forget about him."

"But he is very good man, if you would just meet him!" I pleaded.

"I'm sure he's a good man, I didn't say he isn't, but he's not suitable for you," Shahram repeated.

"He is. I promise if you meet him and talk to him, you'll change your mind," I said.

"Are you listening to me or not? No more discussion! You are too young and naive. Do you know why he divorced his wife? Have you ever asked him or his wife why they divorced?" Shahram was getting edgy as he tried to get into my head.

"I don't need to ask his wife. He already told me why. They both were very young and different. They argued all the time. Nothing more," I responded.

"This is his version. It doesn't matter anyway. I repeat, he is not suitable for you and that's it. Forget about him," he finally demanded firmly.

"But please, just meet him once. Talk to him to see if you still think he's not good for me," I begged.

"It's not necessary. It will not change his situation whether I see him or not. He can be the nicest man. But it is his life situation, not him as a person that bothers me. No more discussion about this. Tomorrow, you will tell him that whatever has been between you is over. That's it!" Shahram was getting frustrated, and I was on the edge of crying.

"Please give him a chance," I begged again.

"Tomorrow you do what I just said," he demanded. Trying not to get angry, he left the room.

Shahram was kind and flexible, but he would remain rigid in his stance once he made up his mind. Knowing that, I decided to put him in an unavoidable situation to meet Dariush.

*   *   *

The next morning, I met Dariush in the cafeteria. Sitting in a less-crowded corner, I told him the conversation of the night before.

"It is not fair. I made a mistake in the past and your brother wants to punish me for that?" he said.

"He is not punishing you. He is just worried about my future," I said.

"I know, but I love you. Just because of a childish decision I made when I was too young, isn't it my right to be happy again?" he asked.

"I don't know what to say. My brother thinks that I am too young and too naive," I said.

"You are not naive, and I am not a monster. Now what do you think? Do you want to listen to your brother?" he asked.

"You know I don't have any choice. He is like a father to me. I love you. But if he does not approve of you, no one in my family will," I told him.

"Then you mean that … that's it? We just give up? Is this what you want?" he asked.

"You know it's not what I want. I have not given up yet. He has not met you. If he meets you and talks to you, I'm sure he'll soften." Having believed what I said, I suggested, "Today, when you drive me home, I will invite you in. Then I will ask Shahram to come and talk to you."

*   *   *

That evening, Dariush drove me home as usual. But this time, he parked the car close to Shahram's house and waited in the car while I went into the house.

I was so nervous and could hardly breathe. I paused at the door to take some deep breaths to calm down before ringing the doorbell. Shahram opened the door.

"Hello," I greeted.

"Hello, dear. How are you? Come in," Shahram said.

"Shahram jan, Dariush is here to meet you. Will you please let him to come in? Please just for a few minutes," I begged in a wobbly voice.

"What? Why is he here?"

"I asked him to come. Can I ask him to come in?" I asked desperately.

"No, you can't. I don't have anything to say to him. We talked about it last night. Go back and send him home." He tried to be calm, but the color of his face had turned red.

"Shahram jan, okay. Would you just come down and talk to him at the street for a moment. I just want you to meet him," I said.

Frustrated, Shahram said, "I don't want to see him. Don't you understand? It does not matter for me how he looks or how well he speaks. Go and send him home."

Our heated discussion brought Tara to come to the door. "What's happened? What are you two arguing about?"

"I just want Shahram to see my boyfriend. He's waiting outside," I answered while Shahram left us and went to the kitchen.

"Your boyfriend? Who's your boyfriend?" Tara asked.

"Shahram knows about him. But he does not want to see him. Please, Tara jan, ask him to let Dariush in just for a few minutes to talk to him."

"Why doesn't Shahram want to see him?" Tara asked.

"He thinks he's not suitable for me. Will you come down and see him?" I tried desperately to find a way to ease the situation.

"Wait, I'll go see what I can do," she said and went into the kitchen to talk to Shahram.

I heard Shahram's irritated voice from the kitchen. "No, I won't. I told her I won't. That's it. She has to end this and I already told her …."

Tara's efforts did not work. However my desperation made her to agree to come outside. "Okay, let's go see him," she said and put her jacket on and followed me.

Dariush got out of the car as soon as he saw us coming. He shook hands with Tara and introduced himself. After the greetings and introductions, there was silence. It was a very tight circumstance.

It was a breezy, cool evening, and we just stood outside in the cold. I was not able to find anything for us to talk about to ease the atmosphere. I felt a pain in my heart. The whole situation was painful and crazy.

"It was nice meeting you. I don't want to keep you out in the cold," said Tara while she reached out to shake hands with Dariush.

I asked Dariush to wait for me and then followed Tara into the house. "What do you think about him?" I asked her

"He is handsome, but I don't know anything about him," she responded.

"Will you please ask Shahram one more time? Please!" I begged even though I was not optimistic about the outcome.

"He won't, Niki. I'm sure he has a good reason. Don't be so stubborn. Let him go now. I'll talk to Shahram later," she advised me. But childishly, I insisted she should try one more time. Finally, she agreed to do so.

Shahram sat at the kitchen table and seemed very uptight. He was annoyed when Tara asked him to give Dariush a chance. "You don't know that he is divorced with a child," he informed Tara. His demeanor was still calm, but he was irritated.

Tara cast a disappointed look at me as she said to Shahram, "Oh, she didn't tell me that."

By then, I knew that I would have no one on my side. I went back to Dariush, who had waited in the car. I sat beside him for a while in silence. It felt as though an expected dark cloud would storm into our love at any moment, and there wasn't any shelter to protect it. At least, we'd be safe in the car for a short time.

*   *   *

That stupid idea of mine worsened our situation. Shahram demanded that no more attempts were to be made to keep that relationship alive.

The next morning, I met Dariush. We sat at the same table in the cafeteria that we had sat at the prior morning, but now I had no inspiring ideas. "I'm sorry about last night," I said.

"We both tried, but it didn't work," he said sadly with a snide tone in his voice.

"No. Not only that but it made things worse," I said.

"We are where we were before," he added.

"My brother made it clear that there would be no future for us," I said.

"It's what he thinks!" he said.

"Yes, but what he thinks is what my family thinks. I think it would be better that we end seeing each other. It is painful for me, but ..."

He interrupted me and asked, "What are you telling me? Why? Just because your brother has the final word?"

"I'm sorry. You know it's not what I want ...."

He interrupted me again, "If it is not what you want? Then, why? We still can get married and have everything we talked about."

"You know I can't do that. I love you, but I don't want to lose my family." I struggled to make him understand.

We talked for hours about the hopeless situation. Finally, he accepted my decision and said, "I don't agree with you. I think it is unfair that others should decide for us. But if it is what you want, then I have no choice but to accept it."

We broke up and tried to avoid each other. Shahram would come to college every day to pick me up after my classes to make sure that our relationship was totally over.

And we did make a great effort to stay away from each other for a while. It was a real challenge to see each other every day in college and try to keep our distance. But we were not able to keep up with the torment for long. Before we knew, we ended up together again.

The end of the college term was nearing. Dariush would graduate and I would finish my second year. We still saw each other secretly and had a passionate romantic relationship.

*   *   *

One day, I was home alone. My mother was at Souri's. I thought it was a good time to call Dariush, and we talked for a long while. In the middle of our phone conversation, we heard noises in the phone. That was not unusual as telephone line interference occurred at that time in Tehran. Both of us ignored the noises and kept on talking.

As soon as we ended our phone conversation and I hung up, the telephone rang. "Come here right now!" the angry voice of Souri ordered me.

It was not hard to guess that the reason she was angry had something to do with me and Dariush. I walked a couple of blocks to her house and found my mother and Souri extremely mad. As my mother cried, Souri shouted and yelled at me. "You are not ashamed of yourself, are you? You are just an egotistical, self-centered girl. You never think about others! Do you know what you are doing?"

I let her release her anger at me before protesting, "What are you talking about? Why are you shouting? Have I done any crime?" I asked.

"Don't play innocent with us please! We know everything," Souri scoffed.

"Know what?" I was pretty sure what she was talking about, but I pretended to be surprised.

"You still are seeing that guy. We heard you two talking on the phone," she finally said as she imitated my voice and my expression.

By then, I realized that while Dariush and I were talking on the phone, her telephone line had interfered with ours. That was really a rare, shocking coincidence. While my mother cried and asked me to end this relationship before Shahram would learn of it, she suddenly passed out. Panicked at seeing her in that condition, I burst into tears and said, "*Mamman jan*, please, wake up. I'm sorry. I promise you, I will do whatever you say. Just wake up."

Souri ran to the kitchen and brought some water and sprinkled it on our mother's face. When she opened her eyes, I embraced her and repeated my promise again.

In a very weak voice she asked me swear to Quran that I would keep my promise. I was so emotional and scared that something might happen to her, I did what she asked of me. Then she smiled and hugged me back.

Souri did not seem convinced. "Now we'll see how long this promise will stand," she stated doubtfully.

The next morning, without the slightest hope of changing the situation into our favor, I told Dariush about the bizarre incident of the night before and added, "That's it! I think it is the end of the story. There is no way. I've promised my mamman, and I can't see her like last night again. I just can't hurt them."

"They are hurting both of us! They don't act rationally. It's your life. You should decide, not them," he argued, sounding very distressed.

"I know, but I can't. You know that. I can't marry you without my family's approval. Not in this society anyway. Let's be realistic about it and choose the easiest way," I said while I felt the warmth of my tears run down my cheeks.

"The easiest way for me is to get married right now," he said as he looked into my eyes. His eyes were full of tears too. That was a very sad day for both of us. After spending the morning in the cafeteria discussing the situation, we chose the easiest way, which meant breaking up.

Fortunately, it was Dariush's last term, and he graduated shortly after we broke up. On the day of his graduation, he repeated his proposal for the last time. It was torturous for me to say no to him when I wanted so badly to say yes. On the edge of saying yes, I overpowered my desires and feelings.

"I still think you are wrong, and this isn't the easiest way—at least not for me. But it's your decision," he said as we stood on a stairway in the middle of a large throng of happy graduates.

"I'm sorry, Dariush jan," I replied while trying to hold back my tears.

"I love you, Niki," he stared at my eyes for a long moment and said, "Good-bye." Then he walked away.

That day was the last time I saw him. I lost him in the crowd and forever. It was months before I stopped crying at night over losing him.

Chapter 5

Social Unrest

The year 1978 was my final year of college. It was also a year of significant disorder and social restlessness that indicated drastic political changes would come about in the near future. The first spark of the revolution's flame ignited from the universities. Gradually, the heated and intense atmosphere spread across the country.

On my campus, I witnessed some of those unusual events, which started to occur when Islamic activists replaced the existing workers in the library and cafeteria. Prior to that time, there had been isolated incidents and unsuccessful demonstrations on the campus. Those gatherings and protests were stifled before they had any chance to spread. Moreover, the protesters were usually student activists and certainly much different from the Islamic activists.

Among the new workers, some were noticeably Islamic eccentric characters, who caught attention on the campus as well as other places. Some were bearded young men and veiled young women. Their appearance stated a strong religious belief that was quite unusual on the campus.

The workers behind these new faces tried to control the behavior of the students step by step. A few times, they approached me and my friends in the cafeteria as we were laughing, chatting, and having fun. They asked us not to laugh loudly. The reason for this request was based in their belief that the sound of women's laughter could have a stimulant impact on men that the extremists considered a sin.

In order to make the point that we were not going to listen to those nonsense, we did continue chatting and laughing louder than before.

There were also some acts of violence by a group of unknown Islamic young men and women. Most of these acts occurred in the library or cafeteria. The aggression led to injuries for some girls and increased the tension on the campus.

On one occasion, when we were in the crowded cafeteria, we suddenly heard a crashing sound that was followed by darkness. While all the lights were off, we heard shouting and the sounds of items being broken in the uproar. Everyone rushed to get out of the place.

Not knowing what had just happened, Sayeh and I held hands and tried to push ourselves through to the exit. The desperate and frightened crowd dragged us along. We had to cross the narrow, long hallway to get to the stairs, which would lead us to the ground level of the campus.

Once we were out of the madness and darkness, we saw the campus police attempt to pass the mass to get inside the building. The uproar lasted until the police got everyone, including some injured girls, out of the cafeteria. The ambulance carried the injured, some of whom were badly beaten, to the hospital. Interestingly, we noticed that the girls who were harassed and beaten harshly were those who used to wear provocative clothes and makeup.

*   *   *

The signs of a future revolt gradually became apparent inside the universities—although it was not so broadly visible in the society. The reality became more noticeable in our college when the small praying rooms of the college gradually began to be filled up. The praying rooms were two small, separate, closed spaces in the campus for students who practiced namaaz, the daily praying ritual.

A few students used these small rooms for praying on a regular basis. However, very soon, the new cafeteria staff workers occupied these rooms at noon for namaaz. Increasingly, other students and some unfamiliar faces joined the prayers. Within a couple of months, these small rooms became overcrowded. The long line of prayers extended out across the hallways.

In addition to my classes and studying, I had a part-time job in the campus administrative office. Oddly, even the office staff had no idea who those prayers were and where they had come from.

Initially, a prayer would be read quietly as it was intended to be read. However, as soon as the line of prayers filled up the hallways and stretched up the stairways, they began praying louder and louder.

From my observation of the situation, no fortune teller was needed to foretell that a revolt was on the way soon. The same kind of gatherings and protests surely took place in many other universities and public places. However, as odd as it may sound, the government-controlled media hardly reported any of these events.

*   *   *

I graduated from college in the summer of 1978. Shortly after, I began working as an account auditor for the financial company IRA. At that time, two years of military service was mandatory for men and working women. Employers were not allowed to hire anyone who had not completed the military service. I had not done my military service, so I was employed as a freelancer.

On my first day of work, six young auditors, including me, and one older supervisor were sent to a client for a financial audit.

The client, Mr. Mohseni, was the new director of the financial department of one of the largest newspaper firms in the country.

About to make major reforms to the firm's financial system, Mr.Mohseni needed to have the books audited before starting the process.

We, the auditors, worked on the books for more than three months. We made little progress because the financial accounts of such a large company were too complicated for inexperienced auditors to handle. Thus four of the young auditors, including myself, were fired and replaced by more experienced auditors.

During these months working in the firm, I realized that I would like to work there as an employee and build my future career. My personality fit well with the dynamic and lively environment. So, I made the decision to apply for any open position the company might have available. Having decided that, a couple of days after being fired from IRA, I made an appointment with Mr. Mohseni.

A short, young man in his early thirties, Mr. Mohseni was soft spoken but vigorous. I nearly had to run to keep up with his quick pace. However, he had no idea why I had made an appointment with him. I explained that I was interested in getting a job in his department. Luckily, he told me that my timing was perfect. He was about to make some changes in the accounting system of the firm. In order to accomplish his plans, he needed to expand his staff by hiring new employees.

However, Mr. Mohseni had to hire me as freelancer as well due to incompletion of the required military service.

*   *   *

On the day I started my new job in the newspaper firm, I was so excited it was like flying to the moon. It was a beautiful Saturday (the beginning of the week in Iran) in the autumn, which is my favorite season. Exactly one week earlier, I had been fired from IRA. That day had been a depressing, sad day for me, not only because I lost my first job after such a short period of time, but mostly because I would not go to the newspaper firm any longer.

The accounting department where I was to start working was located on the seventh floor. Desks were set next to each other with a narrow distance in between them; there were no cubicles. The department had more than thirty employees. Mr. Bahrami, who was one of the owners of the firm, worked in an office on the same floor as well.

A very gentle and kindhearted man, he always had a nice smile on his face. He was very well liked, by all employees of the firm.

On my first day at work, and to my surprise, no work station had been arranged for me. Mr. Mohseni welcomed me and guided me to his office where he explained the current situation in the department. Apparently, most of employees of the financial department were so-called old timers. They were comfortable with the old financial system and their routine tasks at work. They would resist any attempt at changes that might jeopardize their routine and their job security.

However, confident that a young, energetic team would help him implement the new system, Mr. Mohseni intended to hire more people to build up the team. He had no intention of laying off any of the older employees.

With that explanation of the current situation, Mr. Mohseni set up a desk and a chair for me in his office. At least I had somewhere to work temporarily. Later, I was relocated to a small office that was attached to Mr. Mohseni's office. My tasks were not clear and I had little to do. Mr. Mohseni asked me to be patient; we would have many hectic months ahead of us.

Susan, who later in time became a good friend, was hired as Mr. Mohseni's secretary. A sweet, young, petite girl, she was hyper and talkative. We shared the office for a while. But since Mr. Mohseni was going to hire four more people, we definitely needed more space. For that reason, a larger office was created by consolidating two small offices and one storage room.

The preparations to hire four young men took nearly two months. During this time, the auditors continued to analyze the financial reports and audit the accounts.

Finally, the new team was in place and ready to start its task. We were instructed and trained by Mr. Mohseni; our tasks and positions were set. In order to make progress in the project, we needed the cooperation of the old-timers to share their information and knowledge with us.

However, from the viewpoint of the other employees of the department, we, the usurpers, were rivals and should be ignored. Mr. Mohseni needed their cooperation in order to achieve his goals. To encourage them to accept us as part of the staff, Mr. Mohseni acted as cautiously and gently as possible. That was the reason he selected me to make the transition smooth and clear the entrance for the others.

I was positive, easygoing, happy, and friendly. The fact that I was a pretty, young woman might have been one of the many reasons Mr. Mohseni selected me to be sent out from the isolated office space to join the other employees on the floor.

My desk and all the files that I had been working on were moved to the main hall in the middle of all the other desks. Although everyone, especially the older employees, resented the ongoing changes and some regarded me as part of the trouble, they soon accepted me.

Over a short period of time, the other four teammates joined me on the floor. Gradually, the old work method was converted to a modern and computerized one. Fortunately, as Mr. Mohseni had promised, no one was laid off—but some had little to do. I was devoted to my job, my company, and my coworkers. Over time, the new and old employees acted as a large, friendly, supportive team. Looking back, I have to admit that the most enjoyable period of my working life was in that firm.

*   *   *

In 1978, the country was on the cusp of a major revolt against the so-called political dictatorship of the Pahlavi monarchy. Demonstrations and marches occurred on the streets; strikes at various companies became more widespread and intensive.

A strike in the power company brought darkness to the whole city at nights. Shortages of daily essential items caused by the strikes led to long lines in front of every bakery, supermarket, etc. People patiently waited in lines to obtain fuel for the heater to warm their houses. They spent hours standing outside in the freezing temperatures with no complaints.

Automobiles lined up for kilometers in the streets, waiting for gasoline. Astonishingly, no one complained or criticized the circumstances. People had become nicer and friendlier to each other. Everyone struggled and sacrificed for the same cause. The atmosphere of the city was amazingly emotional. The experience of solidarity made the people feel safe in the middle of hazardous rallies. People were united to achieve their common goals—independence, democracy and freedom.

The newspaper firm, like other media centers, was a gathering place for public protesters, who expected their voices would be conveyed to the rest of country through the media. But, due to the strict governmental censorship, no news regarding those demonstrations and rallies were published by any media. So the people, hungry for news, turned to the foreign media and radio stations, which broadcast in the Farsi language. Newsletters and flyers that secretly circulated around the country were the other sources of obtaining news.

*   *   *

In the throes of the revolution, daily life was unpredictable. Every morning, one would wake up to face new challenges. One advantage of working in the newspaper firm was that it was the best place to get news about the rallies. I was in the middle of current events and the news, much of which would never be published due to censorship.

Street demonstrations increased widely day by day and soon spread throughout the entire country. The political parties, which until then operated secretively, began to resurface and joined the revolution. Various groups of people, such as religious minorities, members of the labor unions, and even governmental authorities, united and came out to the streets to announce their support for the revolution and demanded democracy.

During this period of time, Ayatollah Khomeini, who had been forced into exile in Turkey and then Iraq approximately fifteen years earlier, was deported from Iraq by the request of Saddam Hussein. After being refused entry into some countries in the region, Khomeini finally was accepted by France. From the city of Neauple le Chateau, he was free to convey his messages to the Iranian people and, by default, was nominated as the revolution's leader. Soon he was known amongst Iranian politicians and refugees and around the world. Journalists from across the world interviewed him and broadcasted his words in Farsi through foreign radio stations. Gradually, the slogan Islamic Republic of Iran replaced the initial one that called for freedom and democracy.

During this time, foreign radio stations such as Voice of America, BBC, and Voice of Israel, which people used to listen due to lack of other sources of uncensored news, spoke positively about Ayatollah Rohollah Khomeini. They began broadcasting his speeches and his bulletins. They created a hero of Khomeini for young people in particular, like me, who had no knowledge about him due to the political restrictions throughout the shah's era.

However, media censorship was still in effect; no media was able to publish the entire cycle of events. We, the staff and workers of the firm, were time by time called to a large assembly room during working hours to listen to revolutionary speeches.

When the Iranian Nation Oil Company and also the business owners (known as the bazaar), who were said to be the heart of the country's economy, went on strike, it was obvious that the shah's regime would not be able to ignore this serious situation of the country.

The media finally joined the strike as well. People were so determined to go on that they were willing to sacrifice whatever was needed—financially or their lives—for the cause. During the period of the strikes in private and public sectors, employees were paid by donations from people. This included my salary when our firm joined the general strike.

During the winter of 1979, due to the department of electrical company's strike, we experienced a primitive way of living. Most of the people used a kursi[7] to keep themselves warm. The lantern was needed to lighten the rooms at night and also the primus[8] to cook.

Iranian radio and TV had stopped their regular programs. No one would talk politics or exchange news by phone because the government controlled the lines.

At night, like most of the people, we sat around the kursi and discussed politics. During the day, Shahrooz and Ramin followed me and Tara to participate in the rallies. The number of demonstrators increased every day. Pushing aside their different ideologies and beliefs, Muslims, Christians, Jews, and others marched shoulder to shoulder demanding freedom.

The shah's endeavors to cool the heated atmosphere of the society down by making changes to the governments and appointing new prime ministers had no effect on the protesters. The ultimate attempt of the desperate shah to stave off the revolution was his appointment of Shahpour Bakhtiar as his prime minister. (Appendix D)

---

7   **Kursi**, a square table covered with quilts and blankets with a brazier under to keep it warm.

8   **Primus**, small portable oil cooker.

Unfortunately, this act was too late. The uproar was beyond control. The people had already lost the trust to any of the shah's promises and his appointees. Moreover, Ayatollah Khomeini, by then, had taken command of the revolution as leader.

Bakhtiar had spent many years in jail during the Pahlavi regime for opposing the shah. Despite his enmity to the shah, he accepted the position in order to save the country.

Newly appointed Prime Minister Bakhtiar immediately began reforms.

Ayatollah Khomeini had already demanded overthrowing the shah; and sadly enough, the people believed in Ayatollah's promises to bring them democracy and a blooming future.

Ayatollah had promised that he would lead the revolution up to the victory and then he would reside in the holy city "Qum," and have nothing to do with politics.

Simply, he lied and fooled not only the regular people but even the experienced politicians, whom people trusted.

The mottos "Shah must leave," "Down with the Shah," "Viva Khomeini," and "Islamic Republic of Iran" were added to the slogans of the demonstrators.

The demonstrators demanded Ayatollah's return to Iran.

In order to seize people's trust and respect their wishes, Bakhtiar allowed Ayatollah Khomeini to return to Iran after fifteen years of exile. However, Khomeini refused to return while the shah was in Iran. He demanded the shah's departure prior to his own arrival. The shah was forced to leave the country on January 16, 1979.

The day the shah left the country, I rushed to the street. There were no military or police in the streets. It looked as though the streets had been left free to the people to relieve their hearts and express themselves freely. The sounds of blowing horns of the automobiles and the cheering of the people mixed in the air. Posters of the shah and his family were set on fire. Some people even set their bank notes with the picture of the shah on fire.

The shout of joy, and call for the death of the shah, could not encourage me to join them and express happiness because I was not happy. I experienced emptiness and an unfamiliar wretchedness in my heart. I stood among the cheering crowd. Confusion and uncertainty brought me a mixed feeling.

Although I had followed the masses in most of the marches and had repeated the slogans, I did not believe in them. I had done that only because of the unity. Most of the people had done so for the same reason. Christians, Jews, Communists, Democrats, and others had not participated in the riot for Islam. They, as well, had repeated the same slogans over and over for the same reason—unity.

The days at work, we watched through the windows to witness the ongoing revolution. Groups of revolutionists carried corpses covered with blood on their shoulders, and shouted, "Allah-O-Akbar." The sounds of guns firing were followed moments later by scenes of people carrying bloody corpses.

Khomeini's speeches, bulletins, and declarations had significant impact on the military to join the revolution. The large number of lower-ranking officers of Homafaran (the Iranian Air Force) and some army officers and soldiers of the Imperial Army were among the first military branches to announce their allegiance to the revolution.

Once, I followed a group of demonstrators to a military garrison. When we arrived, a large number of people had already surrounded the area. Some offered flowers to the soldiers. Slogans such as "Soldier, my brother, why kill me, join me" and "God is Great" filled the air. Some of the soldiers took the flowers and put them in the tips of the barrel on their guns; others furiously aimed their guns toward anyone who approached them.

$$* \quad * \quad *$$

The shah's departure was not enough to satisfy the majority of the people. The uproar increased. Khomeini declared Prime Minster Bakhtiar a traitor and his government illegal. At the same time, people marched on the streets across the whole country demanding the return of the ayatollah to Iran.

Meanwhile, Prime Minister Bakhtiar pursued reforms actively. He freed all the political prisoners, lifted censorships off media, and dissolved *Savak*, the Secret Police of Iran. He brought the gift of freedom for the first time ever to the people of Iran.

By encountering the people on the streets of Tehran, I could feel the freshness and joy of the free life. This was a spectacular scene to view. At the newspaper stands, people lined up for hours as they waited for the daily uncensored papers to arrive. The throng of people thirsty for real news was incredible. The newspapers were just barely sufficient in quantity to meet such a huge demand. Those who were fortunate to buy a newspaper shared it on the sidewalks with many others.

Bakhtiar moved the country toward the direction of freedom and democracy as was the goal of the original uprising. Obviously, it was not what Khomeini and his Islamic extremists were after to gain.

Bakhtiar pleaded with the nation to give him more time to hold an election to determine the fate of the future form of the government. But no matter how sincere he was and how effective the remedy would be for the ailing country, it was too late. The revolution had already been hijacked by extremists. There was no way to save the country.

Finally, Prime Minister Bakhtiar was forced by the people's demand to let Ayatollah Khomeini return to Iran on February 1, 1979, two weeks after the departure of the shah. While on the airplane with Khomeini, ABC reporter Peter Jennings asked the ayatollah about his feelings of returning to his homeland after so many years in exile. Khomeini smiled and calmly replied, *"Hichi"* (nothing). That response disappointed most of the people and some of his followers. Some doubted his loyalty to the country. The issue was the topic of discussion for a long while.

Still, Khomeini was welcomed by millions. He was escorted to the *Beheshte Zahra* cemetery in Tehran where the body of some opponents and activists, killed by the shah's regime, were buried. There, Khomeini made his famous speech and uttered that the shah had destroyed the cities and flourished the cemeteries. Ironically, soon after the establishment of Islamic regime in Iran, this cemetery overflowed with graves of the protesters and opponents killed by the Islamic Republic regime and later on with the soldiers killed in the Iran-Iraq war.

Khomeini was openly belligerent toward the current government of Prime Minister Bakhtiar, so as soon as he entered the country he declared the Bakhtiatiar government was illegal and that he, himself, would appoint his own government.

*   *   *

Khomeini resided in a school in a slum area of Tehran. The religious dignitaries, political leaders, and other groups visited him daily. Most of the companies and businesses sent representatives to meet Khomeini to announce their loyalty and unity with the revolution.

The return of Ayatollah Khomeini made an uneasy situation worse. Not just in Tehran, but all over the country the revolt had turned to a real revolution. Khomeini freely encouraged the people to overthrow the Pahlavi monarchy. At most of the cross streets in Tehran, posters of Pahlavi were set on fire. Groups of revolutionary arms and activists stopped the cars and preventing them from passing through unless the occupants shouted, "Down with the Shah." Clashes between revolutionists and military became nasty.

By announcing the government of Bakhtiar "an illegal government," Khomeini appointed Mehdi Bazargan, long-time pro-democracy activist as prime minister of the Interim Government of the Revolution parallel with Bakhtiar's government.

By this time, revolutionary guards (Pasdaran) had been formed and fought side by side with other armed revolutionists on the streets.

Prime Minister Bakhtiar declared martial law in Tehran on February 10. Khomeini immediately countered that everyone should break the martial law and stay on the streets.

The next day, the military announced its neutrality to the political events. Street fights intensified.

The last bloody fight between revolutionists and the royal army took place on February 12, 1979. Many people from both sides were killed. This also was the date the Pahlavi Dynasty collapsed, putting an end to monarchy in Iran after more than two thousand five hundred years.

Since Khomeini made the decision to bring down everything related to the shah, he discarded the reforms of Bakhtiar. Very soon, Prime Minister Shahpour Bakhtiar lost control over the country. His government had lasted only thirty-seven days.

* * *

A referendum was held in March 1979. The Islamic Republic was the only alternative for replacing the monarchy. The voters had to vote "Yes" or "No" to the establishment of an Islamic Republic. Approximately 98 percent of the votes were yes. My vote was no.

In a matter of months, after the establishment of the new regime, the prosperous future promised by Khomeini, showed its ugly face to the betrayed people. The clerics took over the country and a religious dictatorship was established.

* * *

The period between the victory of the revolution and the establishment of the Islamic Republic was less than two months. During that period, the hot revolutionary atmosphere of the country was still alive. Political debates and numerous meetings and speeches were held all over the country. People were enthusiastic and actively involved in the fate of the country.

During those days, each day began with new rumors. One of the rumors was that the shah's loyalists had contaminated the city's drinking water reservoirs. A brave TV anchor man drank a glass of tap water on camera to test if it was really contaminated. He asked the viewers to wait for the effect on his body before drinking the city's water.

Most of the people were optimistic about the future while others doubted it. The appearance of the clerics on the TV screens, shortly after the victory, was an unquestionable sign of their future authority.

Despite what was happening, life returned to normal. On the first day back to work, everyone happily congratulated each other on the victory of the revolution. After exchanging experiences from those historical days, an ordinary working day started once again.

I heard the familiar echo of Saeid Khan's (Mr. Saeid's) cart from the distance. A pleasant, polite, middle-aged man, Saeid Khan served employees hot tea and sandwiches four times a day. The sounds of rattling tea cups were pleasant to my ears and a sign of normality. However, as the days passed, it became more and more obvious that life would never be normal again.

Mehdi Bazargan, the prime minister of the revolutionary interim government, had already failed to control the country and the Islamic extremists. Ayatollah Khomeini had the ultimate power over the government; his word was above the law. He would appoint his own men and make policies and decisions without consulting Prime Minister Bazargan.

Khomeini's primary agenda was to increase the pressure on women and gradually abolish their rights. He announced that, per Islamic law, women could not be appointed as judges. All women working as judges had to step down and take an office job. He also declared that per Islamic law, husbands have the exclusive right to divorce. And finally, he announced that women had to wear hijab.

He deceived and misled the entire nation, particularly the women who had sacrificed and never left the front during the hardest period of the revolution. Now women who were pushed toward a society that would be ruled by zealots fired back at Khomeini's statements. Women quickly held massive demonstrations against those statements. One of those rallies was held on March 8, 1979, International Women's Day. The demonstrators marched to different government buildings. Some went to the office of the Prime Minister Bazargan to deliver a written manifest, while others headed to the Ministry of Justice for a sit-in strike.

I was at work when Tara called me about the sit-in strikes at the Ministry of Justice. I told her that I would be there soon.

I arrived late; everyone had already entered the building. The streets around the building were blocked and surrounded heavily by security guards and police. I tried to pass them and get into the building, but they would not let me through.

While I tried to find another way to get into the building, a group of mace bearers shouting "ya rosary, ya tosari," meaning either hijab or thump on the head, approached me. Terrified to death, I looked for a way to escape them. But another group of mace bearers approached from the opposite side. As these thugs moved closer, I suddenly felt a hand around my waist lift me up and drag me. The hand belonged to a policeman who hid me between himself and another policeman.

I stayed with those policemen, trying to hide myself from the groups of mace bearers until they passed by. My rescuer asked me to leave. "Go home. If they find you, they will kill you. We can't deal with them, how can a tiny girl like you handle them?"

I was exasperated by those thugs. They were my countrymen, and I never knew that they existed. I was frustrated over not joining the protesters, so I decided to go back to work. I walked toward the main street to hail a taxi. A few hundred meters away from the policemen, I turned into another blocked street. Suddenly, I heard loud and boisterous noises, shouting the same slogan about hijab. The voices were getting closer to me; I had no way to escape. Scared and confused, I ran around, seeking a safe place to hide. I heard someone calling me. I looked back and saw an old man inside a parked bus, leaning on the door and telling me to get into the bus. I ran into his bus and hid behind a seat. The old driver asked in an angry tone, "What are you doing here? Are you crazy or do you want to get yourself killed?"

I told him that I was late for the strike and was trying to get away from there.

I ducked down behind the seat until the men passed the bus shouting crossly.

When they were gone, the old man told me it was safe to come up from behind the seat. Then he told me to run. I thanked him and got out.

Running, I finally made it to the main street, which was heavily jammed with traffic. I was a mess and breathing heavily. No empty taxis were available. I heard the sound of a car horn. I looked to that direction and saw a young man in a nice car point at me to get into the car. I made a quick assessment that he seemed to be a decent man.

As I approached his car, he opened the passenger side door and said politely, "Please get in. It is not safe for you here. I'll get you away from here."

Without any hesitation, I got into the car. None of the cars were moving. A few moments later, he turned to me with a smile and said, "What's the matter with you women? Just wear the hijab. It's just a rosary—a piece of fabric. This much boisterous noise is not worth it ...."

I could not listen to anything more he had to say. With resentment and anger, I opened the car's door. While getting out, I shouted at him, "I misjudged you. Your appearance fooled me. I thought you were a decent, intelligent man. If all decent, intelligent men of this country think like you, I feel pity for all of us."

Since the company was not far from there, I decided to walk to ease my anger. I had not gone far when a group of women covered in black chador encircled me and cursed, using swear words I had never heard before. They shoved me around and called me a whore. I struggled to fight back, but they were much stronger than me. Finally, I succeeded in breaking away from them and ran as fast as I could until I was breathless.

I finally arrived at the firm. It was around six o'clock in the evening; the building was nearly empty. I rode the elevator to the seventh floor. The only person on the floor was a middle-aged muscular security guard. I sat at my desk. I was worn out and distressed about everything that had happened, particularly the fight with the nasty women. Uncontrolled tears fell down on my cheeks.

Then I broke down and cried heavily. The shocked security guard tried to comfort me. He offered me a cup of tea and a glass of water. I told him about the various incidents and the women. He shook his head and in a fatherly tone said, "My daughter—dear, there are many more good and kindhearted people than the bad ones in this world. But unfortunately, bad people are the noisiest and that's why we think most people are cruel. In reality, it is not the fact. Don't worry. Just be patient with bad people."

He was so wise and kindhearted—just like the majority of good people he was talking about. His words calmed me down. He then escorted me to the street, called a taxi, and sent me home. And I realized that I was blessed. Several good men—the policeman, the bus driver, and the security guard—had been there when I needed them.

As I learned later, those at the sit-in strikes were attacked by hard liners and mace bearers. Many women were beaten and injured. As my savior policeman had honestly admitted to me, the police could not handle those cruel thugs.

The rally carried on for days. Tara and I actively participated in most of them. The demonstrations were held at different places and were organized by women's organizations throughout the country. Every day, a new group of women, nurses, teachers, workers, and others announced their unity and joined the huge crowd of protesters, mostly women. Men, from different political parties, volunteered to protect female protesters from attacks by extremists by making a body shield around us. The attackers were entirely mace bearers—fanatic groups and women covered in black veils. They threw stones at us and the other demonstrators. They also attacked us by clubs and chains.

After days of demonstrations, the government realized that the women would not give up. In order to ease the tension, Prime Minister Bazargan, who had his hands full with enormous other issues, stated that wearing hijab was not compulsory.

But, it was just another trick as mace bearing men and women were organized to attack unveiled women. Gradually, not only did wearing the hijab become mandatory, but most of the women's rights became null and void.

However, up to the present time the women have not given up the fight. The Iranian women activists intend to get back their rights, despite of the cruelty of the Islamic regime.

Chapter 6

⌒⁓⌒

Crisis and Brutality

After a few months of a honeymoon-like period, during which the Iranians could enjoy freedom of speech and relief, and right after establishment of the Islamic regime, spiteful brutality dominated the society.

On March 1979, a Revolutionary Islamic Court was established. Ayatollah Sadegh Khalkhali was appointed as the Islamic judge of the court by Ayatollah Khomeini.

Khalkhali was a cruel mullah who executed thousands of men and women in just a few days after the establishment of the Islamic regime—later on after Khomeini died he admitted that all executions were ordered and approved by Ayatollah Khomeini personally.

Numerous high ranking civil officials, military generals, ex ministers, executives officers and civil servants who were working for the past regime, and those who were against the Islamic regime or were suspected of being an opponent, were sentenced to death by Khalkhali in the summary trials.

The men and women were brought to the court, which was broadcast on television. Some of the men's heads were covered in bandages or covered with blood. Their trial lasted only a few minutes before they were found guilty of various crimes such as "seditious and treacherous to Islam" or "the most vicious person on the earth" or "battling God." the terms was used at that time and unfortunately still are used to justify executions of the opponents. They were sentenced to death by Khalkhali, and were executed just minutes later.

*   *   *

While in exile, the shah was fighting a losing battle with cancer.

As his medical condition became more critical, he needed instant medical care. President Jimmy Carter reluctantly permitted the shah, once a close U.S. ally, to enter the United States for cancer treatment. Very soon after the shah was admitted into a New York hospital, Ayatollah Khomeini demanded his extradition to Iran for a trial. The U.S. government rejected this request, but the shah was asked to leave the U.S. soil. Simultaneously, an anti-American sentiment was supported by Khomeini to force the United States to extradite the shah.

Intensive anti-American demonstrations were held and led to an invasion of the American Embassy in Tehran on November 4, 1979, by a group called, "The students in support of the Imam's policy—Khomeini's policy." The name Laaneh Jaasoosi—Nest of Spies—was given to the American Embassy. Fifty-two American diplomats and embassy staff were taken as hostages.

News of the occupation of the American Embassy spread immediately. Curious, I went to the location of the embassy to see what was going on.

I got there late in the afternoon. A huge crowd at the gate of the embassy shouted, "Down with the America." It was an unusual form of gathering. The crowd was much different from those I used to participate in protests during the uproar of the revolution.

The air was filled with hatred and rage. The expressions of the masses were not only harsh but even loathing. The slogans were not chanted in unison. The mobs appeared to be spontaneous rather than well organized. Reporters and cameramen attempted to make reports and take pictures, but they were pushed around by the mobs. On that day, for the first time, I heard the slogan "Down with the America" and saw an American flag burning in Iran.

I passed through the throng and reached the closed gate of the embassy. Through the bars, I tried in vain to look inside the building. Despite the brightness of the street lights and the lights of the embassy's yard, it was difficult to see inside. My attempt to climb the gate was not successful. I was stopped by some youngsters who had surrounded the gate to block the entrance.

Disappointed at not being able to see what was going on inside the embassy, I stood among the other spectators and witnessed the chaotic scene. Since the slogans were not chanted in unison, it was difficult to understand what the furious crowds were ranting about.

I pushed through the mobs to free myself and put all the raucous blast behind me. The stream of traffic a few blocks away from the embassy was the same as on other days. People heading home after a normal working day were not aware of the chaotic madness that was going on some kilometers away. However, very soon the entire nation would be aware and fed up.

*   *   *

Prime Minister Mehdi Bazargan's attempt to release the hostages remained unsuccessful due to Ayatollah Khomeini's support of the action. That resulted in the protest and resignation of Bazargan and his cabinet.

Approximately two months after the taking of the hostages and the resignation of Bazargan, the first president of the Islamic regime, Bani-Sadr, was elected.

Numerous negotiation and military attempts failed to release the American hostages. President Bani-Sadr's effort to resolve the crisis failed as well. Ayatollah Khomeini and his Islamic Revolutionary forces had the absolute authority, rendering the president powerless to keep the matter under control. Eventually, in 1981, Bani-Sadr resigned. After his resignation and disputes with religious leadership, he escaped the county and went to exile in France.

After 444 days; and months of behind-closed-doors negotiations, the hostages were released on January 20, 1981, the day of President Ronald Reagan's inauguration.

Since the first day of the hostage crisis up to this point, hostility between Iran and the United States had been elevated.

*　　*　　*

The chaotic and bloody years began with the establishment of the Islamic Republic regime after of the shah's regime toppled. I witnessed closely a fraction of the cruel face of Islamic extremists and the misery that spread over the entire country.

After the revolution victory and before the establishment of the Islamic regime, people still enjoyed freedom. The University of Tehran and many other places around the country were the meeting venues for gatherings and demonstrations. Prominent Muslim clergies as well as politician from every party and group could deliver speeches freely. The radio and TV media were still able to broadcast uncensored news. Numerous new and unlicensed newspapers and bulletins were published and distributed.

However, very soon cleric domination and new Islamic rules revealed its real totalitarian nature. The outcome of the revolution was a major disappointment to most of the people. Uprisings and demonstrations across the country intensified. Political parties, nationalists, religious and ethnic minorities such as Kurdish, Azeri, and all the other groups who had participated in the revolution and sacrificed, would have to fight for their freedom all over again.

*　　*　　*

Ayatollah Khomeini authorized the establishment of a paramilitary force called Sepaah-e-Pasdaran—the army of guardians of the revolution—which was loyal to the revolution and clerical leaders. Its task was to keep the country stable. Other paramilitary forces were established, such as the Revolutionary Committees, which acted as police. They were authorized to make illegitimate arrests, confiscate property, control and guard the urban areas, and interfere in people's private life and daily business.

The regime's intention was to eliminate unwanted individuals and all opponents' activities from the work places. This began with massive layoffs in both public and private sectors. *Paksazi*—purification—was a new term that would be used as a reason for layoffs. In this way, the companies would expel men and women based on their religious and political beliefs and the loyalty to the new Islamic regime.

The newspaper firm where I worked continued to experience its dynamic, but volatile atmosphere. However, there was no doubt that sooner or later the storm of the cleansing would hit our company as well.

Mr. Mohseni, who had succeeded in setting up the new financial system, was now ready to lead the entire financial department in an energetic and enthusiastic manner. As Mr. Mohseni's coworkers were accepted by the other employees of the floor, all of us were now to work side by side as a larger team.

But it did not take long before things changed in the firm.

There was a large storage room in our department behind Mr. Mohseni's office. One day, we noticed that file cabinets were moved out and replaced with desks and chairs. No one had a clue of who would occupy this large room.

A couple of days later, four women covered in black Islamic veils appeared on the floor and were led to that room. Thereafter, they came every day to the office and did little other than wait. It was not difficult to determine that they were waiting to replace the unveiled women.

At noon, these women used to go to the restroom to do vozo,[9] and then return to the storage room, their office, to do namaaz. We had never seen anyone perform namaaz at a work place before.

We, the unveiled women of the department, followed them to the restroom to mock them. It was childish, but quite fun. They always ignored us and said nothing. In silence, they did vozo and returned to the former storage room.

This became a kind of cold war between us, the war in which the enemy was confident of her victory, and we were aware that we would come out of this battle as losers. But it felt good to express our disgrace.

*   *   *

On one particular morning, after exchanging the news and rumors of the day with my colleagues, I went to my work station. Suddenly, the sound of heavy steps filled the air. Everyone looked at each other with amused faces. Shortly after, a group of Pasdaran—young military men in uniform with stern, bearded faces, equipped with large machine guns hanging on their shoulders, reminding of German's Gestapo—entered the department.

Ignoring the stunned, curious eyes of the employees, they headed straight toward Mr. Bahrami's desk.

Mr. Bahrami, one of the owners of the company, was very popular among staff of the firm. He was not only polite and kindhearted, but he possessed a tender manner. The company had been founded by his late father. Mr. Bahrami and his brother had taken over the company from their father. His brother had left Iran at the beginning of the revolution.

We watched as the rough faces of those young Pasdars approached Mr.

---

9   **Vozo**, an Islamic ritual to wash the face, the hands, and the feet, before performing Namaaz.

Bahrami's desk. Mr. Bahrami stood up, puzzled, but calm. In no time, our department was filled by the workers and employees of other departments.

The atmosphere of the society was filled by fear and terror. Since the daily news reported arrests, tortures, and executions, no one dared to protest. The employees who had crowded on the floor watched quietly as Pasdaran surrounded Mr. Bahrami to arrest him.

I never understood what he was charged for. On those days the Islamic regime did not need to give any reason for arresting people. The newly formed system just needed to replace regular people with loyal ones in the media.

Mr. Bahrami had a short moment to say good-bye before being escorted out. He looked at the silent eyewitnesses and sadly said, "I trust all of you to take a good care of this company." Some of the spectators shed tears while others dejectedly shook their heads. No one knew where they were going to take him or if his company was the only asset that would be confiscated.

An hour later, everyone had returned to their departments. We were still furious and in a state of shock when once again we heard the sound of heavy steps. A middle-aged, short, small, and bearded man entered the floor surrounded by four other bearded Pasdars.

The men stopped in the middle of the hallway and turned to us. The shorter, small man introduced himself as Mr. Taheri and announced that he was the new president of the company. He advised and urged us to respect and adapt to the new Islamic rules. At the end of his speech, he addressed the female employees, "From tomorrow, you sisters come to work in suitable dress."

Since Muslim men are not allowed to look at a woman's head and body if she is not completely covered, he avoided looking at us the entire time he spoke to us.

He and his entourage left; we remained, distressed, disappointed, and quite puzzled. In small groups, we talked about the day's unfortunate events. A couple of hours later, cheering news spread across the floor. Apparently some workers, who were angry about Mr. Bahrami's arrest, had beaten Mr. Taheri on his head with a piece of wood. Mr. Taheri's head was fractured, and he was taken to the hospital. That joy was short lived. The next day, he returned to the company with his head wrapped in bandages.

Over a matter of weeks, many employees, including key personnel, journalists, and writers, were terminated. The young women in hijab, who had occupied the storage room, were sent to different departments to replace other female employees. Our financial department remained untouched. Since we were involved in the company's finances, this gave us an impression that we were spared from the mass layoffs at least for a quite long time. We were wrong. The storm finally hit our department.

One morning, Mr. Mohseni called the six of us, his original team, to his office. Even though nothing was unexpected during those days, the call for a meeting was unusual. As we entered his office and sat around the conference table, we noticed that Mr. Mohseni was nervous. Generally, he was a speedy man but not a stressed person. He talked, walked, and worked in high speed.

However, he behaved differently that day in his office. He glanced at each of us and in a trembling voice said, "They are coming to get me. We've been together from beginning. We are a team. Can I count on your support?"

Coming after him was not his imagination; we believed him even though it had not been expected. Since he had transformed the financial system to a much more efficient and smooth system, the company still needed him. The new computerized system was still unfamiliar to most of the staff; he was needed to maintain it. Apparently, it did not concern Mr. Taheri, the new president of the company. It was sad and heartbreaking to see how frightened Mr. Mohseni was, and his request for our support was painful for me.

None of us had ever said a word when Mr. Bahrami, the nicest person in the company, had been taken away. He had many more supporters than Mr. Mohseni but not a sound of protest was heard that day. Since then, I felt ashamed of myself *Why didn't I say anything? Why was everybody waiting for the next person to protest?* These questions had bothered me ever since. Now this was the right opportunity to ease the burden of guilt. I made the decision to stand up for Mr. Mohseni. All of us assured him that he could count on our support. He thanked all of us, but apparently our words were not enough to comfort him. He seemed worn out.

We left his office and returned to our desks as our coworkers curiously looked at us, wondering about the meeting in Mr. Mohseni's office. They quickly grasped the situation when minutes later another episode of the demonstration of power played out before their eyes.

With his head still wrapped in bandages, Mr. Taheri led two Pasdars to Mr. Mohseni's office. Nobody moved. I jumped up and looked at the other members of Mr. Mohseni's team and waited for them to join me. They just looked back at me. Disappointed, I realized that I would not get any help from them. I ran to Mr. Mohseni's office and joined Susan.

A Pasdar stood on each side of Mr. Mohseni and forcefully dragged him out of his office. He eagerly wanted to know where they were taking him and why. He received no response, but he was insistent in getting an answer. His face had turned pale. Susan and I protested, asking why and to where they were taking him. We defended him by loudly saying that he was an honest and qualified boss.

Mr. Taheri and none of the bearded Pasdars even looked at us. It was as though we did not exist. They continued to drag Mr. Mohseni away as Mr. Taheri followed.

Susan and I stubbornly ran after them asking to let him go. Suddenly Mr. Taheri stopped and turned to us. In an insulting tone of voice he said: "Go back and remove the colors from your lips and put some clothes on instead of being so nosy."

Susan and I by looking at each other revealed our shock and anger. I was so furious that I could give him another blow to his head. I felt the heat of anger captured me.

Our effort was useless. Our feelings of disappointment and anger made Susan and I go to the other teammates, demanding an explanation: "Didn't you guys promise to support Mr. Mohseni? Why didn't you join us instead of leaving us alone?"

The only excuse they gave us was that nothing and no one could change the situation to help Mr. Mohseni.

*   *   *

The society outside of our company was changing in the same way but on a much larger scale. Adjusting to an Islamic society had a very high price that was paid by thousands of innocent people. There was a period of time that people were even scared of each other. By saying or doing something against the regime, it put you in a dangerous position of being arrested, tortured, and even executed.

Chapter 7

Secret Life

"Miss Bahara, I have a message for you from Behzad Sani," Saeid Khan shyly said as he served me a cup of tea.

"Who is he?" I asked, while picking up the teacup.

"He is a journalist working on the fourth floor," he responded quietly. "He asked me to tell you that he would like to call you for a date, if it would be okay with you."

"I don't know who this person is. Tell him that I will not go on a blind date," I replied and asked Saeid Khan to give him my response.

The same day, on the second round of tea servings, Saeid Khan came to our floor followed by a young, tall man, whom I had never seen in the firm before. He looked handsome, and I guessed he was in his late twenties. He walked alongside Saeid Khan and passed me without saying a word. He paused for a moment in front of Susan's office, which gave me a clear view of him. Then he turned around and left the floor.

This act looked funny to me, but I liked it. I was thinking of telling Susan about what had just happened, when she came to me to say: "Niki, come to my office. Someone is on the phone and wants talk to you."

"Who? Why would they call your number and not mine?" I asked as I followed her.

"How could I know? I asked him to call your extension, but he insisted to talk to you on my phone," she answered.

I sat on the edge of her desk and lifted the handset, "This is Bahara," I said my last name, using only the last name is the custom at work in Iran.

"Hello, I'm Behzad Sani. I hope I've not bothered you and not interrupted your work," the caller said in a deep raspy voice.

"I'm not at my desk. Am I?" I answered playfully.

"Then I have bothered you," he confirmed and laughed.

"Yes, you did. Now what was the reason?" I asked, still teasingly.

"I've been thinking about you since I saw you. Can we meet after work? We can go wherever you like …"

I interrupted him and in the same teasing tone said, "Wow! Not so fast! I just saw you for a few seconds. How do you know I liked you?"

We continued chatting for couple of minutes in the same humorous mode, but we did not meet that day. After several phone conversations, we started seeing each other nearly every day.

At first, we tried to keep our relationship secret at work. Despite utmost caution, the news spread. To my surprise, I received some anonymous phone calls. The callers labeled Behzad Sani a con artist and advised me not to be fooled by him. They recommended that I not become involved with him. In addition, some also claimed that Behzad had many wives and children in different parts of the country. Even Susan received some calls. She was asked to keep me away from Behzad. She took those calls more seriously than I did and asked me to be careful. The firm was huge with many departments and hundreds of employees. It was nearly impossible to trace who the concerned callers were.

I was twenty-three years old and somehow, in a crazy way, I enjoyed those calls. It was like a game to me, which made me even more curious to find out why so many people cared. Finally, I told Behzad about those warning calls. He laughed and simply said, "They are jealous. These lampooners are lying only because they are jealous."

The only call I took seriously was from one of the well-known and respected writers. He was the only one who identified himself to me when he called and said, "You are like a sister to me, and I don't want you to be tricked by this guy. He's not good for you. I know him very well. He is a charlatan and can fool everyone. You are not his first victim. Do you know that he has several wives in other cities? He changes his identity all the time. I'm telling you, like a brother, get rid of him." He sounded very sincere.

I was speechless and was not able to say a word. I just listened to him until I finally pushed myself to say, "Thank you, Mr. Abedi."

I sensed these painful allegations that came from Mr. Abedi might be true and confirmed the other calls. It was certainly not a jealousy call, as Behzad had claimed the calls were. I believed Mr. Abedi even though I did not want to face the truth.

*   *   *

That same evening, while Behzad drove me home, I told him about Mr. Abedi's phone call. I tried to be as calm as possible and not to show any emotion in order to see how he would react.

He looked at me and smiled. Then he shook his head and scornfully said, "How could he lower himself to call you with such accusations?"

"Like the others, he is very jealous!" I mocked, trying to stay composed.

"Can you find any other reason?' he asked.

"Oh no, I can't find any other reason at all! Everyone in this company is after me and everybody envies you!" I said in a sarcastic tone.

"Don't tell me that you believed him. Did you?" he asked.

"I just told you he is jealous, didn't I?" No longer able to stay cool, I added, "Do you think I'm stupid? Mr. Abedi has no reason for lying and telling me exactly the same things that the others have said. By the way, he said that he knows you very well and that you know it."

He turned to a smaller street and stopped the car.

"I have to go home. Why did you stop?" I protested.

He said nothing. He turned off the engine and stared at my eyes.

I stared angrily back at his eyes and said, "It's getting late, and I don't have time for you to tell me the same nonsense. If you've decided to tell me the truth then tell me, otherwise I will take a taxi home."

He took his eyes off me, leaned forward, and rested his forehead on the steering wheel so that I could not see his face. Finally, he lifted his head. With his eyes filled with tears, he took my hands and looked through the window, trying not to look at me. I was not sure what to do. I felt bad, somehow guilty.

Still not looking at me, he said, "I don't want to lose you. I love you more than anything in this world. Niki, please promise me that you'll stay with me. Please, Niki!"

"What? Everything they've said is true? Are you telling me that?" I asked. I had already been convinced by then that there was some truth in what I had heard.

"No Niki, not everything. I wish I was brave enough to tell you earlier, but I was not. I was scared. I'm still scared of losing you. Please, please say that you forgive me," he pleaded sadly.

"Tell me the truth now. Whatever it is, I want to know!" I demanded anxiously and prepared myself to hear the worst.

After a few moments of silence, he finally said, "I was eighteen when I married a girl the same age. We were both just kids, which made her parents interfere in our life. That's the reason we divorced after two years. Now, I have an eight-year-old daughter, who lives with her mother ...." He was talking and talking, and I could not hear him anymore. I was not able to say a word.

"I beg you to forgive me, Niki. I wanted to tell you many times before, but when you told me about the other guy and your conflict with your family, I was scared. I love you more than my soul. If you leave me I'll die ...." Words and sentences burst forth from his mouth but did not reach my ears. They evaporated in the air. The only sound I could hear was my heartbeat.

"Niki say something! I know I should have told you earlier, but I didn't want to let a mistake that I made when I was just a kid ruin my chance for being happy for the first time in my life ...." He continued to babble.

Infuriated, I freed my hands, which he was still holding and shouted at him, "That's enough. Save your tears. I don't need to hear more."

"Please wait! I'm so sorry that I didn't tell you sooner. I knew you would leave me. Don't go! Please. Let us talk! I love you, Niki." He grabbed my hand as I reached for the car door.

"Okay, just drive me home. I have to go home. It's getting late. If you have anything else to tell me, say it on the way." I said forcefully as I sat back in the car seat.

During the entire drive to my house, he repeated again and again the same excuse and persisted to ensure me that it was the only secret he had kept from me. For couple of days, I tried to keep my distance from him. He kept calling me, but I did not answer his calls. Realizing I wouldn't talk to him, he called Susan and through her asked me to forgive him. I was too confused to think clearly. Susan was the only one I talked to about Behzad. She was aware of my weakness for him and tried to talk me into not going back to him, "Let him go! He has not been honest with you. How do you know he's telling you the whole truth now?" she asked as she tried to reason with me.

"I don't know! Why should I believe that the others are telling the truth? If it is the truth, why don't they tell me what he has done that makes him such a bad person? How do they know that he has a wife in every city? Have they followed him everywhere? It's just crazy," I told her.

"It doesn't matter what he's done or not. He's not good for you anyway. You know that your family would never let you marry him. Then, why do you want to create another headache for yourself?" she asked.

Susan was right, and I knew it. But every morning when I got to work, I still wished that he would call me, watch me, and try to find an opportunity to ask for another chance, which he did. He never gave up until we were together again. This time, we did not try to make our relationship secret in the company. We went to work together, had lunch at the company's restaurant, and left work together. We openly demonstrated that we stayed together despite all warnings. That helped. I did not get any phone calls after that. It seemed that those who were concerned about my future had simply given up.

*   *   *

Months passed. Society and my life had changed. Behzad and the unexpected events of the aftermath of the revolution had occupied my time. I enjoyed my life at home, at work, and being in the middle of how life was changing.

My relationship with Behzad became more serious. Both of us were aware of the fact that once my family found out, it would be a dead end for us. We tried to find a solution to ease the situation for us. The only way out was to keep his past a secret.

I decided to tell Shahram about Behzad without mentioning anything about his past. I forced myself to give a brief version of Behzad's life. I told him that I was seeing a nice twenty-eight-year-old journalist and that we were thinking about marriage.

Shahram let me talk before giving me his opinion. "I'm sure he is a nice guy, as you say. But the problem is his occupation. Being a journalist is a very good job while you are single and don't have any responsibilities at home. Journalists typically have no steady family life. That's why I think he would not be a good match for you," he stated firmly.

Puzzled and not expecting this response, I said, "You mean that journalists should never get married? I'm sure there are many journalists who have a happy family life of their own."

"Certainly there are some, but in that kind of life one partner would be away most of the time because of work. This would not be so easy. That is not the life I wish for you. Be a wise girl and end it as soon as possible," he requested nicely.

I was so in love that nothing would make me think about ending my relationship. This time, Shahram was not too hard on me. I still had a chance to change his mind. "We've been talking about getting married for a while now. I can't just end it. I know that you want the best for me, but I want to take a chance. Will you just meet him and talk to him? Maybe you would change your mind," I suggested, hoping for a sign of flexibility.

Shahram was silent for a couple of long minutes. His serene face had turned into pensiveness. It was impossible to guess what kind of response I would receive. Finally, he looked back at me. In a soft, uncertain voice, he murmured: "Khahar Jan—dear sister—when I say something, I know what I'm talking about. I know people. It's not that I am against your will; I just don't want you to take the wrong steps in your life. You still are too young to get married. Give yourself some time to find the right person."

"I'm not getting married tomorrow. We are just talking about marriage. I promise if you meet him you'll see that he would be the right one. You'll like him. Just let him come and talk to you."

"Okay, I'll see him, but no promises," Shahram stated doubtfully.

I kissed him and thanked him happily. At the same time, I felt guilty about not telling him the whole truth.

*   *   *

Behzad came to our house several days later. Shahram preferred to talk alone with him. After I introduced them to each other, I left the room.

After the men had talked for a while and Behzad had left, I asked Shahram excitedly about his opinion. He tersely answered, "He knows how to talk. He is a good talker. I have to think about it. I'm not sure. Let me think for a couple of days."

After some days passed, Shahram gave me his final opinion about Behzad. "Don't think about him ever! He's not the person you think he is. He's not trustworthy and is not good for you. End it Khahar jan!" he said compassionately but decisively.

I knew that Shahram had checked Behzad's background and surely had heard the same stories as I had. I felt an unpredictable hostility and anger toward those anonymous persons who had ruined my plans. I just simply did not want to believe any of those allegations. To me, he was a caring, tender, and passionate person. I was convinced that since nobody knew him as well as I did, the finger-pointing had no basis.

All those warnings and antipathies made me more determined to keep the relationship alive. My mind was made up to stubbornly resist every one so that, not even for a moment, I thought about breaking up with him.

I also realized that Shahram would never approve him. I no longer thought about our future and was happy with my secret relationship for the present time. However, Behzad seemed not to have given up on the notion of a shared future for us even if he did not talk about it. I understood that the day he surprised me with a suggestion.

While driving me home after work, he chose a different pathway and stopped the car in front of a *mahzar*—the matrimony office. "This is the only way!" he said as he pointed to the building.

"What? What way?" I asked puzzled.

"What does the sign say?" he asked and pointed to the building.

"There? Here is a mahzar," I read the sign and protested, "Oh no, we can't do that!"

"Why not? Do you know a better way?" he asked.

"No I don't, but I can't. It is not right," I responded.

"It is right. What are you scared of?"

"I'm not scared. I'm just … I don't know what I am. My mamman and Shahram, what should I tell them?" I said.

"I promise they will come around after we get married. At first, they will be upset, but finally they would have no choice but to accept me as your husband. Don't you want this?" he asked.

"Of course, this is what I want, but not in this way," I answered.

"There is no other way," he argued.

We discussed that particular alternative that day and for some days afterward. It was easy for Behzad to make his decision, but it was not the same for me. In those days and in that society, getting married secretly and without the family's blessing was an inappropriate act and not common at all. I did not want to disappoint my mother and Shahram. I loved them and was aware of the consequences, but I pictured different scenarios in my head. Behzad also tried to convince me that if they really loved me, they would forgive me and respect my decision. He tried to comfort me by talking about a happy loving life together, which would satisfy my family as well.

Finally, I decided to go through with a secret marriage. I had ridiculously convinced myself that by getting married my family would be in an irrevocable situation and consent to a real ceremony before anyone was aware of a secret marriage. In that scenario, we would have a happy ending to our love story with no family drama.

We set a date. According to the rules, we had to do blood tests prior to the marriage. Also, I needed my father's death certificate. Per Iranian law, women were required to have their father's permission to get married. In my case, I needed my father's death certificate to prove that my father was not alive.

I searched through my mother's papers and found the death certificate. Now we needed two people as witnesses. Behzad's family, as he told me, lived in Abadan, in southwest Iran. He also mentioned that his family would not participate in the ceremony because they did not like the idea of a secret marriage. So, he asked a friend, who was a middle-aged woman, and her son to be our witnesses.

Everything was set and the wedding day arrived.

*   *   *

"Get up, it's morning. The sun will be up soon. You'll be late for namaaz," my mother's soft voice woke me up like every other morning. But this was the morning of my wedding day.

Mixed feelings of nervousness, agitation, and excitement had kept me up through most of the night. The beautiful image of the future, which Behzad had pictured for me, had soothed my anxiousness to let me fall asleep during the last hours of the night.

My mother's kind, soft voice and the brightness of the morning opened my eyes to the reality that awaited me. I did not feel well. Everything seemed unreal. I was not able to bring my feelings under control. I did not want to get up. My bed was the safest place. *Should I get up? I can call in sick and stay in bed. No, get up. Don't be chicken. Today is a good day. It's your wedding day. My God! Help me. Am I doing the right thing? Oh, God, please!* I remained motionless in the bed fighting my uncertainties.

I heard my mother again, this time complaining: "Get up girl! As usual you're late for namaaz. Now the sun is up. Don't you have a job to go to? It's getting late!"

She sounded somehow disappointed that I had missed my morning namaaz, which supposed to be done before dawn. Although I did not believe in religion, I continued to practice namaaz as long as I lived with my mother in order to make her happy and avoid any possible confrontation.

Nonchalantly, I got up to the fresh aroma of sangak, which my mother used to buy early in the morning before waking us up. The scent of fresh bread and brewed tea used to make my mornings enjoyable, but that morning everything was so different.

I put on a beautiful red dress, which Behzad had given me as a present, and got ready for the day. I sat at the breakfast table, still dealing with my distressed thoughts. Seeing my mother's kind and bright face with a pleasant smile on her lips made my guilt more painful. I tried not to show my inner distress, but Ramin realized something was wrong,

"What's wrong with you? Today you look funny," he asked with his hoarse, teenaged voice.

"You're funny yourself! It's nothing wrong with me. Why do you say so?" I asked him.

"I don't know! Have you seen a ghost?" he teased me.

"Yes, I've seen you!" I teased back.

"Don't argue! Have your breakfast! Are the two of you starting your morning by arguing again?" my mother said delicately with a smile. We continued to tease each other for a few more minutes as I tried to hide my anxiety.

At the door, ready to leave the house, I lied to my mother, "Mamman, I am going to a movie with my friends in the afternoon. I'll be late. Don't be worried!"

I had told her many other lies before as an excuse for coming home late, but this time was different. This lie was really big. This lie made me not just a big liar but also a big sinner. I felt like a criminal.

$$* \qquad * \qquad *$$

Many times on the way to work that day, I was so close to turning around, going back home, and calling in sick, but I didn't.

When I got to the company, Behzad was already waiting for me. Seeing him replaced all my uncertainties with optimism. Any doubts and guilt vanished. My fragile confidence was boosted. We stood in front of the company's gate and went over our plan for the evening.

The day felt extraordinarily lengthy as though time had stopped. I was dying to talk to Susan, but I was strong-minded about my decision, and I didn't want anyone to color my decision with doubt.

In the afternoon, Behzad and I went to the mahzar that we had sat in front of just a couple of weeks earlier. Once inside, we found Behzad's friend, a nice, cheerful lady with a large bouquet of flowers and a box of pastry. She and her handsome, young son were waiting for us.

To explain why we were not having a real ceremony with the whole family participating, Behzad made up a story. He explained that my family lived in the other province; we would celebrate there later.

The lady sympathized that my family was not with me at such a happy moment. She was curious and asked many questions, for which I did not have any answers. Each time, Behzad stepped in to help me by making up stories. Finally, we were led to a smaller room where we would be married. We waited for the mullah.

I was worried about getting home late. My impatience in repeatedly checking my watch astounded the lady and her son. It was hard for me to concentrate and comprehend what was happening around me. My only concern was being late and what excuse I would give my mother. I told her I was going to a movie, which bought me some hours. Those hours had already past. I should have been home by this time. My thoughts quickly shifted from being late to what would happen afterward.

Behzad handed all the necessary documents to the mullah. Every movement in that room seemed to be in slow motion. The mullah slowly checked the papers and took notes in his book. I was anxious to be done with the whole process as quickly as possible.

Finally, he began the sermon. Everyone in that room seemed to be happy and enjoying the moment except me, the bride. "*Aroos khanoom*—lady bride—Niki Bahara, ... am I your appointee to marry you to Mr. Behzad Sani?" the mullah asked me.

"Yes, you do!" I replied with no hesitation and hoped that we were done. But we were not. He had to recite some verses from the Quran and go through the whole ceremony.

After signing the marriage documents, the lady insisted, "You have to sweeten your mouth." She offered the pastry she had brought and invited us to her house to celebrate. She insisted and would not accept "no" as an answer. She finally gave up, but she was very disappointed since she had made a wedding dinner for us. I needed to rush out of there, which I nearly did. I apologized and thanked them, letting Behzad create another story for them. Finally, we left them stunned.

Behzad drove me home as fast as possible and dropped me a couple of blocks away from the house. I ran toward the house and found a worried Shahram on the street waiting for me. The guilt I felt was enormous. I apologized for being so late. He did not protest or complain. He just said that he was worried.

As expected, I found everyone at home had worried about me. Souri did not buy my story about going to the movie. She kept asking questions about which movie I had seen and the story line. When I said that I did not know the name of the movie because I did not care about the names, she mocked me, "You say so and expect me to believe you!"

My mother did not ask why I was late; she just thanked God that I got home safely.

That night was the most bizarre and distorted night I ever experienced. I could not go to sleep. Nothing in the day seemed to be real to me.

*   *   *

The next morning, I went to work as usual. We decided to keep our marriage secret at work. Susan was the only one that I told. I had to talk to somebody. The secret was too big for me to be able to hide from Susan. She did not congratulate me as I expected and was not surprised upon hearing the news.

Instead, she clearly disclosed her disappointment. "I had my own suspicions about you two, but I was hoping that I was wrong. If you had told me yesterday, I would have tried talking you out of this craziness. Now it's too late, and I'm sure there was no way you would listen to me anyway!"

Over the following days and weeks, Behzad and I tried to build a life together although its future was uncertain. Even with the limited time we had together, which amounted to the short hours after work, we looked for an apartment to rent and some necessary bits and pieces for the place.

Weeks passed. Everything was ready for us to start our life together, but I did not know how to break the shocking news to my family. I was not even sure what I was expecting to happen.

Behzad seemed to understand my situation. He never put any pressure on me to set a deadline to tell my family. He even respected the rules of our society where girls are supposed to save their virginity until after marriage. So, we did not have sex. The reason for refraining from sex, even though we were married, was due to the uncertainty of the reaction of my family. Behzad was concerned about me and my future. He wanted me to be a virgin in case something forced us to divorce.

I could feel that his love and devotion was deep and sincere. Even with those worries and an uncertain future, I was happy. I loved him, and I was waiting for a miracle to happen that would turn everything around in our favor.

*   *   *

Three months passed since Behzad and I had married. The only times we could manage to spend together were a couple of hours in the afternoons and half a day on Thursdays. In Iran, most of the companies and businesses were open only half a day on Thursdays due to the weekend which is on Fridays.

One Thursday afternoon, I was in Behzad's car as he drove through a very busy street heading to our favorite restaurant. To my surprise, I saw Shahram's car next to ours in the middle of the heavy traffic. Shahram looked at us and drove toward the side of the street where he stopped the car.

My first reaction to that surprise encounter was to take off my wedding ring. We followed Shahram to the side of the street and stopped behind his car. Not knowing what to do, I asked Behzad to stay put in the car as I talked to Shahram.

I got into Shahram's car. He ignored my greeting and without a word, he started the car and headed back into traffic. No words were exchanged during the drive home. He, Tara, and Neda were scheduled to leave for Spain for a two weeks' vacation the following day. It was very unfortunate that he had to come upon us a day before his trip. I was embarrassed and unable to think clearly. Silence was the best for that moment.

"Dear, we'll talk about it after we come back," Shahram said calmly before he dropped me off at home. Kindly and fatherly, he added, "Try to be a wise girl."

The next day Shahram and his family left for vacation, which gave me some time to find the courage to break the news.

A secret marriage could indeed be labeled as a revolt for a traditional Iranian family. My inconsistent feelings of guilt, confusion, and uncertainty had made me ashamed. My wishful illusion, on the other hand, calmed me down and took me to a magical world of fantasy. In that world, Behzad and I would live together as a happy couple, and my family would share my happiness. In the world of my dream, we had three kids—two girls and a boy. Our children would happily run around my mother's house, chasing my niece and nephews.

However, the reality was far from my dream world. I had to decide whether to continue my secretive life or tell the truth and face the consequences. Behzad had left the final decision to me regarding how and when to reveal our secret to my family. He promised me that whatever the decision would be, he would support me.

"I'll tell Shahram when he's back," I told Behzad resolutely even though deep inside I was still uncertain about it.

"Are you sure you are ready for that?" Behzad asked.

"No, I'm not. I don't think I would ever be ready, but it's time. Let's do that. Whatever happens, it happens. Nothing would change with time," I said.

"I'm concerned about you. Are you sure their reaction won't affect you and make you change your mind about us?" he wanted to know.

"No, I will not change my mind. Are you crazy? Of course, they will get very angry. It won't be easy at first, but now that we are married maybe they'll come around and let your family come for khastegari.[10] As long as no relatives and friends know that we're married, we can have the real wedding party," I stated, revealing my wish and hoping it would be the reality.

"I doubt it. If it doesn't happen the way you hope, what will you do?" he asked.

"I don't know. They want my happiness. I'm happy with you. Maybe they'll change their mind about us now that we are married." I could not give him a straight answer.

"You didn't answer my question. In case they get so angry and ask you to choose between them or me, what would you do then?" Behzad asked and waited for an honest response.

Without giving him the answer he needed to hear, I responded, "They will never ask me to do that!"

"I think they will. But if you remain determined and strong-minded, I promise you that with time they will come around," he said.

"I am strong-minded about us. There is no other way; I have to tell them soon or later," I said.

"Do you want me to be with you when tell them?" he asked.

---

10 **Khastegari,** an Iranian tradition, when the parents of the groom go to the bride's parents to ask the bride's hand in marriage.

"No, no, no, it'll be better if I tell them. I think I will tell Souri first. Maybe she could help me with it," I replied.

"Don't count on anybody on this. Just be strong and don't show any weakness. Please be strong for me," he advised.

*   *   *

Having decided to break the news to Souri first, I asked her to come to me one day when no one else was there. Curious about what I was going to tell her, she came over. I was unexpectedly very calm with no feeling of dread or anxiousness. Once I opened the door, she quickly asked, "What's happened? What do you want to talk to me about?"

"What a nosy sister! How did you get here so fast? Did you run?" I teased her.

"I'm not as slow as you are. No, I just walked. Now tell me," she teased me back.

"I was kidding; I don't have anything to tell you. I just felt lonely and needed some company!" I said.

"*Baseh, baseh* —it's enough—tell me whatever you have to say, I have to go back home." Souri had left her three-year-old son, Arya, home alone with their maid Fati.

"Okay, let's go for a walk. I'll tell you," I suggested.

We went for a walk. Once on the street and before the fear would capture my guts, I blurted out, "I'm married."

Souri stopped and stared at me, trying to see a sign of a joke in my eyes, "You are kidding, right?"

"No, I'm not joking. It's been more than three months now," I responded.

"You are not joking! You are married! Did I hear correctly?" she asked again.

"Yes," I answered.

"With the same guy?" she asked.

"Yes," I answered.

She paused and leaned against the wall. She was trying to digest the news. Suddenly her face changed color, her lips trembled. She furiously yelled, "Just like that? Married? No shame? Nothing? What about Mamman and Shahram?" and strode into the house. I followed her inside. She called Shahrooz, who had just arrived home. With a shaky voice, she said, "Shahrooz, come here, listen to what she's saying. I don't get it."

Shahrooz didn't capture the shock and importance in her request as he replied, "I have to pee now. Later."

"No need to pee! After hearing this, your pee will stop by itself!" Her sense of humor had mixed with her anger.

Shahrooz hesitated. He turned and looked at us. "What? What's up?"

"I don't get it. She says she's married," Souri responded.

"Married? What does that mean?" Shahrooz asked.

"Don't ask me, ask her," Souri said flatly.

Perplexed by the unexpected news, he looked sharply at me. With his mouth open, he shook his head. I had to say something. Now my heart started beating hard. I felt like a thief, trapped during a robbery. "I've been married for three months now," I quietly stated, confirming Souri's news.

Souri, who paced aimlessly, asked Shahrooz, "Can you believe it? What can we do now? I don't know what to do." Then she turned to me asking, "You tell me what to do. How could you do that? How?"

Shahrooz's nervous glances shifted from me to Souri. He had not yet digested the news. "What did you say? Married? To whom? Why?" he asked again, making sure the news was true.

"Who cares to whom? Let's think what we should do now," Souri rushed to answer him before I could say anything.

By then, Shahrooz was convinced that it was not a joke. He burst into anger and yelled at me, "No shame? How can you face Mamman and Shahram now? Is this the way you show your gratitude to them? Is this what Shahram deserves after so many years of sacrificing? If he hears this, he'll have a stroke. You'll kill him. Dumb girl." He became more and more frustrated and asked unanswerable questions while calling me "an irresponsible and selfish, dumb girl."

After the initial shock was over, they tried to cool down. They did not yell at me or talk to me anymore; instead they consulted each other to decide how to deal with the disaster. All of a sudden, Souri, who seemed to have come to a good idea, turned to me asking, "Are you still a virgin?"

"Yes, I am," I answered.

She shook her head victoriously, turned to Shahrooz and said, "Thanks to God! She's a virgin! Now we can get her divorced before Shahram gets back."

Oh God, what can I do now? I thought to myself and remembered Behzad's warning about exactly the same situation.

Shahrooz appeared satisfied by my answer and Souri's idea. He turned to me to ask, "Can we trust you? You're telling us the truth, aren't you?"

I did not answer.

He got up and ordered, "I want everyone to get into the car."

"Where are we going?" Souri asked.

"I don't trust this girl. We're going to the doctor to see if she is really a virgin. We have to be sure about it."

We got into the car and headed to the doctor's office. I sat quietly in the backseat as they were talking and planning about what they should do next.

*   *   *

The doctor checked me and reported the happy news to Souri and Shahrooz that confirmed my virginity.

"Now we're going to see this guy. Before Shahram is back, we have to end this foolishness. This guy must divorce her," Shahrooz said as we left the doctor's office. Then he turned to me and said, "That was really good news. Despite your stupidity, you didn't close all the doors behind you. Now tell me where we can find the guy."

"I think he's in our apartment now," I responded.

"What do you mean by 'our apartment'?" Souri asked scornfully.

"We rented an apartment," I said quietly.

Shahrooz smirked and shook his head.

"How did you find time?" Souri asked again in the same disdainful tone. I did not answer.

"Where is the apartment? Do you have a key?" Shahrooz asked

"Yes," I answered.

"Okay, show me the way" he insisted.

*   *   *

"You'll shut up and not say a word while we're inside. Do you get it?" Shahrooz demanded of me in a harsh tone. We were inside the elevator and headed to the third floor to see Behzad.

Shahrooz looked me in eyes and said, "You two must get divorced before Shahram is back. I will make sure that this happens."

Souri tried to calm him down and begged him to control himself before we entered the apartment.

*   *   *

Behzad jumped up as he heard the door open and saw the three of us standing in the doorway. He had just come out of the shower and had tied a bath towel around his waist.

"Hi, sorry, I was not expecting you to come over today. Please sit down." He tried to be as casual as possible.

"That's fine. We are not here to party. We're here to discuss your marriage," Shahrooz said. It was obvious that he was trying to control his temper.

"Okay, we can talk. Just let me go put some clothes on," Behzad said and turned to me to see if I was okay. I was not. I was a mess.

"I wonder, when did you have time to furnish this apartment?" Souri asked as she looked around the apartment while waiting for Behzad to change and come back.

"We rented it furnished," I said even though she had not directly asked me.

Annoyed by Souri's curiosity, Shahrooz said, "Nothing matters now. Just concentrate on getting into the guy's head."

*   *   *

Once Behzad came back dressed in jeans and a T-shirt, Shahrooz calmly said, "What's done is done. Niki is naive and made a big mistake. We expect you to help to correct it. The only way to correct this is for the two of you to get divorced,"

"I don't see this as a mistake. I didn't get married to get a divorce," Behzad answered determinedly.

"Getting married is not a mistake, but the way you did was a big mistake. This way is not appropriate for our families. While nobody knows about it, let's do the right thing," Shahrooz said in the same solid tone.

"Niki knows that I would do anything for her. I don't want a divorce, but if she thinks that we should, I respect it and will do it for her," Behzad said as he looked at me.

This response pleased both Shahrooz and Souri. They fixed their eyes on me, waiting for my response. I remained silent. Behzad had thrown the ball into my playground. He seemed so confident about the decision that I would make. All eyes in the room were on me, cornering me for an answer, but I was not ready to make a decision. The whole situation was so vague to me that I wished I had not revealed my secret.

I avoided their gazes. My lips were closed. My silence lengthened. I saw satisfaction on Behzad's face. He was confident. Nobody pressured me to say anything at that moment. Indeed, both sides were convinced I was on their side.

As soon as we left and sat in the car, Souri and Shahrooz gladly and hopefully talked about the visit and how well it had gone. Their happiness vanished when I announced that I would not file for divorce.

During the entire drive home, both Souri and Shahrooz tried many different ways to talk me into filing for divorce. Their tone changed from kind and compassionate to harsh and rough. Finally, Shahrooz decided to send me to Rasht, a city along the coast of the Caspian Sea in northwest Iran, to stay away from Behzad to think and come to my senses.

I was so confused and felt so ashamed of myself that I did not resist, and tamely let Shahrooz to take me to Rasht that same day. By letting myself doing as I was told, perhaps I tried to soften the hard situation to let both Shahrooz and Souri cool down a bit.

After five hours of driving, we arrived at his girlfriend Mahtab's house late at night. He stayed the night. In the morning, before leaving for Tehran, he instructed Mahtab how to handle me. She had to make sure that no phone or key should be available to me. He disconnected the phone and locked it inside a cabinet. He also took my purse with him to make sure I did not have any money.

I stayed with Mahtab about a week. Every morning, she would do exactly what Shahrooz had instructed her to do before leaving for work. I never protested. Mahtab talked to me for hours to help me understand Behzad, my family, and my future. I was confused. All the warnings and advice I was given only made me more stubborn. I had acted like a slave, a dumb slave. I had said no to a divorce once; but after that, I did just what they asked me to do. I obeyed what I was ordered to do. I naively waited for some miracle to clean up this mess.

*   *   *

Shahrooz brought me home the same day that Shahram and his family were scheduled to return from Spain

"You dumb girl, don't you get it," Shahrooz berated me in the car. "You don't get how you hurt Mamman and especially Shahram. You're so selfish."

In his last attempt to get into my head, he continued, "You don't understand now, but you will regret it someday when it's too late. This guy is bad news. No one has said anything positive about him. You will ruin your future and you'll have no one to help you then. Think about it."

My silence and stubbornness got on his nerves. He put on music and said no more until we were in front of our house. "Souri and I decided not to tell Shahram and Mamman for now. We still have faith in you. Think! It's your own future, don't ruin it," Shahrooz said before we got out of the car.

*   *   *

It was late in the afternoon when we entered our house. My two aunts had come from Isfahan—a large, historical city in Iran—to visit. They were in the kitchen helping my mother prepare dinner. Ramin was doing his homework. Souri and her family arrived shortly after. Shahram and his family would join us later. The whole family was gathering for dinner.

Those family nights used to be pleasant and enjoyable for me, but that was not the case on that particular night. I was distraught, but I had to play it cool and pretend to be my usual self. I was positive that Souri and Shahrooz had to do the same. As we ate dinner, Shahram and Tara told us about their trip. I tried hard to act as normal as possible. The easiest way I found was just to be quiet and laugh when everyone else laughed.

*   *   *

That night, I had a nightmare in which I was stuck between two walls that pressed in on me from both sides with no way out. Frightened, I woke up. Scared to go back to sleep again, I stayed awake the rest of the night to avoid more anxiety. The next morning, a bizarre incident changed everything for me.

It was a Friday morning, and my mother, my aunts, Shahrooz, Ramin, and I were having breakfast. Suddenly, we heard a loud shout followed by quick footsteps from the stairway. Seconds later, the door to our house jerked open; Shahram nearly threw himself inside. He had Souri in tow. She desperately begged him to calm down, but he was in his utmost anger. "Where is this stupid girl? I'll kill her. I'll kill her ...," he shouted.

His face had turned pale. He was in a terrible state of shock. He moved his hands hysterically up in the air. Shahrooz tried to hold him to calm him down. My mother, while trying to catch his hands, begged him to cool down and think about his health.

Shahrooz had to slap him to get him out of the state of shock.

I stood there and watched, unable to move.

My aunt took my hand and pulled me along and out of the house. She left me in the street and asked me to stay there until Shahram calmed down. I sat on the ground—frightened and helpless. So many thoughts ran through my mind. *It was not supposed to happen like this. What had occurred since the night before? Shahrooz and Souri had decided not to say anything to Shahram yet to give me some more time to think.*

I was scared to death seeing Shahram in such a condition. I had never seen him like this before. *How could I turn a calm and peaceful person to his climax of insanity?* I prayed to God that nothing would happen to him.

As much as I wanted to go back inside to see how he was doing, I knew if Shahram saw me it would only make things worse. It seemed as though I was living a nightmare. *Oh, God, let this only be a nightmare, so that when I wake up this will be over.*

Finally, Souri came out. She threw the key to her home to me and headed back inside. I ran after her to ask how Shahram was doing. She turned to me and looked directly in my eyes. With scorn in her voice and in her body language, she sharply responded, "Nothing matters to you but you and that husband of yours. Don't act like you care!" With that said, she turned and walked away.

I went to her house. Arya, my three year-old nephew, happily ran to me, and I embraced him. He gave me a bit of comfort. Disappointed that I didn't play with him, he left me alone and went back to Fati, the babysitter.

Every minute that passed seemed like an hour. I am not sure how long it was before Tara and Souri came to me. Souri seemed to have recovered from her state of shock. She looked calm, but Tara was furious. She rushed to me and harshly said, "I swear to God, if anything had happened to Shahram, I would have killed you! He is not just your brother, he's my husband. He was at the edge of a stroke. You were killing my husband."

She was right, and I knew it. "I know, and I'm sorry. I didn't want it to happen like this. How is he now? How is Mamman?"

Souri jumped to answer, "Don't bother! You should have been concerned about them before, not now."

"Please tell me," I insisted.

Ignoring my question, she said, "Niki, you've hurt Mamman and Shahram enough. Now it is time for you to correct your mistakes. If you really care for them, prove how concerned you are."

Silence was my answer. This was not the time to argue. *Indeed,* I thought to myself, *the worst is over. Now both Shahram and Mamman know about everything.*

"Don't just sit here and look at us! We are not here to entertain you. Say something and end this craziness," Tara insisted.

"Now that Shahram and Mamman know, it doesn't matter anymore. They're already in shock and …" I began to explain.

But Souri interrupted me and asked, "Who said that they know? They don't know anything about your marriage. Shahram was shocked that you were still seeing the guy."

Tara took over to help Souri make her point, "Think what would happen to him if he heard how stupid you were and what you've actually done."

Despite their anger, both still tried to trick me into making a decision. "I don't believe you. Shahram saw us together the day before the trip," I said quietly.

"Okay, he knows now, but you still have to get the divorce. It's the only way," Souri confessed.

"No, now that they know, I don't see any reason for a divorce. Behzad sends his family officially for khastegari and we … , " I was suggesting my imaginative plan as they listened to me with their mouths hanging open.

"You are really an unreasonable, dumb girl! You are not ashamed at all. How dare you suggest something like this when you saw what happened today," Souri said in a stunned, low tone.

Tara, too, seemed to become more irritated over my suggestion and said, "Wake up Niki, the problem is not khastegari or the ceremony. Why can't you understand?"

The harder they tried to get into my head; the more disappointed they became. I would listen to both of them, but I would repeat my first response, "Now they know. It makes no difference if I divorce him."

Both women were extremely mad. Souri turned to Tara and said, "Let's go. She's not living in this world. Talking to her is just a waste time. It's like talking to the lifeless wall."

They left me. Souri was right; it was like talking to the wall. I had turned into a wall. My entire body was a lump. My senses had been transformed to a tight mass and made me unable to feel anything at the time.

Souri returned with my purse. She handed it to me and quite unsympathetically said, "Go. Go wherever you want and never look behind." Then she left.

With my purse in my hand, I sat there, unable to think. I looked for Arya and found him in his room playing with his toys as Fati watched over him. He ran to me. I embraced him and kissed him. He asked me to play with him. I kissed him again and held him tightly against my chest and said, "Auntie Niki has to go now. I promise next time. Okay?"

I heard myself saying: *Auntie Niki has to go*; then I had to go. My instinct or maybe my stubbornness influenced my decision to leave. I put Arya down and watched him go back to Fati. I hung my purse over my shoulder and stomped out of Souri's house.

*   *   *

I leaned against the door of Souri's house, which I had just closed behind me. It was Friday. On Fridays, my whole family usually gathered together in our house for lunch or to drink tea and chat. But this Friday was completely different, and I could hardly digest the events of the day. A painful knot tightly blocked my entire throat. I wished I could cry to ease the pain.

Hesitantly, I started walking to the main street. I turned back after every couple of steps, looking back, hoping someone would call me to return. It felt as though I had betrayed everyone, and I kept going. I turned to the main street and no longer turned to look back. I found a telephone booth to call Behzad. He was not at home. I took a taxi. Since it was Friday, the traffic was not very heavy. The driver drove fast to get me to a completely new life—as fast as the speed of the events of the day were leading me to my destiny.

Chapter 8

~~~~*

Drastic Change

On that fall night in 1979, the moment I opened the door to my apartment, my life took its course toward a series of drastic changes. Once inside the apartment, I felt a dreadful anxiety that had not only controlled my soul but my entire body as well. Impatiently, I paced around until I heard Behzad's steps in the hallway.

He was not surprised to see me there. I felt he was expecting me. He knew that I would be there soon or later. He came to me and hugged me. No words exchanged between us for some minutes. He held me tightly against his chest. I had not shed a tear from the time I had told Souri the truth about my marriage even though I needed to cry to ease the pain.

Suddenly, the curse of heaviness in my heart burst open and my tears began to flow. I cried hysterically while Behzad held me in his arms and caressed my hair affectionately. I cried throughout the entire night. Behzad sat by me and talked about the bright, happy life before us. He tried to convince me that our life together was worth the hassle. But no consolation made me stop crying, not even his.

*   *   *

I started a passionate and loving life with Behzad. He easily expressed his love and made me feel loved. He was a devoted and supportive husband. He cared for me and treated me like a princess. I was very happy with him, but losing contact with my family, Shahram in particular, was hard on me. My mother was the only one who never lost contact with me or left my side.

"Why Niki? Why did you do that? Did you ever think about Shahram? Why did you leave home like this? You are a part of me, how can I cut you out of my life?" my mother had asked as she expressed both her love and her disappointment the day after I left home. She could barely handle my punishment and being "cut out of her life" as she phrased it. So, less than a month later, she came to see me and remained in contact with me while the others did not even answer my phone calls. They hung up on me as soon as they heard my voice.

I badly needed to call Shahram to hear his kind voice and tell him how sorry

I was to disappoint him, but I could not. Many times I attempted to call him, but before he could pick the phone up I hung up.

*   *   *

Later, my mother told me about the day I left home. "The day you left, Shahrooz followed you in his car and waited outside your place for a while," she confided. "After that, and for some weeks, he or Shahram watched you to make sure everything was fine with you. They did not trust Behzad to let you just go to him."

I was curious to know how Shahram had found out about my marriage and asked my mother about it. She explained that Souri went to Shahram and Tara's home in the morning to have breakfast together. Once, after they had been away for two weeks, Shahram had casually asked Souri what they should do about me and the guy. Confused, Souri mistakenly thought that Shahram knew about the marriage and responded that I had to get a divorce. That unexpected response to his innocent question shocked Shahram terribly and made him so furious that he lost control.

After hearing how Shahram found out, I was amazed how a simple misunderstanding turned everything upside down. "Everything happens for some reason," I told myself to justify my deeds.

*   *   *

In Iran, family bonds are usually very tight. People always have contact with each other even though they are not physically close. I needed to feel the sense of love and security from my family. My thirst to be back among them was unbearable. However, having family or friends around seemed to be the least of Behzad's concerns.

Months had passed since Behzad and I officially began living together. Naturally, I was expecting to meet his family and friends. Our only visitors were my mother and my friends. I did not meet anyone from his side at all. I had my doubts whether or not he really had any friends. So I raised the question and his response was a promise that I would meet them soon, which never happened.

"I'd like to meet your family. Why don't they contact us? Have you ever told them about us?" I asked him once.

"What a question! Of course I have. You know that they are not living in Tehran," he responded.

"This is not an excuse. They don't live on the top of the mountains or in the desert! Wherever they live, they could certainly phone. And if they really care, a short trip would not hurt anybody," I asserted.

"They are like your family. They are still angry with me because of the way we got married. But don't worry. That will pass sooner or later, and you'll finally meet them," he explained.

Not believing him, I said, "This is ridiculous. First of all, you are a man and, generally, families are not as tough on boys as they are on girls. Secondly, this is not your first marriage."

"Still, they are angry with me for whatever reasons that they have. They are my least concern. I know they'll make peace soon," he said.

"What about your sister? She lives here in Tehran. Is she upset too?" I asked.

"She is like the others," he answered briefly.

"You told me that you were living with her when we were dating so she knew about us. Didn't she?" I asked.

"Yes, but it doesn't change anything," he said.

"Why don't you call her and invite her to visit us?" I asked.

"I'll never do that. I never beg for love. Remember, love is something that you never beg for. If she cares, she'll call," he stated.

"Give me her number. I'll call her," I suggested.

"No, she has to call you!" he disagreed.

"I don't care who calls first. I just want to see them," I insisted.

"But I care, and I want them to call my wife," he replied.

Some months later, I finally met one of his sisters, Jila, a tall and cute young girl, who had just returned from London, where she had been living many years. On her first visit to our home, I found her to be a very warm and humorous girl. At the time, she lived in Tehran with one of her sisters, Homa. I was delighted to meet one of his family members, though I still could not understand why the others never called or visited us.

*　　*　　*

I had never heard him talk about his daughter. He had told me that his daughter lived in Ahvaz, a city in southwest Iran, with her mother, but he never visited her. Not having any contact or even a phone call with his child was very bizarre to me. "Have you had any contact with your daughter recently?" I asked him once

"Why do you ask?" he wondered.

"Why not ask? She is your daughter. I was wondering if you have any contact with her," I repeated.

"I've told you that she lives with her mother who does not want me to see her," he said.

"It is your right to see your own daughter. She can't stop you from seeing her," I said.

"I don't want to cause any trouble for her mother," he said.

"What kind of trouble?" I asked.

"She doesn't want me to be involved in my daughter's life, and my daughter has a good life with her. So why bother?" he tried to justify.

"Don't you miss your daughter?" I asked.

"She was just a baby when her mother and I divorced. I haven't seen her for a long time. Actually, she is just my biological kid," he said nonchalantly.

"What? Just your biological kid! How can you say that?" I asked stunned at his response.

"I haven't been with her to see her grow up. That's why. Now please don't talk about my past. I don't want to bring any part of my past life into our life together. Please forget that I even have a past. My life started with you. I have no past. I don't want anything from the past to get into our life. Please, Niki. Please end this talk," he replied.

"Everyone has a past, and no one can forget the past. Why should your past disturb our life?" I asked.

"I want to concentrate only on our life. Just that! Please, you do the same," he said to end the discussion.

But I remained curious. From time to time, I insisted that I meet his family.

Chapter 9

~~m~~

Iranian Kurdistan

In 1980, shortly after Mr. Bahrami arrested, the new president of the newspaper firm, Mr. Taheri, began a mass lay off, or *paksazi,* of "undesirable" employees. The displaced employees were replaced by those who were loyal to the Islamic regime.

Behzad was among those journalists who were displaced. Before enforcing the restricted Islamic media laws, and prior to being laid off, he had been sent to Kurdistan by the firm a couple of times to report about the turmoil and uprising against the central government in that region. (Appendix E)

*   *   *

On his various trips, Behzad interviewed some leaders of Kurdish opposition, including Abdol Rahman Ghasemlou,[11]" Sheikh Ezzeddin Husseini,[12] and Jalal Talibani[13].

During that period of time, society changed drastically. It was clear that the crucial social and political restrictions were getting worse.

Meanwhile, the media kept their freedom. Many newspapers and magazines were published, including some without publishing licenses. Political parties were still able to publish their own bulletins. On Fridays, Tehran University was the meeting place for various political parties and other groups to exchange their opinions and also distribute their newsletters and bulletins.

Before the Islamic regime took total control over the media and enacted restricted media laws, Behzad decided to publish his own newspaper, *Persian Kurdish.* From my viewpoint, his trips to Kurdistan had aroused his interest in Kurdish political matters. His newspaper supported the Kurdish autonomy policy of an independent Kurdistan governed by the central government.

---

11 **Ghasemlou** was the leader of the Democratic Party of Iranian Kurdistan. He was assassinated in 1989 by the agents of the Islamic Republic of Iran. (Source Wikipedia)

12 **Sheikh Husseini** was the spiritual leader of Iranian Kurdistan autonomy movement.

13 **Jalal Talebani** is the current president of Iraq. He is the leader of Democratic Party of Iraqi Kurdistan. At that time he fought against Saddam Hussein.

He made trips to Kurdistan for interviews and to report on the Kurdish uprisings for his own newspaper, which was distributed mostly throughout Kurdistan. Behzad and I distributed any remaining copies among the activists in the Friday gatherings at Tehran University. The *Persian Kurdish* newspaper was published as long as no publishing permit was required.

*   *   *

The clashes between Kurds and government forces, the Pasdaran, intensified and reached its peak. In addition, the fights throughout the other provinces changed course to more violence and acts of terror. In Tehran, as well as in other cities, mullahs and other men in power were assassinated by different political groups, who claimed responsibility for the terror actions. The Islamic regime's desperate attempt to survive and remain in power led to mass executions, terror, prison sentences, and torture. The executions included not only activists, but even those suspected of opposing the regime. Violence and fear dominated the society.

In this fearful atmosphere, Behzad and many others stopped publishing their newspapers. Instead, Behzad decided to obtain a license to legally publish a newspaper in the English language. Per law, individuals who had at least a bachelor degree could obtain a permit or license to publish a newspaper. Since Behzad did not have an academic degree, he asked me to apply for the permission in my name.

However, I was not comfortable about becoming involved in something that I had no idea of its purpose and principle. Indeed, the political direction of the newspaper was not clear to me. Therefore, I hesitated to apply for a license.

In order to win my trust with his idea, Behzad suggested that as soon as the license was issued, I would give him a power of attorney. That would make him, officially and in writing, the only responsible party. The plan sounded logical and safe to me; I agreed.

I applied for the permission, and it was approved. According to the plan, on the same day we went to a law office. I officially gave him authority to use the license to publish a newspaper. The document indicated that I was the owner; but as the publisher, Behzad was entirely responsible for the paper's content.

The process went smoothly and soon after, Behzad started running the newspaper. He rented an office in a nice, central part of the city. He made a pleasant office for himself by furnishing it in a very short time. He hired two young girls who were proficient in the English language and a young boy as his assistant. The two girls would translate his articles and news from Farsi to English. The boy would run the office tasks. Behzad would be out of the office most of the time to collect the news to report.

In the meantime, I was busy with my regular job and passionately participated in many anti-regime gatherings and rallies. Sometimes I followed Behzad to his interviews with politicians and religious leaders.

*   *   *

Behzad and his employees enthusiastically worked late hours to get the *News in English* papers out. After publishing a few issues of the newspaper, Behzad came up with an idea. He wanted to hire journalists to work abroad and send reports to him for the newspaper. The journalists would pay their own fares to Europe. Their salaries would be on a commission basis. The idea seemed perfect.

In no time, Behzad put an advertisement in several major newspapers of the country to hire journalists to report from Europe. The chance to go abroad in those days of crisis and an unpredictable future was an opportunity for many young journalists. In less than a week, hundreds of resumes streamed into the office.

Most who had applied for the job were not qualified. It was difficult to choose the right person for the job. Behzad came up with a solution. He put another advertisement for a group test. The date and the place were announced; participants who passed the test would be invited for an interview.

All the plans and ideas made the atmosphere of the office vigorous. I impatiently looked forward to going there after my work day to be a part of the adventure. The three young employees were enthusiastic about the entire project as well.

With the help of a TV reporter, Behzad prepared the test questions. The test was given in an amphitheater in a college. I was proud of Behzad. It was amazing that he was able to manage everything so quickly and was so organized. His employees were also impressed.

A week after the test, the results were ready and the interviewing process began. Behzad conducted all the interviews and selected a few qualified journalists. Those selected came to the office every day, expecting to be sent to the various sites as soon as all travel documents were prepared and available.

Chapter 10

⟶

Reconciliation

It was nearly eight months since we had been married and about five months that we had lived together. I was still dealing with my conscience to overcome the guilt of betraying my family. However, enjoying a passionate life with Behzad convinced me that despite all pain, I had made the right decision by marrying him. Unfortunately, one day another unexpected incident filled my spirit with turbulence.

Automobile license plate numbers in Iran usually indicate the province in which the car was registered. The plate number of Behzad's car indicated it was registered in Ghazvin—a city in northwestern Iran. It did not seem to be a big deal until one particular Friday.

On that beautiful, spring day, we decided to go out for lunch. We parked in front of our favorite restaurant. As the host escorted us to a table, Behzad suddenly took my hand and drew me toward the door and out of the restaurant.

Quickly, he opened the car door and asked me to get in. As we quickly drove away, I asked, "What's happening? Why did you do that?"

"There was a person that I didn't want to see me," he said calmly as though it was not a big deal.

"Who was that person?" I asked

"Not an important person, I just didn't want him to recognize me," he responded casually.

"The way you ran away from him shows me that he is important to you," I said.

"I didn't run away. Let it go. Don't think about it. We'll go somewhere else to eat," he said nonchalantly.

His coolness and denial made me uncomfortable. I pushed the matter. "I don't want to go anywhere. Just tell me why you ran away? The way you behaved was like you were a criminal who had seen a policeman."

"I told you why. It's nothing more to it. Now tell me where do you want to go?"

"Nowhere! I will not go anywhere. I know it is something that you don't want to tell me. I have to know whatever it is. I will not let it go so easily," I insisted.

"You have to tell me."

While Behzad tried to calm me down, he said, "I'm not a criminal and no one is after me. The thing is that I know people. Some are like lizards. They make your life miserable. The guy I saw inside is one of those people. I did not want him to bother us."

"How could he make our life miserable?"

"Niki, I don't want to take any chances when it comes to our life. I prefer to avoid problems. Maybe I overreacted in the restaurant and made you suspicious. You still don't understand how precious you and our life are to me. I haven't gotten hold of this life easily, and it would be easy to lose that hold."

"I care about our life too. The thing I don't understand is why someone can put our life in danger. We are not from another planet. We are regular human beings, like others. At least I am! What makes us so important to lizards, as you call some people who want to harm us?" I insisted on getting an explanation.

I had learned from experience that it was not easy to get a straightforward answer from him. Then, the conversation would get me nowhere. I remembered Shahram's smart observation after talking with Behzad for the first time, "He knows how to talk," Shahram had said. "He is a good talker."

I, too, had begun to realize that Behzad was the master of manipulation. But this time, I was determined to learn the truth. So, I stubbornly demanded an explanation about the ridiculous episode in the restaurant. Again, Behzad gave me the same silly reason over and over and insisted that I should put it behind me.

My frustration affected our relationship. The tension and coolness remained for days, which made him understand that I was not about to give up. He had to tell me the truth, whatever the truth was.

"Niki, I wish you would let it go, but it seems like you won't. So I'll tell you, but I need some time. I promise you I will tell you. Just give me some time," he told me one day.

"Why do you need time?"

"I just need time. Please give me some time."

"How long do you need?"

"I'll tell you on the day of my birthday. It's not too long to wait."

I agreed, giving him the time he asked for. His birthday was two weeks away, two days after the Iranian New Year. I was convinced that it had to be a serious matter; otherwise he would not choose that particular day to talk about it. I understood why he had chosen that day. He expected the truth would have a milder affect on me, and my reaction would be not so hard on him out of respect for his birthday.

*   *   *

March 21, 1980, was the beginning of spring and also the Iranian New Year. Having lunch the day after New Year in my mother's house was a family tradition as long as I remembered. This was a good opportunity for my mother to bring the family back together. She had tried to convince everyone to put away their anger and make up with me. However, none of them would do so as long as Shahram was not ready for reconciliation.

Three days before the New Year, my mother called to give me the news I had been wishing for. Her attempt to gather the whole family for the New Year finally was successful, and Shahram had agreed to reconcile with me.

I felt so enormously relieved to be able to return to my family. My happiness was beyond my concern about my issues with Behzad. I promised myself that I would not let anyone or anything ruin the joy of this family reunion for me.

The day finally arrived. I felt like a prisoner released from jail, not knowing if I would be accepted again as a regular, honest citizen. I rang the bell and heard my mother's jolly voice followed by the familiar sound of her steps behind the door. She opened the door, embraced me, and invited us in.

Souri, Hamid, and little Arya were already there, as were Shahrooz and his girl friend Mahtab. Ramin seemed taller than the last time I saw him. I embraced everyone and wished them all a happy New Year. The welcome was not particularly warm, but I had not expected it to be. However, Arya made me feel welcomed when he cheerfully ran to me and gave me a pleasant hug.

When I heard the bell door ring, I felt a flow of heat throughout my body and my heart started pounding fast. Ramin opened the door to Shahram, Tara, and little Neda, my happy three-year-old niece. She was my sunshine. Once they entered, I was not sure what to do and what to say. Sweet Neda saved me. She was so surprised at seeing me there that she nearly screamed to Tara in her sweet childish voice, "Mommy, Mommy look Ameh Niki—Aunty Niki—is here."

I went to her and lifted her up. I was so enormously caught in the moments of joy that I forgot how nervous I had been just a few moments earlier. Shahram kindly hugged me and kissed my cheeks. He was still my wonderful and kind-hearted brother. I was ashamed. I wanted so badly to tell him how sorry I was to have disappointed him, but I couldn't. Deep inside, I did not want to spoil the moment. I wished for everything to be forgotten and to be as it was before. It felt as though Shahram wished the same. He acted as though nothing ever happened.

He shook hands with Behzad politely. It seemed that the long period of misery was over. I was back in the bosom of the people I loved and was on top of the world. Behzad, who was treated like a family member, seemed to be comfortable and enjoying a good time.

We sat on the floor, around the sofreh, talking, joking, and teasing each other as we used to. Since politics was the subject of discussion in those days, our conversation turned to politics. Shahrooz passionately tried to convince us that we should stop criticizing the regime. To stop his tirade, and since we still were in a light mood, Tara and I teasingly carried him outside, left him on the street, and shut the door on him.

My mother opened the door to let him in, while everyone was still laughing. Shahrooz back inside, sat at sofreh, laughed and said, "You girls will never understand the meaning of logic."

Not for the first time, I noticed how different Shahrooz and Shahram personalities were. Shahram is peaceful, ethical, and caring. Shahrooz follows his own principles. Moreover his allegiance to Ayatollah Khomeini made him a very different person.

That was a wonderful, pleasant day. I hoped the time would stand still, but life had to go on. The memories of this brief happiness cheered me up for many years after.

*   *   *

The morning after my reunion with my family was supposed to be a happy day for me, but I woke up with anxiety. Behzad was already up and ready to go to the office. As usual, he was cool and jovial. His humor, and the way he put his words together to say a funny phrase, used to make me laugh, but it didn't that morning.

He came to me with his hands across his chest and humorously said, "My highness is up. How can your servant make your morning as bright as fluorescent lights?"

I ignored him.

He sat on the edge of the bed, stroked my hair, kissed me, and said, "Good morning. A tiny smile could make my day."

"Good morning." I looked at him and smiled, realizing the day was not just the day he had promised to tell me about his secret. The day was also his birthday.

"Happy birthday! I'm sorry I should have gotten up earlier to make you a birthday breakfast," I said while getting up.

"Oh, you do remember!" he said, pretending to be surprised.

"Of course, I remember. Now you sit put, I'll go get your present."

"There is a present for me! Should I close my eyes?" He was rubbing his hands together to play up his excitement.

*   *   *

After he left, I got ready for work. I still felt ill and uneasy. I thought about staying home and going back to bed to sleep the day away, hoping time would go by faster, but I did not. Instead, I went to work and straight to Susan's office. I needed to talk to someone to soothe my anxiety. Contrary to my belief, Susan not only did not ease my concerns, but she even tried to warn me. "I don't have a good feeling about it either," she said quietly. "You know that I can never trust him. You better prepare yourself for anything."

"You don't know him, Susan. You don't live with him. He is a very nice person. Why are you so negative about him?" I asked, criticizing her instinct.

"No, I don't know him the way you do, but I've heard enough about him. You have too, but you choose to ignore the talk."

"I am over those times and talks. Now he's my husband and is very good to me. That's why I'm afraid to hear what he is going to tell me. I don't want anything to mess up our life together."

"I don't know what to say, Niki. But he has lied to you before and still has more secrets."

"You're not helping me. You make me more nervous. I'll talk to him tonight. I'll let you know tomorrow."

"Be prepared for another surprise," she advised me as I left her office. "Don't fool yourself this time!"

My day at work was the same as usual, but the time seemed to pass slowly. I was so impatient that I left early. I stopped on the way home and bought a cake and some flowers. At home, I set a nice dinner table and waited for him. As we celebrated his thirtieth birthday, I looked for an opportunity to remind him of his promise. Amazingly, the moment I decided to ask him, all my worries and anxiety turned to a kind of coolness. "Do you remember your promise? I'm ready to listen to what you have to tell me."

"Yes, I remember. I still wish you could let it go." The expression on his face and the tone of his voice had changed.

"No, I can't. Now tell me," I said.

I decided not to say a word or show any emotion while I listened to him. I was determined, as Susan had asked me, not to fool myself anymore and put emotions aside to allow myself to see reality.

*   *   *

He dropped his head down and held it in his hands for some minutes. I could hear his long, loud breathing. He lifted up his head and with eyes filled with tears he stared at me. I had seen the very same scene and exact play performed before; the precise repetition of the same phrases echoed in my ears, "Niki, you are my whole world. I would die without you. Please try to understand me. I have kept this from you because I love you so much that I've been scared of losing you …."

I did not need to listen to this part of his justification, but I calmly sat there and listened. After finishing his excuse as a premise, he was silent for several moments before speaking again. "I told you that I used to work in Ghazvin for some time. You know the city is small. I didn't know anybody there. Loneliness was hard on me. You know what small cities are like. Having any relationship with a girl out of marriage is a sin, and no parents let their daughters have boyfriends." He paused and looked at me from the side of his eyes; his head was still dropped down.

Even though I could guess the next part of his story, I had to force myself to stay in control. I did not feel any kind of rage toward him. I was as still as stone.

After not seeing any reaction from me, as he had expected, he continued, "Then I met a girl. After dating a couple of times, her parents found out. Her father was wealthy and in a very high governmental position. He was angry. He was distressed over his reputation in the city.

"Then he put pressure on me to marry his daughter. I did not love the girl, but I had no choice but to marry her. From day one, a quarrel started between us. I did not want any children; I wanted out of that marriage. But she became pregnant. Before the baby was born, I divorced her and left the city." He paused once again, lifting up his head and looking in my eyes, waiting for any reaction. He got nothing.

"Niki, please say something. Please try to understand me. I know that I should have told you before, but …."

I knew by heart those phrases he was saying. I got up and left the room. He followed me, stopped me, and took my hands. I let him hold my hands and hug me. I did not have any energy or desire to resist.

"You are the only one I love and care about. Believe me; I did not love that woman. The kid is just my biological son. I haven't seen him, and I don't have any kind of feelings for him. That part of my life is dead to me," he said as he held my head against his chest.

"Enough! Two biological children! Two forced marriages! How many more biological children and compulsory wives do you have?" I asked mockingly while I tried to pry loose from him.

He let me go, and in a sad voice pleaded, "Don't talk like this, Niki! I made two big mistakes in my life. Please don't let my mistakes ruin my life. Whatever you say, just forgive me."

"How many other mistakes have you left in other cities and run away from?" I asked in a scornful tone.

"I swear to God this was the last thing I had kept secret from you. You know why I did that. How can I prove it to you?"

"You don't need to prove anything to me anymore. Everything will come out by itself. Tell me, who did you run away from in that restaurant? Why did you run away from that person?"

He did not say anything. He kept his eyes away from me for a while. I repeated my question, "Tell me who that person was?"

He cast a quick, sad look at me so I could see his tears. Then he whispered, "Why do you torture me? Why don't you believe me? I'm not running away from anyone. The person in the restaurant was a relative of my ex-wife in Ghazvin. I didn't want him to make any problems for us."

"Nobody can ever make your life a mess better than you can. You know what? It's enough for me for now. I am not in a mood to talk anymore. If you have anything new to add, say it, if not I am going to bed."

"Before you go, just tell me that you've forgiven me."

"Don't worry. When you tell me about other biological children and wives in other cities, I will simply forgive you," I said in a very sarcastic tone and walked away.

"Niki, please don't do this to me. I'm sorry," he said as I left the room.

"I'm tired, good night!" I murmured.

*   *   *

Years later Jila, his sister, gave me completely different story. As she told me, Behzad left his wife the day after their son was born. While she was still in the hospital, waiting for him, he took all the money, jewelry, and other valuable items from their house and disappeared.

*   *   *

Now that I was aware of another truth about his past, at least another part of his past, what should I do? My body was drained of emotions.

What's happening to me? I wondered as I hesitantly went to the bedroom and slowly lay down on the bed. All of a sudden, I felt the weight of my head. Its heaviness was so unbearable that I tried to squash it into the pillow. Minutes later, the heaviness was replaced by a terrible headache. I had never experienced this type of headache, but later on, and for many years to come, I had to deal with these horrible headaches. This time, through the pain, I heard the voices of those at the firm who tried to warn me, whispering intensely in my ears. I thought, *what if he is a con artist as I was warned that he was? What if he is a bad person? Where is his family? Does he really have any family or friends? Why is he so secretive? ...*

Behzad sat beside me. He caressed my hair as he used to do. I asked him to get me some pills. The headache was unbearable. I am not sure how long I remained motionless in the bed before falling asleep. I woke up with anxiety many times during the night and saw Behzad still sitting there and watching me.

When I woke up in the morning, the headache was gone, but the heaviness was still there. I heard Behzad in the kitchen, preparing breakfast. I got up and tried to get ready for work. I was confused and tired, but I felt an urge to get out of there.

Behzad entered the bedroom with a breakfast tray in his hands and said, "Good morning." I looked at him and felt only hatred. I had never felt that deep hate before and never experienced it again.

I rushed to him, took the breakfast tray, and threw it forcefully against the wall. Then with all my strength, I pounded him on the chest repeatedly and furiously shouted at him to get away from me. He took my hands and tried to calm me down. I pushed him out of the door. Then, I quickly dressed for work and left the house.

He followed me quietly like my shadow. His car was parked on the street. He rushed to the car and opened the door for me to get in. I ignored him and took a taxi to work. I went straight to Susan's office. Without any control over my feelings anymore, I started crying hard. Susan hugged me and tried to comfort me. I forced myself to control my crying and briefly told her what Behzad had disclosed to me from his past. That did not surprise her. Indeed, I was terrified that all the accusations I had heard about him might be true.

In that moment, I was unable to act normal in the office, and I did not want to draw the attention of my coworkers. I was not in the mood for working either. I called Sayeh to go to her place, but she was not at home. I decided to go for a walk. Susan was so worried about my condition that she offered to join me.

When we stepped out of the building, I saw Behzad standing by the gate. He came to me, but I went back inside. I didn't want to see him or hear his voice at that point. Susan asked him to leave me alone for a time and promised him that she would take care of me. He left.

While walking with Susan, I was the sole talker and she listened. She did not have any answers to my concerns. I was confused. I did not know how to handle this situation. I knew that my family would welcome me back, but I could not see myself moving back home. How could I tell them that I was an idiot?

Talking with Susan helped me ease the pain to some degree. On the way back to the company, we saw Behzad still sitting in the car waiting for us. When he saw us coming, he came forward and asked if everything was fine. I said that it was and he should go.

Back at work, I tried to keep myself busy. In the evening, I pushed myself to go home. I felt betrayed and being in the apartment didn't feel like home anymore. Behzad was not the same person to me whatsoever.

From then on, my feelings and behavior toward Behzad changed dramatically. He tried hard to repair our damaged relation; I thought about a divorce. Many times, I thought of talking to Shahram or my mother about it, but my pride wouldn't allow it. Besides, since Behzad had been accepted as my husband by my family, our marriage had already been announced to relatives and friends. That was another barrier in my decision for a divorce and put me in an awkward position. Per tradition, my relatives and friends had already started inviting us to their homes and coming to visit to our home. The timing made it all the more difficult.

I simply could not trust him anymore. He was thirty years old and had revealed two unsuccessful marriages. I was not sure if he had other marriages and other secrets for me. My colleagues had tried to warn me that he was a con artist and a dangerous man, but no one ever told me why he was dangerous. Nonetheless, now it was like the light of the day and clear to me that there had to be some truth in all those allegations. I started having serious doubts about his personality. How could he be so emotional, affectionate, and caring to me while he claimed no feelings for his children and called them, "just my biological kids?"

By time, my anger eased, if not faded. But my passion and love for him had turned to apathy.

Chapter 11

~~

Unpredictable Circumstances

It was May 1980 and President Bani-Sadr failed to grasp the necessary authority to govern. He had tried to disband revolutionary organizations, namely revolutionary courts and committees as well as revolutionary armed groups such as the Pasdaran. These organizations were under the influence of clergies, supported by Ayatollah Khomeini.

Since Khomeini and his Islamic forces would not give up the power to the central government, it was impossible for any president to be in command. In addition to suffering the social disorder, Bani-Sadr faced two other major problems: the issue with Kurds and other minorities and the hostage crisis in the American Embassy.

President Bani-Sadr had made many unsuccessful attempts to compromise with the Kurdish leaders. His efforts to resolve the hostage crisis were fruitless as well. As a result of his failure, the number of executions escalated and a state of terror and brutality dominated the society. Mass arrests and killings of the anti-regime activists and protesters or any other movements reached its peak. Khomeini was determined to safeguard the survival of the Islamic regime by wiping out the opponents, whom he called Islam's enemies.

*　　*　　*

Under unpredictable circumstances, Behzad took another trip to Kurdistan to make reports from that area. The trip lasted a few days. He held interviews with Sheikh Ezzedin Husseini, spiritual leader of the Komoleh Party of Iranian Kurdistan, and Abdol Rahman Ghasemlou, leader of the Democratic Party of Iranian Kurdistan. Both leaders were opposed to the regime, and Khomeini had declared jihad, a holy war, against them.

Behzad also interviewed Jalal Talibani, the leader of the Democratic Party of Iraqi Kurdistan at that time.

After returning from Kurdistan, Behzad published the interviews with those leaders. Obviously these leaders had strong words against the Islamic regime. Jalal Talebani had also criticized Saddam Hussein.

Behzad was excited and pleased about those interviews and looked forward to distributing them. I, however, cared little about what he was doing as I was still angry with him. The day the newspaper was supposed to be distributed, Behzad called me at work. It was a very strange, short call. He told me that he had something to tell me and asked me to see him outside the building.

I found him stressed and worried at the gate. As soon as he saw me, he said in a quiet and fast tone, "Let's walk!"

"What's happened?" I asked curiously as I followed him.

"Today, I received some nasty calls," he answered as he looked over his shoulders to make sure nobody was around to hear him.

"Nasty calls? Why? Who did call you?" I asked.

"The Islamic committee. They called and threatened me."

"How did they threaten you? What did they say?"

"They just said, 'It seems your head is too heavy for your neck to carry. How dare you have contact with the enemy of Islam?'"

"How do you know that they were from the committee?" I asked.

"They told me that they were from the Islamic committee," he answered.

"Why should they come after you? The newspaper is not out yet. How is it possible that they already know about the contents?"

"I don't know how, but they already knew about it."

"You say 'they' all the time. How many people have you talked to?"

"I got three calls from different people. They did not want to talk. They just swore and called me 'hostile to Islam,' we have to do something, Niki. They'll kill both of us." He sounded scared.

"Then don't distribute the papers for now. Let's wait and see what happens," I suggested.

"I'm not sure what to do. Go back to work now. I wanted you to know and be prepared," he said.

"Prepared for what?" I asked.

"I have to think about what we need to do. It's not a good sign. We have to take it seriously," he said.

"Did you tell anybody in the office?" I asked.

"No, I didn't want to scare them," he answered.

"You should have told them. They work with you and if you are in trouble, so are they," I said.

"No, they are not in trouble. Only you and I are," he insisted.

"Me? I don't have anything to do with it. Why me?" I asked.

"You say so! But the Pasdaran don't see it that way. You are the owner of the paper," he explained.

"But I don't have any responsibility," I said.

"Let's talk about it later. Now go back to work. I'll think of something," he added.

"Where are you going now? Are you going to the office?" I asked.

"I think so. I'll call you. Don't say anything to anybody. Act normal. I'll find a way, don't worry," he advised me as he walked away.

I looked around. We had walked quite a way. The streets were busy; the people and automobiles were commuting as usual. Everything looked normal. It was just my life that was about to change forever. A long, rocky road was waiting for me to cross and take me to a different world, separating me from everything and everyone I loved and cared about.

*   *   *

On my way back to the company, I wondered how the Islamic Committee had found out that the newspaper would contain those interviews. I tried to pinpoint someone inside the office as an informant, but it was not likely anyone of them could possibly be the informant, since they were young and enthusiastic about their jobs, and more important; they were not fans of the Islamic regime. I thought about the printing house, where Behzad printed the papers. I had never been in the place. I never knew where it was located either. According to Behzad, the place was safe and he knew the workers very well.

Actually, it did not matter how they had found out about it. The reality was whether it was true. If Behzad had been threatened, it was a very serious matter. Nevertheless, I still could not trust Behzad. I sensed something was terribly wrong; not knowing what it was made me agitated. I could not understand why he had to publish such provocative articles and interviews. He was aware of the cruel character of the current regime and the terrifying atmosphere its army and supporters had created. He knew very well the consequences of this kind of act; still, he was willing to jeopardize our lives.

I needed to talk to someone. Susan was just a few steps from me, but I could not make myself talk to her. In my entire life, I used to have confidence in my friends to keep my secrets private. I had many friends, but I usually trusted one friend as a close one in every period of my life, in school, college, and now at work. I freely talked to them about everything.

I had discussions about trusting people with Behzad many times before. He used to advise me, "Never talk about our life to anybody. You should never give information about yourself to people, even if they are friends."

"I trust my friends, and I always talk to them. If you can't trust your friends, then who can you trust?" I countered.

"Don't be such a fool! Friends become your enemies if it benefits them," he had argued with me.

On that day, for the first time, I realized I could not trust anyone—not even Susan.

*   *   *

At the end of the day, Behzad called me again and asked me to wait for him to pick me up. Once I was in the car, I asked him about his day at the office. He said he did not go to the office that day. He still looked very worried.

"Why not? What did you do all day then?" I asked.

"I walked around, thinking." He responded.

"Why did you do these interviews now? You should have known that it would be a great risk at this time. You knew they would ultimately come after you." I questioned his motive.

"Yes, I knew that. But I am journalist, and this is my job," he simply answered.

"But interviewing these people is like inviting Pasdaran to come after you," I protested.

"What's done is done; let's think what we do now," he proposed.

"As I told you this morning, don't distribute the papers." I repeated my suggestion.

"I thought about it too. It is the only way for us now. Let's go to the office to pick up the papers," he said.

"What should we do with them?" I asked.

"We'll take them home first and then we'll think of something," He answered.

It was late in the afternoon and everyone had left for the day. All of the papers, wrapped in bundles, were spread in the corner of the office ready to be distributed. Behzad had some gunnysacks with him, which we filled with the papers. I suggested going outside of town and dropping them somewhere into a river, but he seemed to be too scared to do anything then. Instead, we took the gunnysacks home and decided to wait a few days before getting rid of them.

*   *   *

The next morning was not so different from other mornings; the only difference was the gunnysacks spread throughout the apartment. We tried to be positive about the day. After all, we did the best we could to avoid any further troubles. We got ready to go to work as usual. In the hope of having left the trouble inside and behind the door, we shut and locked the door as left for work.

As I got to work, but before I made it to my desk, the phone started ringing. Since Behzad's office was close to our home, he had arrived at the office much earlier. I was pretty sure that the call was from him. I rushed to pick it up. I was right it was Behzad. He asked me to see him outside again. But this time, he wanted to meet at a street corner further away from the company in half an hour.

I did not have a moment to think about it or worry. I had just arrived at the office, and now I had to act as if everything was normal. I chatted with my coworkers as usual. Saeid Khan came with the tea cart and greeted us with his gentle smile. He offered everyone a cup of tea. I drank the tea and waited for an opportunity and a good excuse to leave. When the moment was right, I left for the street and took a taxi to meet Behzad.

I found him in the same distressed condition as the day before. We started walking. "Niki, they are after us. I saw the committee's car in front of the building. I'm sure they were waiting for me. We have to do something." He sounded and looked very distressed.

"What more can we do? How do you know that they were waiting for you? There are other offices in the building. Maybe they were watching someone else," I suggested.

"Maybe, but I can't take the risk. We have to get away."

"Get away? To where?"

"I don't know. Somewhere."

"I'm not sure about that Behzad. We should wait and see."

"Wait for what? Wait for them to kill us? Are you living in this country or not? Don't you see the executions? It's very easy for them to kill people."

I was frustrated. I stopped and looked at him: "You say it now! It's not something new, and you knew very well that it wasn't the right time to go to Kurdistan. Why did you do that? Your deeds tell me that you were asking for trouble. I just don't know why."

"I'm a journalist. This is my job. But now I'm worried about you. I don't want you to get hurt because of me."

"Don't worry about me. The power of attorney that I signed will prove that I don't have any responsibility for the paper."

"Do you really think that you are dealing with rational people? The power of attorney may have been an effective tool a couple of months ago but not now. For this regime, it's enough that you are my wife and the owner of the paper."

"Whatever! I still think that we should wait. You are overreacting. I think they just wanted to threaten you to scare you. Apparently, it has been working. Now no paper would get distributed. That's exactly what they wanted," I said although I was not sure about that myself.

"They don't play games with people, and you know that. They don't need to do that as long as killing and getting rid of every opponent is so much easier for them. We have to leave while we still have time. This is the only way," Behzad insisted.

"To where?" I asked.

"I'll think about it. Maybe somewhere in Europe," he replied.

"Europe? Do you mean we escape the country?" I asked. I certainly was not expecting to hear that.

"Yes, for awhile, until everything settles down," he confirmed as if it was not a big deal.

I could not believe what I was hearing. I loved my country; I loved my life and all the people in my life. I enjoyed my work. My only problem was him.

He was talking and trying to convince me that we should, at least, consider leaving as a solution. At that exact moment, I thought about divorcing him so that I could be free from all the havoc he had caused. I had lost my faith in him and no longer trusted him. On the other hand, if he was telling me the truth, we certainly would be in an unpleasant situation.

I was not able to think clearly. Who could I talk to? All of a sudden I thought of Mr. Arman, a friend of my family. I had known him and his family for years. He was a good friend of Shahram, and I knew I could trust him. He was an honest and wise man. After all, it was not fair to put my family into more misery by just vanishing. Someone close to them should know my whereabouts.

Behzad did not like the idea of telling anyone and tried to talk me out of it, but I insisted that we go to Mr. Arman to consult with him. Finally, Behzad agreed

*   *   *

Mr. Arman was very surprised at our unexpected visit. He invited us to his office and asked his secretary to bring us tea. He had met Behzad once before. He and his family were the first ones who came to our house to visit after the reconciliation between my family and me.

We sat down and Behzad told him about our situation, the newspaper, the interviews, and the threat. Arman listened to him very carefully. The longer Behzad talked, the more the sign of uneasiness on Mr. Arman's face turned to fear. Finally, when Behzad mentioned that leaving the country would be the best for both of us, Mr. Arman, who was trying to be calm and lenient, lost his patience. He interrupted him and said, "Don't rush, and give it some time. These days, this kind of threat is not unusual. Sometimes they just want to scare you. It was a wise decision not to distribute the papers. Go back to work and act normal," he encouraged us.

"You are right. We won't rush into anything. But you know how the situation is these days, and we have to prepare ourselves for anything," Behzad said.

Mr. Arman turned to me and advised me kindly, "Dear, in any case, you don't need to leave. You stay while Behzad gets away from here for awhile until the situation gets better. If he has to leave the country, you can join him legally later on."

"You know that I am the owner of the newspaper," I reminded Mr. Arman.

"Yes, I know. Maybe you are responsible too, but your charges would be minor because the publisher is someone else."

Behzad disagreed, "We don't know what will happen if they get Niki. They don't care about her. The owner of the paper is also the enemy in their eyes."

Arman hesitated for a moment before responding. "Why did you go to

Kurdistan and make those reports as you were aware of the consequences?"

Behzad gave the same reason that he had given me: he was a journalist and reported the current news.

It was obvious that his response did not satisfy Mr. Arman, "This is your job, why did you involve Niki?"

"My only regret is that I put her in this danger. It was not my intention. That's why I officially declared that all responsibilities would be mine. Unfortunately, there is no use for it now."

Behzad continued to talk and tried to explain further. Mr. Arman impatiently interrupted him, "My advice to you is not to rush. Whatever happens, it will be better for Niki to stay here." Then he turned to me, looked straight into my eyes and urged firmly, "Niki jan, I still believe you don't need to leave, but think carefully before deciding anything."

"I will, Mr. Arman, I will try my best," I promised.

*   *   *

Years later, when I saw Mr. Arman again, he described his feelings about the situation on that particular day. "That day, when you left me, I lifted the phone. I held it in my hand for long minutes, confused and undecided. I could not trust Behzad. I wanted desperately to save you, but I did not know how. I thought of calling the Islamic Committee and having him arrested. I even dialed the number. I was terrified that if I did that, it could put you in danger. I had a fight with my conscience. Finally, I hung up the phone and trusted God for your safety and destiny. Completely aware of the dangerous and unpredictable situation, I decided it would be safer for your family if they were not aware about your whereabouts, in case of any ongoing investigation by Pasdaran. That's why I never told them about your visit to my office."

*   *   *

My greatest concern was for my family. It was not fair to keep them in the dark and suddenly disappear. However, having told Mr. Arman about the trouble we were dealing with lessened the complexity for me to prepare myself for the worst.

Behzad stopped me once we were outside of Mr. Arman's office. He looked in my eyes to make sure that I was still aware of our situation and said, "Niki, we have to be very careful not to tell anyone else about our situation. We are in danger, and we should decide what to do as soon as possible. I'm still thinking about leaving before its too late."

"Why do we have to rush? Today is Wednesday. You don't need to go to the office until Saturday. Let's just wait a couple of more days." I suggested

"We can't go anywhere right away. I have to make some arrangements. It'll take some time," he said.

I had a feeling that he had already made up his mind. Now it was up to me to go with him or stay and face the consequences.

Thursday and Friday passed without any danger. That weekend was the same as other weekends; at least I tried to think it was. The only thing unusual about it was our effort to hide the newspapers. We hid them in every corner of the house, even inside the oven. On Friday afternoon, we went to Souri's. She had invited the entire family to her house for dinner. This was a very happy gathering. However, I had a concerned feeling that this family gathering might be our last.

Neither I nor Behzad mentioned anything about our problem. We pretended that everything was just as usual. I tried to forget about our situation. To me, any world outside my sister's house didn't exist that night. I wore a red, short-sleeved summer dress, which concerned my mother. Attacks on women for not wearing hijab had become a new phenomenon of the Islamic society.

As we were leaving, my mother turned to me. "Niki, for God's sake be careful. Please put on more conservative clothes. Anything can happen these days," she advised me in a begging tone of voice.

"Okay Mamman. Don't worry. I will." I promised her as I kissed her good-bye before leaving Souri's house.

*   *   *

It was Saturday morning, the beginning of a new week, and a bright spring day. I looked around calmly. Nothing had changed. The light blue curtain covering the small window did not hold back the brightness of the sun as it found its way into the room. The picture of a young, beautiful girl sitting under the shade of pine trees gazing at a flying pigeon hung on the wall. All the familiar objects in the room gave me a sense of peace. The agitation of the last couple of days seemed like an illusion. I remained in bed, feeling weak. The last few days had been so intense that I nearly forgot about my shock and frustration over Behzad's dishonesty, but it still bothered me.

Behzad was already in the shower. The sound of water boiling in the kettle from the kitchen was like a call for me to get out of bed and make tea. But I didn't. I felt a pleasant stiffness in my entire body. A bizarre sensation held me back, allowing me to stay motionless in the moment.

Behzad's voice startled me and reality set in again, "Good morning. Don't you want to go to work today?" He looked unconcerned, which surprised me as he had been very worried lately.

"Are you going to the office today?" I asked him, ignoring his question.

"Yes, I am. Let's see what happens today. As you used to say, feel the pain first then cry. I got to feel the pain first," he said offhandedly.

I said nothing. I was not in the mood to talk. I needed to hold on to my silence.

*   *   *

That morning at work I was prepared for another annoying call from Behzad, but he never called. It could be a sign indicating there were no further problems. The frustration that had prevented me from acting normal was gone. With my cup of tea that Saeid Khan brought me, I walked around and chatted with my colleagues. I felt really good and needed to keep it that way.

The brief break from reality was over the moment my phone rang when Susan and I were getting ready to leave for lunch. It was as though an alarm bell had sounded. Somehow, I knew something was terribly wrong. I tried to ignore that call. I let it ring a couple of times before answering it hesitantly. I heard Behzad's voice, "Niki, meet me at Razz's restaurant. I'll be waiting for you there."

"I'm going to lunch with Susan …"

He interrupted me and firmly said, "Niki, listen, come now. I can't wait."

"Okay, see you there then."

I sat on my chair with the phone still in my hand. I was completely undecided about everything. I could feel something was going to happen that would change my life forever.

Susan was ready to go and waited for me in front of her office. I put the receiver on the phone and took my purse.

"Order from the boss?" Mr. Amiri, my colleague, who had heard my conversation asked teasingly.

"Yes, it was. You men! We women are never at ease when we have you around," I responded laughingly.

"But you women can't live without us," he retorted in the same joking tone.

"What an honor! But you know what? I can say the same about men," I responded as I walked toward Susan.

*   *   *

After apologizing to Susan that I would not be able to accompany her to lunch, I left the building and took a taxi to the restaurant where Behzad waited for me. Traffic was not heavy, so it did not take long to get there. Behzad stood in front of the restaurant. Despite the urgency of his phone call, he seemed calm.

We entered the restaurant. He chose a table in a corner far from the other tables. Without exchanging any words, we sat down. Strangely, I was not so curious to hear what he had to say. I was comfortable with not knowing anything. In silence, we waited for the waiter.

Once the waiter took the order and walked away, Behzad brought his head closer to me and whispered, "I got a call this morning from the Islamic committee. They asked me to go to the committee and get some articles against Ezzeddin Husseini and Ghasemlou to print."

"What did you say to them?" I murmured.

"I said yes. I said I'll go and get them this afternoon."

"What do you want to do now? Do you go and get them?"

"No, I can't do that. They won't give up Niki. If I don't go there today, they'll come after us."

We both sat silent for some moments; Behzad broke the silence and said, "We have to leave today."

"And go where?" I asked.

"I'll tell you later. Be quiet now, the waiter is coming," he said as the waiter brought our meals.

I already had lost my appetite, and I had nothing to say. Behzad seemed to be in the same condition. After minutes passed in silence, he looked into my eyes and in a sad, soft tone said, "Niki, I'm sorry to put you in this unfortunate situation. Please forgive me. I know I put you in danger. But I promise you I will protect you and not let anything or anybody hurt you. I will protect you with my life, I promise."

"No, it's not just your fault. I could have said 'no' to many things, but I didn't. Now it's too late," I admitted.

"I should not have involved you in this mess. I regret it. I want you to know that whatever happens I love you more than anything in this world. I will do whatever to keep you safe. Trust me! I …" He kept on talking, but I could not hear him anymore.

My body was present but my mind was not. Consumed by my own thoughts, I tried to get a clear picture of the circumstances in order to be able to trust him again. Oddly, images of our small apartment, which we had decorated beautifully, and the colorful fishes in our aquarium moved like a slideshow before my eyes. I thought of the lovely relationship we had not too long ago.

These images were replaced by a clear picture of my mother's concerned face when I left Souri's house in that red dress. The exact emotional moment when Shahram gave me a warm hug on the day of our reunion circulated in my thoughts.

"Hey, where are you? Are you listening to me?" Behzad touched my hand to bring me back to reality.

"I'm here, just thinking."

"We don't have much time. Eat something. We have to leave."

"Where?"

"Kurdistan, there are people there who can help us."

"We must go home to get some clothes and other things."

"We don't have time for that. Our documents are important, which I have with me," he said hastily as he motioned to the waiter to bring the check. I said nothing. I didn't argue. He paid and we left the restaurant.

"Come, we have to get a taxi," he said.

"Why a taxi? Where is your car?"

"I left it parked in front of the apartment. In case they are watching me, they would think I'm home."

He called a taxi to take us to the bazaar.

"Why to the bazaar?"

"To exchange some money."

"Why? You said we're going to Kurdistan."

"In case we have to leave the country, we're going to need money."

"You don't have a passport," I reminded him. "How do you think you can enter another country without a passport?"

"I'm not sure about anything right now. Let see what happens."

"Do you have my passport?"

"Yes, I have it."

We caught a taxi and stopped talking. The silence in the taxi made me think and doubt about everything once again. *What am I doing? Why am I following him? Is my life really in jeopardy? Can I trust him? Is it possible that he's just a liar and no one is after him? Do I still love him? What will happen if I stay? Is it possible that I may get arrested or killed? What should I do? Please God, help me decide.*

I could still turn back if I decided to do so. I had two options before me. I could trust Behzad and follow him, or I could leave him and be ready to face any challenges or dangers. Neither of the choices was optimal. It was a dilemma that nearly made it impossible for me to choose.

*   *   *

The bazaar was crowded. I wasn't really aware of my surroundings. I was like a blind girl who had trusted a man to lead her. I had my arm tight around his and let him lead the way. Indeed, he was in charge of my life at that time.

He stopped at a small, exchange currency store. The entrance to the store was narrow, and he wanted me to enter first. I suddenly turned back and hung about outside the store while he exchanged his money for U.S. dollars.

As I waited on the crowded sidewalk, I wished that the crowd would take me with them or that I could get lost among my own people. I just wanted to say, *"No!"* to everything and go back home.

I was drawn into my thoughts when I felt Behzad's hand around my shoulder leading me through the crowd and out to the street. He hailed a taxi and asked the driver to drive us to Sannandaj, the capital of the Kurdistan province in Iran.

Chapter 12

⌒◌⌒

Iraqi Mountains

Feeling empty inside, I watched the city I was about to leave behind through the car window.

During the entire trip to Sannandaj, we did not exchange a single word. It was a long drive, and I was getting farther and farther away from my city and my life while getting closer to a new and uncertain fate.

It was late at night when we arrived in Sannandaj. From there, we hired another taxi to take us to Mahabad, another Kurdish city, where the foremost clashes between Kurdish activists and Islamic regime army occurred.

A couple of hours later, the taxi dropped us off on a corner in Mahabad at Behzad's request.

After passing through some small alleys, Behzad stopped at a house with an old, metal door and rang the doorbell. A young man opened the door and happily embraced Behzad and shook my hand. He led us through a small yard to a bright and simply decorated room; his wife warmly welcomed us. Our unexpected arrival did not surprise them. It seemed that we were expected guests.

Behzad introduced them to me as his best friends, Manooch and Mino. They had a one-year-old baby girl, who was sleeping in the other room. Meeting that nice and cheerful couple and the smell of freshly made food brought a sudden change to my mood and stimulated my appetite.

Mino spread the sofreh on the floor and set up the dinner. Manooch was a humorous man and made the dinner time pleasant for us. He joked and made me laugh so that I nearly forgot why we were there. His attractive young wife, Mino, may have been a couple of years older than me. Her smiling, friendly face made us feel comfortable in her house. However, it seemed strange that politics were not a subject of our conversation that night. Even more interestingly, they never asked why we were there. Thanks to our hosts and their hospitality, I had relaxed and broke my silence.

When they left us to get ready for sleep, I asked Behzad, "Do they know why we are here?"

"Yes, I mentioned it briefly to Manooch when I called him this morning."

"I didn't know you had such nice friends. I didn't know you had any friend at all." I pretended to be surprised.

"I have good friends!" he said with emphasis.

"I'm happy you do. Now we are in Kurdistan. What are we going to do here? Are we going to stay in their house or what?"

"No, we won't. Tomorrow, I'll talk to some people to see what they can do for us."

"Do what?"

"Maybe help us to cross Iraq's border."

"Who are they?"

"My newspaper is very popular among people here. Many of them know me. Some helped me with my reports when I came here. I'm thinking about talking to Sheikh Ezzeddin Husseini. I'm sure he'll help us."

"How?"

"He knows reliable folk that can help. I'll see him tomorrow. Nothing is certain right now."

"Okay, we have no choice anyway," I stated.

"Are you okay with it?"

"I'm not okay with anything. But if this is the only way, what can I say?"

"I'm very sorry, Niki. You know I am, don't you?"

"Yes, I know!"

"I promise I will never ever again let you down. Trust me."

"Don't try so hard! You know you can't regain my trust, at least not anytime soon. Please, let us not talk about trust and promises now. Save all that kind of talk for later," I said softly, trying not to be so hard on him.

*   *   *

The next morning, a crying baby woke me up. I needed a few moments to remember where I was and why. I heard Mino talking to her baby in a childish voice to comfort her. Behzad was already up; I could hear him talking to Manooch. Curious, I quickly dressed and joined them.

I was not as sad or distressed as I had been the day before. On the contrary, being in Kurdistan, which was like a battlefield at that time, had turned me to an energetic, inquisitive person overnight.

Breakfast sofreh was spread out. With her baby on her lap, Mino fed the baby small pieces of bread with jam. A samovar, with the teakettle on top of it, was set close to her. With a smile, she bid me good morning and invited me to sit beside her. She then called Manooch and Behzad for breakfast.

After breakfast, Behzad asked me to stay with Mino. He and Manooch were on the way to see some people. I didn't argue even though I was curious to meet those "some people."

I stayed at the house and played with the cute baby as Mino made lunch. Now that I was alone with Mino, I was surprised that she never asked any questions about what brought Behzad and me to Mahabad. Either she was not interested or was a respectful host and did not pry into our business. Whatever the reason, I was happy about it.

Very soon, Behzad and Manooch returned. Behzad appeared to be pleased over the outcome of his efforts of the day. He mentioned briefly to me that he had an appointment with Ezzeddin Husseini in an hour. I offered to go with him. He not only agreed but somehow he seemed satisfied with my suggestion. My guess was that having his wife at his side would make a good impression on Sheikh Ezzeddin, who might then put more effort in to help us cross the border.

*   *   *

As Manooch drove us to meet with Sheikh Ezzeddin, I rolled down the car window to let the wind blow in my face and tousle my hair. It was a beautiful, fresh summer day. Observing a completely different city and its people gave me a sense of joy.

Iran is a vast country with many different ethnic groups who share distinctive cultural traits and languages. The Kurdish people are one of those groups. Being in Mahabad gave me an extraordinary view of that part of my country. The Kurdish men and women in their traditional outfits added colors to the simplistic appearance of the town. This was the first time I had the opportunity to see Kurdish people so closely. I had seen pictures of Kurdish women in colorful, long puffy skirts and men in comfortable, baggy cotton pants in books and magazines, but they looked so different in person.

*   *   *

Manooch dropped us near Sheikh Ezzeddin's house. As we walked toward the house, I felt uncomfortable in my summer dress and high-heeled shoes, which made me look so very different from the local people.

A few young Kurdish men stood on guard in front of the Sheikh's house. Behzad told them that the sheikh was expecting us. We were asked to wait while one of the men went inside. He returned shortly to let us in.

A few Kurdish armed fighters, called Peshmerga,[14] wandered around the small yard. One of the men led us to the sheikh, who was sitting on the floor of the terrace that was covered by carpet. There was a cushion against the wall for him to lean against, but he sat straight, watching us as we walked closer to him.

With a pleasant smile, the sheikh invited us to sit down. We took our shoes off and sat down in front of him. I liked him the moment I saw him. Old and peaceful, he gave me a sense of calmness.

---

14   **Peshmerga** is the term used by Kurds to refer to armed Kurdish fighters. Literally meaning *"those who face death."* Peshmerga forces include women in their ranks. Many Kurds will say that all Kurds willing to fight for their rights are Peshmerga. (Wikipedia)

"Mr. Behzad, I'm happy to see you again. What can I do for you?" The sheikh's kind eyes confirmed his sincerity.

"Sorry, Imam, for the trouble. I know that you are very busy. Thank you for your time," Behzad said to express his gratitude.

"You are a good man and you support us. You are welcome anytime. I always have time for you," the sheikh responded.

Behzad introduced me to him and briefly filled him in on our story. The sheikh listened and shook his head as he looked into my eyes and then Behzad's.

As Behzad neared the end of the story, Sheikh Ezzeddin offered us, with no hesitation, the way out. "Both of you can stay here with us. We need devoted people like you. You stay here and help us with our campaign." He turned to me and in a fatherly tone tried to comfort me, "My daughter, you'll be safe here with us. Don't worry!"

"Thank you, I'm sure I will," I responded.

Behzad, who was determined to leave the country, smiled and revealed his plan by telling the sheikh, "I appreciate your offer, Imam. It would be an honor to stay here and serve your people, but we've thought of going to Europe. I'm a journalist and can be more helpful to your campaign when I am in Europe. There, I'll be able to report freely the true news about this regime and its brutalities." Behzad paused a moment to gauge the sheikh's reaction and response, but the sheikh said nothing; he looked straight ahead and seemed to be in deep thought.

Behzad continued, "We just need to get to Iraq. From there, we can get ourselves to any European country. The only problem is crossing the border. I hoped you would help us to cross it," he said determinedly to show he had made his decision.

"Well, … you have helped us, and I can help you. But are you aware of how dangerous crossing the border is?" the sheikh asked in concern.

"Yes, we know," Behzad confirmed and then added, "Everyone is in danger these days."

"Once you get to Iraq, it would not be so easy to get out. Are both of you sure you are willing to take the risk?" This time, his eyes were on me as he warned us, expecting me to understand the situation that I was going to put myself into.

"Nowhere is safe for us. We are ready to take the risk," I rushed to reply.

Now that I was in Kurdistan and sitting in front of the sheikh, amazingly all my distress was gone. I enjoyed experiencing the new adventure. It was like a movie in which I was to play the main role. I looked forward to starting this new adventure.

Behzad, who had not expected I would be so positive about it, proudly glanced at me. Then he turned to the sheikh and said, "We both are ready. We just need to get to Iraq."

"All right then!" the Sheikh finally said and called one of the peshmerga and said something in Kurdish to him before sending him away. He then turned to us and offered us tea, which had been served a few minutes earlier. He then stated, "I'll ask one of my faithful men to help you."

In no time the messenger, the young peshmerga, came back followed by a tall, vigorous, young man with a chiseled face and a thick mustache. The man was dressed in a peshmerga uniform, which was similar to a military uniform, but looser and thinner. This allowed peshmergas to move around the mountains more freely. He lowered his head and looked downward. Humbly, and in a low voice, he said hello and sat down by the sheikh.

Sheikh Ezzeddin said something in Kurdish to the young man and then turned to us. "Ali is one of my favorite and trustworthy men. He'll help you." The sheikh then turned to Ali. "Mr. Behzad and his wife are my friends. You take good care of them," he said as he pointed at us.

"I know Mr. Behzad well. I've read his paper. I will happily take good care of them," Ali said in his low and humble voice.

Behzad expressed his appreciation to both Ali and the Sheikh, I had a very good feeling. I liked Sheikh Ezzeddin and the people around him. Most of them were strong and powerfully built peshmergas. Despite their tough appearances, I could see in their eyes that a bright and gentle spirit was present behind that outer shell.

Ali asked us to be ready as we would leave within a couple of hours. He added that he would send someone to pick us up. Then he left as fast as he had come some minutes earlier.

We got up to leave too. Once again, Behzad promised Ezzeddin Husseini that he would never stop fighting with the power of the pen.

*   *   *

Manooch drove us back to his home. We were supposed to get ready for our journey, but we were already ready. We did not have any baggage or even any comfortable clothes to change into. Getting ready meant a call to my mother. My plan was to tell her that Behzad and I were out of town for a couple of days. This would buy me some time until I had the right opportunity to call her again. But Behzad did not agree with me. He explained that all phones in Kurdistan were controlled by the government. Making that call would be risky for us and my family. I did not listen to him and called home anyway. I lied to my mother by telling her we were in Mashhad, a holy city northeast of Tehran. The unexpected sudden trip stunned her.

*   *   *

Mino set the sofreh for us. We had just sat down when the doorbell rang. Manooch went to open the door. He came back to tell us that a peshmerga was there to take us to Ali.

There was no time for lunch. Quickly, we said good-bye to Mino and Manooch and kissed the baby before leaving. Behzad promised Manooch to call him as soon as he had the chance.

The pishmarga did not say anything other than hello to us. We followed him in silence. We walked through some alleys. My purse hung over my shoulder carrying some makeup, a small mirror, and a wallet. Behzad wore a small case around his neck containing money and our documents. My high-heeled shoes were hurting me. I wasn't used to walking very far in heels. We followed the guide, who stopped at a house similar to Sheikh Ezzeddin's. The door to the house was open. He paused to let us enter the house ahead of him.

We passed a woman in traditional dress, inside the house. She sat at a small pond in the middle of the yard, rinsing some dishes. She returned our greeting with a friendly smile as her eyes followed us. Our guide said something in Kurdish to the woman as he led us to a room.

The voices from women inside the kitchen at the corner of the yard could be heard.

Once we were in the room, we saw Ali, accompanied by seven Kurdish men, sitting around a sofreh, chatting and eating. It was a very plain room covered with a rug. There were no decorations or extra items.

We interrupted the men as we entered the room. They turned their heads toward us to respond to our, "salaam." Ali stood up and invited us to join them. He made space for us next to him and offered us some food. It appeared as if just enough food had been made for them; we simply tasted some. The men, Ali included, tried not to pay attention to us. They continued to eat and talk in Kurdish.

We were strangers among our own countrymen. They shared a common language and culture that was far different than mine. Probably some of them did not speak Farsi at all. I felt that I was already in a foreign country.

All eight fighters were in good humor—relaxed and cheerful. However, I could not keep from wondering how many of them would survive another fight. Oddly, instead of being worried about the road we were going to pass and its consequences, the unfortunate upcoming destiny of those fighters occupied my thoughts.

I was deep into my thoughts when I heard Ali mention the name of the newspaper Behzad had published in Kurdish. The men's eyes turned toward us. The glances of appreciation that landed on Behzad aroused feelings of guilt in me. I knew I should be proud of Behzad, but somehow I was not. Once again, the annoying feelings of distrust made me uncomfortable.

"*Tashakor,* the paper was good," said one of the fighters, thanking Behzad in his Kurdish accented Farsi.

"It was the least I could do. It was my duty," Behzad responded.

*　　*　　*

Once the men finished their lunch, Ali told us it was time to leave. We followed Ali and two of the men into an old, dusty car. Its driver drove away once we got into the car.

Little was said on the drive to Sardasht.[15] We stopped in that city long enough to drop two of the men off in front of a small store. Then we continued our drive to Piranshahr on the border of Iraq.[16]

The noticeably quiet and empty streets of Piranshahr seemed very strange to me. I was curious to know the reason. Ali told us about the bloody fights between the Kurds and mullah's men (he referred to the Pasdaran of the regime as mullah's men) in Piranshahr and its suburban villages.

It was dark when the driver stopped the car before a motel in a narrow alley of Piranshahr. We followed Ali inside the motel. After a short conversation with the man behind a scruffy counter, Ali paid the fee for the room for the night and got the key. Ali informed us that there was just one room available for the night, so we had to share the room with him.

The corridor that led to the room was crowded. I was the only woman. Most of the doors to the rooms were open, and I could hear noises coming from even the farthest distance. The conversations sounded like Kurdish, and I could not understand a single word. The passing crowd threw swift gazes at us. Even though no one cared about my ridiculous city outfit, I felt embarrassed. The sadness and grief on their faces had caused the atmosphere of the place to be one of gloom.

We followed Ali to the tiny room that we would share with him. It was furnished with a small bed and two worn-out couches. Ali asked us if we were hungry. I said I was not. Ali left and came back with two cups of tea and some water. He advised us to get some rest for we would have a long journey ahead of us the next day. He left us again and didn't return until the next morning.

It was a long, mournful night. Ali had told us about a recent clash between guerilla fighters and the mullah's men. In that fight, many peshmerga as well as many civilians were killed and some villages had been set on fire by mullah's men. Ali also explained that it was impossible to bury the dead bodies during the day due to attacks from the mullah's men on any kind of ceremonies. Families of those who had been killed buried the bodies in the middle of the night.

The wail of the women was heard from the distance. It was heartbreaking and unbearable. Gunfire and unfamiliar humming sounds interrupted the grieving momentarily. Tears ran down my face. I had never been so close to the cruelty of the real world. Up to that point, I had been proud of my participation in some demonstrations against the Pahlavi's regime. I couldn't help but think of my stupidity and arrogance. I was scornful of my idea of a contribution to the revolution.

---

15 **Sardasht** is a city in northwest Iran. It is the first city in the world that was attacked by chemical weapons during Iran-Iraq war, by Saddam.

16 **Piranshahr** is a city in northwest Iran on the border of Iraq. A mountainous area, there the mountains of the Siah Kooh and Sipan lie.

The sounds faded away as the darkness lightened. When the day dawned, a lifeless gloomy silence replaced the grief and mourning of those in emotional pain from the night before.

*   *   *

Early that morning, Ali returned to the room that he had never shared with us. He brought peshmerga uniforms for us to wear and a pair of sneakers for me. We wore the uniforms and put our own clothes in a bag that Ali had with him. I felt comfortable in that uniform even though it was big for me. Now, Behzad and I no longer stood out as two funny looking strangers.

We left the motel to continue the trip. Including the driver, Ali, and two other peshmergas there were six people in that small car. The street still was empty. There was no sign of the mourners from the night before. I wondered what type of disaster came out of the gunshots that we heard throughout the night.

We drove through the street and passed some routes by the countryside. We saw vast areas of tight trees and bushes along the path. The driver dropped us at a mountain slope. We would be walking on the next portion of our journey. My sneakers were too large and not so comfortable, but in that situation, I could not complain. We walked and climbed the rocky mountain with its thick trees and bushes until we reached a more open area where we were joined by men on horses. They had four extra horses and a pony for us. The pony, as we learned, was for Behzad to ride.

On our arrival, everyone mounted on horseback. Ali got up on his horse, and one of the men helped me to climb up to and sit behind Ali. A spontaneous, tidy line of riders was made.

The path was not so difficult for the horses to climb. The riders seemed to have no problem keeping themselves seated steady on the horses. However, while the horse climbed uphill, holding tightly onto Ali's waist trying not to fall was a real challenge for me.

We rode for a few hours before we reached a gully with a small river of clear, cold water. This was our first stop. The fresh and clean air of the mountains was pleasant. The other riders, the peshmergas, seemed not to pay any attention to us. They dismounted and led the horses to the river to drink water. Behzad helped me get off the horse so Ali could dismount.

My back and legs ached, but the journey was something of an adventure. And I enjoyed it. I didn't know where we were heading and what would happen on the road. I didn't know what was waiting for us after we reached our destination, supposedly somewhere at the border of Iraq. The unknown made the journey more exciting. Once the horses had their fill of water, we continued on our way.

Hours later, the sun began to sink down to the horizon. We had ridden almost the entire day when we arrived at a flat area of the mountain. The area was not vast, but large enough for a clean shelter for the peshmergas to rest. The men led the horses to a corner of the area to tie them up and let them rest. One of the men helped me get down. Ali took his horse and Behzad's pony to the same kind of open stall.

The area was roughly packed with stones, and a cavernous opening was located at one side of the shelter. A couple of peshmergas as well as other men and women rambled around. Ali walked over to one of the peshmerga, who was a young girl with curly, brown hair and big, brown eyes. He motioned to us to join him. As we approached, he introduced the young girl as his wife Fatimah. She greeted us with a pleasant, wide smile before disappearing into the cave.

Fatimah came out shortly, carrying an aladdin, a kerosene lamp. She turned it on and put a kettle of water on top of it to boil for making tea. She went into the cave again. This time, she brought out a rug to spread on the ground and invited us to sit on the rug. Behzad and I sat down as she and Ali joined us. It was as though this small spot of the enormous mountain was their home; none of the other peshmergas came close to their territory.

Fatimah poured tea for the four of us, but I was so exhausted and starving that I did not care for any. I drank it anyway. After the tea, Behzad asked me to stay with Fatimah. He was going to meet Jalal Talebani—the current president of Iraq—whom he had met a couple of times for interviews. Talebani was hiding from Saddam Hussein at that time.

I was eager to go with him and meet Jala Talebani in person. Behzad had no objection, but Ali did. He said it would be better if I did not follow. *It was understandable,* I thought. *Ali would not take any unnecessary risk to expose Jalal Talebani's hiding place for anyone.*

I was so worn out that I forgot how hungry I was and fell asleep after they left. I am not sure how long I had slept; but when I woke up, it was completely dark. Behzad and Ali had returned and sat on the blanket at my side and talked. I got up and joined them. Fatimah was not around. The aladdin was on and a pot was on top of it. Peshmergas sat on the ground at a distance from us. The sky burst with stars. It was a beautiful, chilly night.

Behzad and Ali passionately discussed politics, which I didn't care about at the moment. My only concern was my hunger and whether or not we would get something to eat. The pot on top of the aladdin was a good sign to me; I prayed that there would be food in it.

My prayer was granted. Fatimah came out of the cave with some spoons and bread in her hands. She placed them in front of us, took the pot down, and asked us to eat. I did not know what the food was, and it did not matter. I do remember that it was the most delicious food I had ever eaten.

Once we finished the meal, Ali suggested that we get some rest. The peshmergas were already lying down on the rocky ground. Ali mentioned we would need more energy for the next day.

Fatimah led Behzad and me inside the cave where we would sleep. The cave was so dark that it was impossible to see how big or small it was. We merely trusted Fatimah to lead us inside. She stopped at one spot and said we could spend the night there and left us.

I am usually frightened of mice, lizard, and other rodents. Thinking of any possibility, of being exposed to them, scared me to death. But oddly enough, that night I never came close to thinking that those animals existed in the cave, which certainly could have been the case.

We sat on the ground and touched the rocks around us, feeling for a blanket or something on the floor to sleep on. There was nothing but rocks. We were too exhausted to care. We just lay down and fell asleep on the rocks.

I opened my eyes the next morning. Still, all I could see was darkness. It was cold, and my left shoulder ached. I felt Behzad sitting at my side. I turned my head and saw a narrow beam of sunlight that stretched inside through a small opening in the cave.

"Are you awake?" Behzad asked quietly.

"Yes, I am. It is so dark. How can Fatimah find things in here?"

"They can't have much. This is their hiding place. They have to be prepared to get rid of everything in case they have to escape," Behzad explained.

My eyes had slowly become accustomed to the darkness. The only visible thing was a small barrel of water and a broom that leaned against a corner. Everything else was just stones. I still was not able to see enough to determine the size of the cave.

Outside, Fatimah and Ali sat on the rug at the same spot as the night before. The peshmergas, whom I could see more clearly in the daylight, were a group of about ten. Some sat on the ground, some on the stones, and others stood or wandered around to kill time. I was curious to know what was on the agenda for the day, but it was not my place to ask.

Ali was shaving. He had a razor in one hand and a small mirror in the other. A bowl of warm water and a piece of soap were placed in front of him. He greeted us and adjusted the mirror and began to shave. Fatimah asked if we needed some water to freshen us. She went inside the cave to get a pitcher. There was not much water in it, but it was enough to wash my face and feel refreshed.

It was an early, chilly morning. Our surroundings consisted of the mountains. The silence was enjoyable but somehow creepy to my "city" ears. We sat by Ali and Fatimah. We did not say much and just waited for Ali to finish shaving so we all could have tea.

Fatimah poured me tea. We had cheese and bread for breakfast. I was enjoying the dazzling morning of the mountain when Ali announced it was time to leave. He gulped down the last drop of his tea and stood up to set off. We did the same.

Behzad took our bag of clothes and said good-bye to Fatimah, thanking her for her hospitality. She was such a nice, quiet girl that I felt I needed to hug her good-bye. However, the atmosphere was so serious that it left no room for sentimentality and emotions.

Ali and some other peshmergas had readied their horses. Once everybody was on the horses, Behzad helped me up to sit behind Ali again. Then he got up on the pony. Once again, I held on tightly to Ali's waist. Everyone was ready for another day of riding.

*   *   *

By noon, we reached an open area somewhere on the mountain. We had ridden nonstop through the hills for hours and had come across some other riders. It was only later that I learned they were smugglers. I was stiff from sitting the entire time and clutching Ali's waist, trying not to fall off when the horse had to go up and down at ledges.

I understood later that the open area was a kind of encampment and a shelter for smugglers, peshmergas, and other travelers who crossed the border illegally. By the time we arrived, some men and horses were already resting in that area. Some loads were already in piles all over the place; other smugglers were in the process of unloading their horses. At one side of the area, stones were piled up to provide a shady place and shelter.

Apparently that was the place we had to say good-bye to Ali and his companions. From there on, we would trust another guide. As soon as we got off the horse, Ali called to one of the men inside the shelter to join us. Ali assured us that the man was reliable and that he had full confidence in him.

The man came toward us. He was a strongly built Iraqi Kurd with a heavy mustache. Ali had a short conversation in Kurdish with the man before introducing "Ali Arab" to us as a good friend. Ali Arab would get us to Iraq. He reassured us once more that this was a good man and we could trust him. Then he insisted that we be very quiet on the entire journey to Iraq. He explained the importance of the silence—the lowest sound would draw the attention of the border guards, which would create a very dangerous situation for everyone.

Before leaving, Ali told us about a shooting the night before in the very same track we would be on. A couple of men had been killed by Iraqi guards, It was imperative that we were careful and followed Ali Arab's instructions.

*   *   *

Ali left us, and I watched him riding fast on his horse until he disappeared somewhere in the mountain. I felt abandoned among strange men in that creepy atmosphere of bare nature far away from civilization. Now, we had no choice other than trusting Ali Arab. Our new guide gestured toward the shelter area and said something in Arabic. We did not understand what he said, but we guessed that he meant for us to go there. Without a word, we followed him to the shelter. The area was covered by short-napped and coarse carpets. In the corner, I noticed an old metallic table with an aladdin and a samovar organized side by side on it. On top of the samovar, a teapot was kept warm. A young, skinny boy served cooked rice from the pot on top of the aladdin. A few men leaned against the wall, talking and laughing in Kurdish and in Arabic.

As we entered the shelter, the men looked at us and kept their eyes on us for some moments before continuing their conversation. We sat down. Ali Arab, our new guide, said something to the boy then joined the other men to chat. The skinny boy came to us with two cups of tea and some bread and rice, which Ali Arab had ordered for us.

Gradually, more and more men and horses occupied the area. Now there were not enough empty places inside the shelter for all the men to sit. The men spread around. Horses were unloaded and tied. The loads were piled all over. Some men sat or lay on the ground; others groomed their horses.

I sat by Behzad, looking around. Since I was the only woman there, Behzad was concerned and uncomfortable. He asked me to take a nap, but I was not sleepy. I was excited about everything. This was a different world to me; I wanted to be awake to observe everything. Those strangers, struggling for survival in their little world, seemed to be nice and peaceful. Most of them might be smugglers, but not drug dealers I hoped. The way they spoke, laughed, and wandered about peacefully in one of the quiet parts of our world, could easily make one forget about all the nastiness of the real world.

Hours passed. As the sun made its way to the horizon, the men started loading horses. When the sky turned completely dark, Ali Arab came to us, and we followed him to his horse. I would ride with him as I had with Ali. Behzad climbed up on his pony.

Recognizing the smugglers among the numerous men in that place was not difficult. Since their horses were loaded with goods, they had to walk ahead and hold the bridles. The others, supposedly not smugglers, rode on horses.

Everyone was ready to move. After some minutes we set off in a neat, long line.

*   *   *

The mountain was enveloped in dark and silence. The only sound that could be heard was the soft and stealthy friction of horses' hooves rubbing against the rocks. We moved very slowly so that no sound would catch the border guards' attention.

For a time, we moved up the mountain. I held on by tightly clutching Ali Arab's waist when the horse climbed higher up the slope. The trail had not been so difficult at the beginning. We rode some hours on the flat ground until we had made our way down the mountain. Absolute darkness dominated, and the yip of foxes was the only sound that broke the silence of the mountain.

Behzad rode on the pony behind Ali Arab's horse. From time to time, I turned my head to be sure he was behind me, but I could only see a shadow of him. Ahead of us, other men of the group moved forward very slowly.

Going downhill was more difficult, and it restricted the movement of the horses. Some spots of the mountain were so slippery that from time to time the horses tripped so harshly at the ledges that the stones and sands under their feet slid down to the gorge. Thanks to the darkness, I was not able to see either the pathway we crossed or the narrow valley below. Based on the men's reactions, I understood how tough the path was in different spots.

At one point, the pathway was so narrow and slippery that everyone had to get off the horses to lead them. Ali Arab dismounted as well. Behzad and I were the only ones riding. Ali Arab walked next to my horse with the bridle in one hand and the bridle of Behzad's pony in the other hand. Ali Arab's hand was my only savior in some spots when my horse slipped and I lost my grip. I was so frightened that I was close to screaming in some instances.

Once, at one hazardous area and in a fragile moment, all the riders got off the horses to lead them through the rough path. One of the men came to help Ali Arab. The man took Behzad's pony's bridle and let Ali Arab have both hands free to take care of his own horse that I was riding on. He kept the bridle in one hand, and safeguarded me by his other free hand. It was a tough struggle for me to tighten my grip on the horse. Ali Arab was a great help to holding me on the seat.

My horse suddenly slipped and lost its balance. I was close to falling when a hand clutched at my face and held me strongly until the horse regained its footing. Ali-Arab had been walking by my side, but everyone was so close to one other, I was not sure whose hand had saved my life at that moment. The pressure of the hand on my face and the shock of the incident made me lose control. I wept. It seemed that the expression of my fear was not just weeping as Ali Arab put his hand on my mouth to silence me. The hushing sounds from the others reinforced the need for me to keep quiet.

Finally, after many hours, we reached flat ground. Soon after, most of our fellow travelers split and disappeared in the darkness. The others gradually left until only the three of us remained. Behzad was still on his pony; Ali Arab walked holding my horse's bridle in his hand. My legs stung from the friction against the saddle, and my entire body ached. I could hardly stay seated on the horse. I asked Ali Arab to let me walk. He helped me down. I walked a bit, but I had no energy left to walk. He helped me up on the horse again. However, rubbing my sore legs against the saddle was painful. I asked him again to help me down. I am not sure how many times I climbed up and down the horse's back.

As we continued along, Ali Arab pointed to the distance where we could see a faint flicker of lightening. Supposedly, that was our destination.

*   *   *

The wind blew stronger as we got closer to the lights. Walking in silence for more kilometers, Ali Arab pointed to one side of the vast desert. I looked in that direction and saw a cottage. By the time we reached the cottage, the blast of the wind was so enormous that I struggled to keep my feet on the ground. The power of the wind made the sands of the desert circulate in the air and slap my face and eyes.

The cottage had a small porch. Ali Arab knocked at the small, wooden door to the cottage. A young Arab came out, and they exchanged a few sentences. The Arab went back inside and handed Ali Arab a mattress and two pillows. Ali Arab gave the items to Behzad and pointed to an iron bed that was a few feet away from the cottage in the open field.

Once we got to the bed, we tried to put the mattress on it. That was not so easy due to the severe wind. After we managed to get the mattress on the bed, we lay down, holding the pillows tightly, and tried to get some sleep. I was so exhausted that in spite of the loud, sandy wind, I fell asleep.

The morning light of the day and the warm wind woke me up. I looked around. There were no other cottages or trees. There was nothing other than a sandy field. The wind was still strong enough to blow away my pillow, mess up my hair, and cover my face with dust. But it was my burning legs that screamed for attention. I rolled up my pants to see how bad the scratches were. The sides of my legs were completely red and irritated. I was dying for some water to wash the dust from my face. Behzad still slept. Ali Arab rested on the porch. The only sound was the blast from the wind. I didn't see any horses, not even Behzad's pony. I guessed they were tied behind the cottage.

I spotted someone approaching from a distance. As he got closer, I woke Behzad up. The stranger was a tiny, short, middle-aged man. This made me think there might be other cottages or villages somewhere close by.

The tiny man woke Ali Arab. They sat on the porch and talked for a while before Ali Arab called us to join them. We carried the mattress and pillows with us to the porch. As we reached the porch, the young Arab, our host we had seen only shortly the night before, opened the tiny door of the room and stepped out. Now in the light of the day, he looked much younger. In his white *deshdasha*—the long, white Arabic dress for men—he looked tall and brawny.

We greeted the three Arabs and handed over the pillows and mattress to the young man. He took them into the room. When he returned, he invited us in. We entered the room; Ali Arab and the stranger followed.

The young Arab's wife, in her red traditional Kurdish dress, sat at sofreh. She looked so young, and her pale, pretty face glowed. She had breakfast ready for us in her small, tidy room. We all sat down around the sofreh to eat.

After breakfast, Ali Arab asked us to change our clothes. We changed from the peshmerga uniforms to our city clothes. The clothes seemed totally wrong for that area; and once again, I felt uncomfortable and embarrassed.

We were ready for our next adventure. I did not feel tired, but I hoped that it would not involve riding a horse. Luckily, it did not. However, now we were to walk. For how long and to where, I did not know.

When it came time to say good-bye to Ali Arab, I wished I could speak his language to thank him for saving my life several times during the journey. I looked at his hands. I would never forget those hands. I was sure that his face by time would fade away from my mind, but I would always have a clear picture of his hands in my mind.

*   *   *

We set off across the lifeless field again on the windy, sunny, hot day. The tiny man moved quickly, I nearly had to run to catch up with him. After going some distance for about an hour, we reached an Iraqi village. The tiny man pointed at a building, said something to us, and quickly left. In a matter of seconds, he was gone.

Behzad and I looked around. We were on our own. Neither of us was certain about what the tiny man meant, but we started walking toward the building that he had pointed to. A few Kurdish villagers, who were coming and going in the empty, small, dirt alley, watched us while they passed. We reached the front of the old, brick building with a worn-out sign in Arabic above its small, metal door. We realized it was the police station.

*   *   *

It was about nine o'clock in the morning as we stood in front of the old building. The door was half opened, and we could hear two men talking inside. I tried to glance through the crack of the door, but it was not open enough for me to see anything. "Can we go in now?" I whispered.

"Yes, I think we should," Behzad replied then added, "Let me talk. Don't say anything."

We entered the building. The police station was just one small room that was furnished with two desks and a couple of chairs. A picture of Saddam Hussein, hanging on the white wall, was the only decoration in the station. As the two policemen stood up and took some steps toward us, one of the men said something in Arabic.

"We don't speak Arabic. We are from Iran," Behzad said in English.

None of them knew English. The policeman continued asking questions in Arabic.

"We are from Iran. We speak Farsi. We don't understand what you are saying," Behzad said in English again.

The policeman gave up his questioning and said something to the other man. Then he went back to his desk, called someone, and talked shortly before handing the receiver to Behzad.

Speaking in English again, Behzad said, "Yes, my wife and I are from Iran. We escaped from Iran." His conversation was very short, and he was asked to give the phone to the policeman. "Certainly, hold on please," Behzad said as he handed the receiver to one of the men.

The policeman spoke a few words before ending the phone conversation. Then he turned to us and pointed at the chairs offering us seats. We sat there, wondering what would happen next.

Both officers were very nice. We were offered tea and later on, at noon time, after hours of waiting, we were served lunch. About one o'clock in the afternoon, a well-dressed young man entered the police station. Unlike the other men I had seen during those couple of days, he was clean-shaven and had no moustache. He did not appear to be Arab or Kurdish.

As soon as he entered the station, he came straight to us and introduced himself in Farsi as "Ali." He was Iranian and the third person by the same name that was introduced to us so far. The only reasonable explanation of using the same name of Ali was to prevent being identified by their real names; since Ali is a common name, it is often used as an alias.

Ali—who for less confusion I refer to him as "Ali Irani"—told us that he was an Iranian but lived in Iraq. We were happy to be able to communicate with someone who could speak our language. Behzad told him briefly who we were and why we were there: "I am a reporter and we've escaped from the regime. We just need to cross Iraq to go to Europe."

That brief statement seemed to be enough for Ali Irani. He never asked any more questions. He just asked us to follow him. His shiny, white car was parked in front of the police station. That luxury car seemed out of place for such a small, humble village.

Behzad sat in the front; I sat in the back seat. Ali Irani ignited the engine with a loud blast. There was no traffic on the narrow road to wherever he was driving. He drove at an uncomfortably high speed. It was as though he was competing on a race track. The thing was that his car was the only one on the track. Sitting in that car and watching his driving was quite scary. Miraculously, after driving for an hour, we reached Sulaymaniah—a city in Iraqi Kurdistan. He parked the car in front of a small, decent-looking hotel.

"It is a nice hotel. Stay here tonight to rest. Don't leave the hotel. I'll come back tomorrow to take you to Baghdad," he said as we entered the hotel. He asked us to wait for him to make sure that we got a nice room. He talked to the receptionist, came back with a key, and escorted us to the room. Before leaving, he advised us one more time not to leave the hotel under any circumstances.

The room was a paradise considering the circumstance. For the first time after days of not having enough water to wash the dirt and sand off my body, water was a luxury. The hotel had just one common bathroom on the floor, but it did not matter to me as long as there was water to wash the dirt and enjoy the freshness. Once I found the bathroom, I took a long shower. Since I did not have any other clothes to change into, I put the same dress on.

I fell asleep on the bed while Behzad showered. When I woke up, it was dark outside. We went downstairs to the small restaurant in the hotel. We ate dinner and talked about calling my mother. I insisted on calling to let her know that I was fine, but Behzad did not like the idea. He reasoned that as long as we were in Iraq, it was risky to give anyone any information. Since Iran and Iraq were not on friendly terms with one another, he believed the phones were tapped. We should be very careful until leaving Iraq. I gave up on the idea of calling home and contented myself with the thought that within a couple of days we would be in Europe. I could call my family from there.

Since the hotel room certainly could be wired and we would be watched, we were very careful of what we said inside the room. The matter Behzad was most concerned about was his connection with Jalal Talebani and his newspaper that supported the Kurds. Sitting at the corner table of the hotel's restaurant seemed to be a safe place to talk.

"You know, they can't trust us. We have to be very careful not to mention anything about the paper and Kurdistan. While we are in the room, we have to be so careful not to mention any names at all," Behzad whispered quietly in my ear.

* * *

The next morning, after breakfast, we sat in the lobby, waiting for Ali Irani. Hours passed with no sign of him. We ate lunch as well as dinner and waited. The waiter was an elderly, nice man and gave us extra attention. I felt comfortable with him around—whether or not he was a government agent. There, in that small hotel, we looked different as well. Once again, I was the only woman in a hotel full of men. I could feel the curious eyes on us. Spending the entire day waiting for Ali Irani irritated us. Finally, we gave up waiting until the next day.

However, several days passed with no sign of Ali Irani; we still waited. As we were told not to leave the hotel, I felt that we were informal prisoners. Each day, new guests checked in and out the hotel while we still sat in the lobby waiting. Behzad whispered in my ear, "They are testing us. They have left us here to see if we would contact anybody. Don't worry, they'll come eventually."

Six days passed. On the morning of the seventh day, while we were sitting at the lobby after having breakfast, a nicely dressed, middle-aged, bearded Arab man entered the hotel and walked straight to us. "I here, go to Baghdad," he said in his limited Farsi.

"Who are you?" Behzad asked.

"I here, you go to Baghdad," he repeated.

"Sorry, but we don't know you and can't go with you. Please send Ali Irani to us," Behzad said.

"Come, you see Ali Irani," the Arab man replied.

"No, we will stay here and wait for Ali Irani," Behzad insisted.

The man gave up and left when he realized that he could not win Behzad's trust.

"Why did you do that? We should go with him. Now we must sit here and wait again. God knows for how long. Ali Irani sent him. Who else knew we were here?" I protested.

"Niki, we have to be very careful. We can't trust anybody. Ali Irani was the one the police knew and he took us from the police station. The only person we can trust for now is Ali Irani. It's safer to wait longer. They will eventually send Ali Irani," Behzad reasoned. "Be patient."

He was right; the next day Ali Irani appeared while we were having lunch and joined us. The nice, old waiter brought him a cup of hot tea. As he sipped the tea, he asked Behzad with a chuckle, "Why didn't you go with that man yesterday?"

"I didn't know him, so I couldn't trust him. You are the only one we know," he replied.

Ali did not argue and Behzad never asked him why he had left us waiting in that hotel for days.

After lunch and before leaving, Behzad headed to the reception desk to pay and check out. Ali Irani took him under the arm and said, "This has already been taken care of. Let's go."

Behzad paused, thinking for a moment; it seemed as if he was not sure how to react. "Thank you," he said hesitantly.

We stepped outside the hotel and breathed the outside air for the first time after eight days. Still, we never got a chance to see the city. Instead, we experienced another car racing adventure in Ali Irani's car. Actually, it was not as scary to me this time. I found it exciting and enjoyed the ride instead of being tense. More traffic on the road made the ride more adventurous.

The sun was about to go down when we reached Baghdad. In a suburb of Baghdad, Ali Irani passed through some small, beautiful streets with elegant, large homes. He stopped the car in front of one of those houses and blew the car horn. In minutes, a young boy opened the gate of the house and Ali Irani drove in and parked his car behind two other cars.

Despite the residential appearance of the building, my first impression was that this could not be a home after all. To the left side of where the cars were parked, there was a garden with some tall trees. A wide balcony off the upper floor extended across and in front of a few rooms with small windows.

The three of us stepped out of the car. Escorted by the young man, we passed through the garden to take the stairs up to the wide patio. The young boy opened a door that led to an entrance off a narrow, long hallway and escorted us into a windowless room. It appeared to be an office. A picture of Saddam Hussein hung on the wall behind a middle-aged solemn officer, who stood up as soon as we entered the room. Two other younger officers stood by his side. We shook hands and sat down on a sofa. The middle-aged officer returned to his desk and sat down. The two other officers sat on chairs closer to his desk.

"Welcome to Iraq. I hope we'll be a good host for you," the older officer said while Ali Irani translated the officer's words into Farsi for us. Surprisingly, before we had the opportunity to say anything, the officer took a large bundle of money from a desk drawer and handed it to Ali Irani. He took the money and politely offered it to Behzad. However, Behzad refused to accept the money and asked why it was offered.

"This is just as a small token of appreciation to you for coming to our country. Please accept it as a gift from us," the officer explained.

"Thank you for your hospitality, but we don't need money," Behzad said politely and explained his real plan for the journey. "We just need to cross your country to go to Europe."

Ali Irani stood in front of Behzad and translated his words to Arabic for the officer. The officer then looked at Behzad and said, "You are welcome to be our guests for how long you wish. The money is your gift. It's our tradition to offer money to our guests. Please take this and enjoy yourself while you are our guests."

"It's very kind of you. With all respect, I can't accept the money. But I'll be more than happy to accept a cigar as a gift," Behzad said as he pointed to a box of cigars on the officer's desk.

The officer gave the box of cigars to Ali Irani to offer to Behzad as he said, "Certainly, please have one." Behzad took a cigar. With his eyes still on Behzad, the officer took a different tactic. "Since the lady does not smoke; then the money is her gift."

It was strange to me that the officer did not talk directly to me but addressed Behzad. Ali Irani still held the bundle and drew out his hand to Behzad again as the officer asked him to do. "I don't smoke, but I'd love to have a cup of tea," I smiled and said before Behzad had the chance to respond. Finally, after Behzad smoked his cigar and I had a cup of tea, the officer gave up. He took the money and put it back in the drawer. That was it. The whole conversation about nothing but the money was over as was our meeting with those officers.

We returned to the car, and Ali Irani drove away. We did not talk much in the car and never asked Ali Irani where he was taking us. Behzad was very careful not to say anything unless he was asked to; he had advised me to do the same. We passed through several streets, crossed some busy parts of the city, and stopped at the front of another spacious house in a nice area.

Ali Irani parked the car on the street and asked us to go with him. We followed him to the door and stayed close to him while he rang the doorbell. He listened to the voice on the other end of the door phone then said, "This is Ali. Mister is expecting me and two guests."

We heard the sound of the door opening electronically. Ali Irani pushed the door wide open. Then he asked us to get back into the car to drive inside. He could have asked us to wait in the car instead of having us walk with him to the door. It was obvious that he was not comfortable leaving us in the car by ourselves—not even for a moment. Once we were back in the car, Ali Irani drove it inside the house's passageway. He parked the car at the side of another nice luxury car inside the house.

The house was very nice and certainly residential. The vast garden in front of the terrace was covered with green turf surrounded by numerous beautiful and colorful flowers. In the middle of the lawn, white chairs and tables were set up for a party. Lights, which were set up all around the garden, had covered the darkness of the night and created a relaxed, enjoyable atmosphere. In the background, Arabic music played as a few guests, men and women, in elegant outfits walked around, chatting and laughing.

We stepped out of the car, uncertain what to do and where to go. A middle-aged woman in her elegant dress and makeup came to us. In English she invited us to join the party, which seemed not have started yet.

Ali Irani stayed by the car as Behzad and I followed the woman. It was interesting that she never asked us who we were yet she invited us to join the party. She led us to a table of beautifully arranged fruits and various appetizers and said to help ourselves.

We treated ourselves with some fruits and sat at a table as the guests would cast discreet glances at us. I enjoyed the gentle, caressing breeze that touched my face and disheveled my hair. Ali Irani disrupted my moment by asking us to go to meet Mister.

We followed Ali Irani up to the terrace and into a vast hall furnished with elegant classic furniture and beautiful paintings. It was a large, two-story house; there certainly would be several bedrooms on the second floor. Ali Irani led us to a set of brown, carved double-doors at one corner of the hall. After knocking at the door, we entered the room to see an older, well-dressed man sitting at a classic desk that was similar to the furniture in the hall.

The old man looked up at us. He appeared to be in very good shape. He stood up to shake our hands and pointed at a couch for us to take a seat. The room, which we understood was his home office, was not decorated as fancy as the rest of the house. We sat down on the couch and Ali Irani sat down beside us.

"Welcome to our country," the old man said softly. "What is the story?" he asked as Ali Irani translated to Farsi for us.

Behzad told him about the escape from the regime and tried to specify that our purpose of coming to Iraq was not to stay.

"You are our guests now. Your happiness and comfort is our duty and pleasure as long as you are our guests," the old man said. While Ali Irani translated for us, the old man reached out to hand a bundle of money to Ali Irani. This time, the bundle was thicker than the one the officer had offered us before. Ali Irani stepped forward to get the money. The exact same scenario was repeated.

"Here you are. This is a small present from us to you," the old man said. As before, Behzad refused to take the offered money and stated the same reason that he had given to the officer in our first meeting. The old man insisted that giving money, as a present, was an Iraqi tradition to respect and honor the guests. He finally gave up and took the money back in exchange for one cigar.

That meeting was as short as the first one. We left the house and once again we found ourselves in Ali Irani's car and heading to another destination.

*   *   *

As we drove away, I thought about those two meetings. The way Behzad handled the situation and did not accept the money impressed me enormously. I suspected that the offer of money by these two men was a test to determine if Behzad was a person to be bought. He proved that he was not for sale.

*   *   *

It was late at night when we drove away. Ali Irani was the only person who could speak our language. He knew what our final destination was for the evening, but he preferred not to talk at all. He stopped the car in front of a house on a narrow street, and honked the horn. After some minutes, the door opened wide and Ali Irani drove the car inside.

"Here you'll stay tonight," Ali Irani said.

"Will you come back tomorrow?" asked Behzad

"I'm not sure, but there are others who'll take care of you," replied Ali Irani as he opened the car door.

The house was small. A tiny pond in the middle of the house was surrounded by green grass and a few flowers. Compared to the other two houses I had seen in Baghdad, this house seemed very small and simple.

We passed the garden and followed Ali Irani inside the house. Two young men came forward. Ali introduced them to us as our hosts, Nasser and Abbas. We shook hand with both young men.

"Don't hesitate to ask them for whatever you need. This is your home now …" Ali Irani was saying when I interrupted him.

"Our home? Didn't you say just for tonight?"

Behzad completed my question by asking, "How long will we be staying here?"

"I'm not sure, but don't worry, you'll be in good hands," Ali Irani replied and left us in the house, which, we had learned, was to be our home for an indefinite time.

*   *   *

Abbas left as soon as Ali Irani was gone. In the short moments I saw him, I found him to be a very solemn, neat, young man. Short and burly, he appeared to be a couple of years younger than Nasser. His penetrating eyes seemed too small for his round, clean-shaven face.

Nasser was a tall, brawny, and good-looking young man. His thick, black hair and mustache did not match his cheery face. He welcomed us in English and gestured to one bedroom and said, "This is your room. Just let me know if you need anything."

The room was small, clean, and windowless. A queen-sized bed and a black phone on a small table in a corner of the room were the only amenities.

The moment we entered the room I argued with Behzad over calling my mother. I was sure that my family was worried sick about me, and I needed to know if Mr. Arman had told them about our visit to his office. I had to be sure that Pasdaran had not bothered my family because of us. As I insisted that I had to give my mother a short phone call, Behzad voiced his concern that the Iranian regime would learn we were in Iraq. Finally, I gave up in the hope that we would leave Iraq soon, and I could call home.

I walked out into the hall to find the bathroom. I came across three bedrooms and a medium-sized living room. It was furnished with two dark green couches and four matching armchairs. A brown, round, wooden table was placed on a colorful carpet in the middle of the room. Light brown curtains covered two large windows, which faced the garden. The dining room shared a wall with our room and was separated from the living room by a white room partition. A wooden dining table with eight chairs was placed in that plain area. The kitchen was located next to the bathroom.

I was surprised to see Abbas in the kitchen; he might never have left after all. I asked him for some water. He did not understand me. Then I pantomimed that I was drinking from a cup. He just shook his head and opened the door to the refrigerator. A bottle of water was the only thing in there. He poured some of the cold water into a glass and gave it to me. He tried not to look at me. I was not sure if he was shy, religious, or an extremely serious person. In any case, I found him to be an awkward person. Actually, the entire situation was strange and made me feel uneasy. However, the reality was that another cycle of unexpected events in my life had just begun.

Chapter 13

⸺✳⸺

House Arrest

The morning sunlight woke me up. It was the end of May 1980. I was getting used to waking up in strange places. I looked at my watch. It was still early. The only sound in the house was from a small, portable air conditioner in the corner of the room. Behzad slept peacefully. My effort to do the same was useless. I sat up in the bed, thinking about the day before and wondering what a new day in our journey would bring.

"Why are you awake so early?" Behzad lifted his head to ask.

"I can't sleep. Go back to sleep," I replied.

"Are you okay?" he asked as he leaned toward me.

"Yes, I'm okay. I'm thinking about yesterday. Why do you think those two men tried to give us money?"

"As they said, it was their tradition," he replied and put a finger on his lips in a gesture asking me not to talk about it. Then he whispered in my ear, "Let's talk later."

I realized that he was concerned that the room might be wired.

"Okay! Now I'm hungry. I hope the guys are awake by now to give us something to eat," I said to change the subject.

*   *   *

Nasser kindly invited us to the dining room for breakfast. He and Abbas joined us at the table. We ate breakfast in silence. We couldn't communicate with Abbas and had nothing to say to Nasser.

After breakfast, Abbas left us. Nasser accompanied us to the living room. He turned on the radio and listened to Arabic music. Behzad asked if he could change the station to Radio Iran to listen to the news. We were hungry for any news from our country. It had been approximately two weeks since we had left, and we were completely unaware of what was happening in Iran. We sat close to the radio and listened to the news.

The news about mass executions of members of different parties and other activists, who the regime called the Mofsede-Fel-Arz—dirtiest souls on earth— was not really breaking news to us. However, reports of Bani-Sadr's struggle to hold onto his fragile position as president and the unfortunate destiny of the shah were heartbreaking.

As we listened to the radio, three Iraqi men came to visit us. Two were middle-aged men with moustaches, and the third one was a young, clean-shaven translator. Strangely enough, the first topic of their concern was my anxiousness to call home. It confirmed Behzad's concern about our room, or maybe all other rooms in the house to be wired.

"Your wife can call her mother if she likes," one of the men told Behzad.

Behzad cast an eye on me to not say anything as he answered, "Yes, she would like to. But, as you know, it might be risky. The phone lines in Iran are under control of the government. She'll call her mother later from Europe."

"Yes, yes, you're right," the man replied and then asked Behzad if he could talk to him alone. I understood that I had to leave them. I said nothing and left the room.

It was a very brief visit. At the door and before leaving one of the men said something in Arabic to Abbas and then turned to us, "I'm sure you need to buy some things. Nasser and Abbas will take you shopping. You can ask them for whatever you may need. They are here for you. You are the guests of our country."

*   *   *

On that hot, summer day, Abbas and Nasser accompanied us to go shopping. I had heard and read much about Baghdad; but this was my first trip to an Arabic country. I expected Baghdad to be a mysterious and obscure city as it was described in the classic stories. However, I found it not only an ordinary town, but a rather dull and boring town.

Abbas parked the car on a busy street. Both Nasser and Abbas escorted us to a medium-sized clothing store where I selected some clothes. At the register, Abbas insisted on paying, and Behzad tried to stop him.

The situation made Behzad uneasy. "You know what?' he asked. "We are good with what we have. I don't want to buy anything. Please take us back. If I want to buy something for my wife, I like to pay for it myself."

Nasser translated to Abbas and they exchanged some sentences in Arabic.

"Please, do your shopping. You are our guests. We're trying to make you happy, but that is fine." Nasser said trying to cool Behzad down. "Do your shopping."

They did not attempt to pay again that day, but they never left our side, not even for a moment.

*   *   *

We remained in that house somewhere in Baghdad. It was as though we had never left the hotel in Solaymanieh. The only difference was that we had two jailers. Nasser was the only person we could communicate with, and he was always around. Abbas was there too, but we only saw him at breakfast, lunch, and dinner. The food was delivered three times a day for the four of us. We sat around the table in silence to eat; Abbas never talked to us. I suspected he knew both Farsi and English, but pretended not to understand.

Behzad and I were cautious and did not speak freely with each other. We were concerned that we might say something that would make our situation worse. It was highly possible that we were kept under surveillance in that house. We restricted our conversations to daily ordinary things. If we needed to communicate on more important matters, we wrote notes to each other.

The days were very hot. Our activities inside the house consisted of listening to the Iranian radio stations and playing some childish games such as the dot game. We filled a piece of paper with dots. Then we took turns drawing lines from one dot to another to make a square, which was called "home." The person who completed more squares won the game. In the afternoons, we walked in the garden.

Nasser was our company and translator when we watched television at night. Most of the programs were about Saddam Hussein. Singers sang about and for him. The news started with reports of his visits to various places. The filmed reports covered the entire visit, which sometimes took hours. He almost always had his little girl with him, which impressed Nasser. He expressed his appreciation and love for Saddam Hussein. Nasser was very nice and goodhearted. He gave me the impression that he really believed in Saddam Hussein.

Abbas was around all the time like a shadow, but I could not describe his personality.

*   *   *

Days passed by. And my frustration grew. My sleepless nights were the most difficult. I needed to call home to make peace with myself, but that simple wish seemed to be impossibility. I cried and prayed many times for my family's safety and well-being—in particular my mother's. I hated and blamed myself for causing her so much distress and hardship.

Behzad stayed awake and kept me company through the long, painful nights. He tried to comfort me by giving me hope that we would be free to go soon. He seemed very confident and positive. I was at a point where it did not matter to me whether we stayed in Iraq or left for another country. I just wanted to know my family was safe and that they knew that I was safe too.

*   *   *

Weeks passed with no visitors. It seemed like we were ignored completely. I started thinking how serious our situation was in Iraq. I had a passport, but Behzad did not. What was he thinking to illegally enter a country with no passport and then ask to leave to another country? How was it possible? We had already escaped one border, how could we escape another one? We were in a very awkward and complicated situation. As each day passed, it became more obvious that we were stuck in Iraq for a long time—if not forever.

Finally, we had a visitor one morning. The short, stubby, middle-aged man with a round and happy face spoke Farsi in a broken accent. His voice was familiar. In Iran, I had listened to him from an Iraqi radio station that broadcast programs in Farsi. That station had broadcast anti-Iranian regimes' news and reports during the shah's regime and now against the Islamic regime. Its main objective was to raise tensions within the country so the outcome would be a revolt by the Iranian people to change the regime.

The radio announcer stayed with us for couple of hours to discus Iran's situation and politics. We passionately discussed the Islamic regime and the revolution. Nasser sat with us. I was certain that Abbas, our invisible host, was somewhere in the house, maybe behind the wall, listening to us.

"I would like you to work with me at the station," the radio man said in the middle of our discussion. "You can write and make reports for the radio," he suggested to Behzad. Then he turned to me and added, "And you can help me read the news."

"We would be very pleased to work with you, but we won't be here for long," Behzad answered for both of us. "But I can write some articles for the station while I'm here," he offered as an option.

"Thank you, I really need you at my side to help your people get rid of this horrible regime. Think about working with me for a longer time! I'll come back to discuss more about it," the radio man said.

"You are welcome here anytime. I'll help you as much as I can while we're here," Behzad repeated his offer and his determination to leave.

Later that day, Behzad began writing some articles against the Islamic regime in Iran as he had promised. He gave the articles to Nasser to deliver them to the broadcaster.

The broadcaster returned a few times with the same proposal, but he stopped coming when he realized that he could not convince Behzad to stay and work for the radio. However, Behzad continued to write and his articles were broadcasted.

During this time, representatives from another group came to see us. Two young, enthusiastic men from the *Mujahedeen Khalqe Iran*—an Iranian armed resistance movement—asked us to join them in the fight against the regime. We were familiar with the organization. They, as did other organizations and parties, played a significant role in the revolution and in fighting the shah. The organization's ideology was a modernized, not so restricted version of Islam—a liberal Islamic regime in Iran. (Appendix F)

The two young men were not curious about our reason for being in Iraq and never asked about our ideology or political views. Their mission was to ask us to join their organization.

"I'm sorry, but I'm a journalist. As a journalist I have to be independent in order to report the facts. I appreciate your offer, but I prefer to fight the regime through my pen," Behzad explained his position to them.

Without an argument, the men thanked Behzad and left. They never came back.

The third attempt to keep us in Iraq came as a request from Dr. Shahpour Bakhtiar's organization.

One evening a middle-aged man named Borzo, accompanied by two women, visited us.

Haide was tall and chubby with a beautiful, round face. She was very funny and talkative.

Zoei appeared to be younger than Haide. She was skinny, not very tall, and quite shy.

Initially, Borzo seemed to be a very formal man, but later on he appeared to be very humorous.

They lived in France, and, as Haide said, they traveled frequently to Iraq. She explained that she would leave for France the next day. Impulsively, I asked her to call my mother from France to let her know that I was alive and healthy and ask after my family. I begged Haide to call as soon as she reached Paris. She promised me that she would. That promise lightened my heart. A heavy, painful weight, which had pressed against my heart, was temporary lifted away.

After some discussion about Iran and speculating on the future of Iran, Haide told us the reason for their visit. "In fact, we are here to ask you to join the campaign. Dr. Bakhtiar personally has sent us to you to deliver his message. Dr. Bakhtiar wants you to join our organization. We all fight in the same front and for the same cause, namely for a free, democratic Iran. We really need to be together in this."

"It would be an honor to fight in Dr. Bakhtiar's front. Certainly! My weapon is my pen and I can use it when I am able to write freely. As soon as we get out of here, hopefully soon, I will proudly cooperate in Dr. Bakhtiar's front," Behzad replied. Once again, he was careful to pinpoint his determination to leave Iraq as he agreed to work with Dr. Bakhtiar.

"I would be very happy to do whatever I can," I added. "Mr. Bakhtiar is the only person we can trust to work for the people. I'm sorry that I was so naive not understanding it before it was too late." It was my genuine opinion and I meant it.

"I will give your message to Dr. Bakhtiar tomorrow when I return to Paris," Haide said briefly and ended the conversation about this matter.

I wanted them to stay longer. As they were about to leave, I spontaneously asked them to stay for dinner. To my surprise, they gladly accepted my invitation. I excused myself and went to the kitchen. I wanted to tell Nasser that we would have guests for dinner. He smiled kindly and promised he would ensure there was enough food for everyone.

Nasser kept his promise. Nasser and Abbas left us to sit with our guests to eat. They did not join us as they had on all the other nights.

Our conversation changed from serious to humorous. We quickly felt like that we had known each other for years. We joked, laughed, and enjoyed the evening until midnight. They left us after promising to come back again, and Haide reassured me that she would call my mother the moment she was back in Paris.

For the first time in a long time, I felt alive. I could still laugh out loud and enjoy the moments. A flash of hope brightened my mood. The reality of an uncertain future and an unbearable present time had seemed remote and untouchable when we were eating, chatting, and laughing.

One week later, they visited us again. Haide comforted me by letting me know that she had called my mother. Haide had relayed my message, and my family was fine. She also gave us a message from Dr. Bakhtiar that he was happy to have us on his side and looked forward to seeing us.

They visited a few more times, and we enjoyed being together. Their visits were the only pleasant events in Iraq that I experienced.

*   *   *

It was late July 1980. Ever since we left Iran, about three months earlier, many unpleasant incidents had occurred in my country. Our only source of news was the Iraqi radio station. We were saddened by the news of the shah's death on July 27. The cancer took his life in the same insidious way as the mullahs took over his country. He passed away in Egypt.

After his departure from Iran, the shah was rejected by many of the allied countries. Anwar Sadat, the president of Egypt at the time, remained the only true friend of the shah. He not only offered him to stay in his country; but also honored him with an official royal burial ceremony.

The news of his death made the mullahs and many others happy, but not me. Even though I did not completely agree with the way he used to run the county, I was saddened and felt an unbearable deep grief.

Sitting on a chair, in a room of a house located somewhere in Baghdad and kilometers away from my homeland, I listened to the radio. I heard the breaking news of the death of the man, who I passionately shouted, "death to," many times during the revolution. Now he was gone, and I was supposed to be happy about it. But I cried tears of sadness and guilt. It was not what I and many others had wished for. I was no longer sure that he was the cruel dictator as had been said. I regretted my participation in "the misleading" of the so-called revolution. I cried for the past and realized that the past was gone forever and nothing would be the same again.

The escape of President Bani-Sadr and the executions of his friends and supporters were two other important and sad incidents of that time. This confirmed that I should not expect anything to get better.

*   *   *

The days passed with no visitors. The agents of Shahpour Bakhtiar never visited us again. The situation was weird, and our destiny was in the hands of total strangers, none of whom was available to us to talk about our future and how long we would be their prisoners.

Behzad and I could not talk freely to each other; scribbled words on paper were our exchange of ideas about the situation. Our daily routine consisted of three meals with our jailers—Abbas and Nasser—listening to the radio, taking a walk in the small yard of the house, and playing the stupid dot game. I was frustrated; Behzad appeared to be relaxed.

Finally, after a couple of weeks, two older Iraqi men came to us. They were accompanied by a younger Iraqi translator. These were not the same people who visited us three months earlier. As soon as we sat down, I was asked to leave them alone with Behzad, exactly the same way that the other Iraqi visitors had asked before.

I left them reluctantly; they understood how disappointed I was. Maybe Iraqis are not accustomed to talking to women when it comes to serious matters. I hated to be treated like a child, but I cared less about that during this situation. I just needed to get out of the house. It did not matter to me where, I just needed to be free to go.

After they left, I wanted to know what they had talked about. Behzad, just as before, reminded me of existing wires in the house by placing his finger on his lips. I brought paper and pencil for him to write down. We always used pencil because we could erase our communication.

I asked in writing, "What did they want?

"They want us to stay here. I said no," he wrote back.

"That was it? You talked for over an hour. Didn't you talk about anything else?"

"No. They were trying to convince me."

"Why?"

"To work with them."

"What kind of work?"

"Reporting and writing for the radio. They want to have another radio station to broadcast in Farsi."

"What did they say when you said no?"

"They asked me to think about it. They'll be back."

"What should we do?"

"They can't keep us here forever. Don't worry! They will have to let us go."

"When?"

"Soon!"

"How do you know?"

"They have no choice."

"Can't they just let us go to France? You didn't say no to Bakhtiar's people."

"It makes no difference with whom we work. They want us to stay here. We have to wait and see."

That kind of communication took time and many pages, which we had to erase over and over.

The visitors returned two days later. This time I knew my place, so I stayed in the bedroom.

After they left, Behzad came to me. To my surprise, he took the pencil. While writing something to me, he said, "I have good news." Then he showed me his note on the paper which was: "Act as if you know what I'm talking about."

"Good news? What?" I asked, trying to act normal, though I was not sure how to react.

"Do you remember that I promised you we'd celebrate our anniversary in Sweden?"

"Of course, I remember," I said even though he had never promised me that.

"We will be in Sweden for our anniversary."

"What do you mean? How?" I asked puzzled. I did not need to pretend anymore; I was really surprised.

"I told them about my promise to you and that our anniversary is in two weeks. They agreed to do their best to get us to Sweden by then."

"Really? Wow! Great!" I shouted in joy and jumped up to hug him.

When I calmed down and digested the news, I handed the paper and pencil to Behzad to tell me more about the meeting.

Our "conversation" returned to writing back and forth.

"I told them that we can't stay here because you don't feel good and that you need to call your mother. I told them that I promised you we would be in Sweden for our anniversary and that you are looking forward to it. Nothing more was said."

I wrote back, "Did they say that they'll let us go to Sweden? Isn't that weird?"

"Why should it be weird? We've been telling them all the time."

"I don't know, but, it doesn't matter, I'm just confused. Never mind, I'm happy just to get out of here."

Behzad scribbled back, "They said they'll see what they could do. They did not promise anything."

"They don't care about our anniversary. Why should they care?"

"We'll see. Don't worry," he wrote.

*   *   *

Early the next morning, as we were getting ready for breakfast, Nasser knocked at the door. He informed us that we had visitors.

"We are popular these days, aren't we? It's ironic that no one comes here for weeks, and then suddenly we have guests before the roosters wake up," I said humorously.

"It's good to be popular. Hurry up! Let's go."

"No, you go, I'll stay here. They will send me back here anyway. I won't be missed."

He left and I sat on the bed anxiously waiting and hoping for good news. It did not take long before Behzad came back and told me that they needed to talk to both of us.

"Oh! Really? Are you sure they want *me* to be present—not the neighbor?" I joked.

Smiling, he grabbed my hand and dragged me along. "Okay, come now. I'm sure they meant *you*, not the neighbor."

With Behzad holding my hand, we entered the living room. The same young translator from the prior day and two other Iraqi men waited. I shook their hands and sat next to Behzad.

"You want to leave us, let's see what we can do for you," the old man said. He was a skinny, short, and gentle old man. He made a very good impression on me the first blink I saw him. He reminded me of the old version of Mr. Arman.

I knew by then that he, the old man, would be the speaker and the other man would just sit and listen. In every meeting with us, there was one speaker, one observer, and one translator.

"You've been very kind to us, and we appreciate your hospitality, but unfortunately we have to leave," said Behzad apologetically.

"We understand. Now the problem is that you need to have a passport ..." the old man said when I interrupted him.

"I have a passport."

The nice man smiled and said, "I know, but your husband does not. So, we have to issue passports for both of you. You have an Iranian passport; we can't give him an Iranian passport, but we can give you both Iraqi passports."

"Thank you; that would be wonderful. Please do what is necessary. We appreciate your help," Behzad said hastily before I could say anything.

"This is the only way. Anyway, we'll need you to have Iraqi identities. We begin with names. You, my daughter, tell me what name you would like to be called," he asked me warmly.

"I like my own name, Niki."

"My daughter, for an Iraqi pass, you need to have an Iraqi name."

"Oh, yes, you're right. I don't know. You choose one for me."

"Not an easy task. Let me think and I will find a nice name for you," he said. He remained thoughtful for some seconds, and then with a smile asked me, "What about Nadia Nader Jamal, do you like it?"

"Nadia is a nice name, but what are the other names for?"

He chuckled and explained, "The other names are your last name. We usually get the names of our father and grandfather as our last name. Now we'll say that your father is called Nader and your grandfather's name is Jamal. What do you think now?"

"Nadia Nader Jamal, it has a rhythm. Yes, why not? I like it," I responded.

"Good, now we have to find a name for your husband."

That nice old man was very different from the other Iraqi men I had met before. He talked directly to me, not like the others, who addressed Behzad when they needed to talk to me even when I was sitting in front of them.

We had more fun deciding on a name for Behzad. Finally, the name of Jamal Hammed Hassan was selected for him.

Before leaving, the old man asked Nasser and Abbas to take us for passport photos. As soon as they left, Nasser, who by then was our closest friend, clapped his hands together loudly and said, "I'm very happy for you. You're going to leave soon. Are you ready now to go and take your pictures?"

Abbas said nothing. He smiled at us, which meant he was happy for us too.

*   *   *

By then it was nearly four months since we had left Iran. Days passed and we were getting closer to the end of August. As we expected our release any time soon, suspicious movements in the house made us impatient and worried. Men would come to the house, walk around, look at every corner of the house, move furniture, and bring in new furniture. It seemed as though they were preparing the house for other guests. They even asked us to stay in the living room while they were in our room. We never knew what they were doing in our bedroom.

We asked Nasser about all the changes; he did not reply. He seldom talked to us anymore. We were served food as usual, but we would be left alone by ourselves to watch television. We felt we were not their dear guests anymore, but a burden.

Nasser had been our only friend we could socialize with, but he was not around most of the time now. The entire circumstance was questionable and weird, which made Behzad tell me to be extra cautious. He wrote me not to start eating at the table before Nasser or Abbas, and to take the same food as they did. He was frightened that they possibly had a plan to get rid of us by killing us in some way.

I did what he asked me to do and ate the same food as Nasser and Abbas. Sometimes, Abbas would not sit with us at the dining table to eat. We thought this was odd. During the months we had been there, both young men sat with us at the table for every meal. That added to Behzad's suspicions and kept him from sleeping at night.

For some reason, I was not as frightened as Behzad. Once, when he was very tense and anxious, I wrote a note to him, "Whatever happens; happens. It is not in our control, just trust God and take it easy."

Another tense week passed. One early morning, Nasser knocked at the door of our room and asked us to quickly get our things together and be ready to leave.

I looked at Behzad, his face had paled. Trying not to show his frustration, he asked Nasser, "Where are we going?"

"To a hotel. You have to be in a hotel for a while," Nasser explained shortly.

Behzad was not convinced and asked, "Why can't we stay here?"

Nasser understood his concern. He smiled kindly and friendly to make us feel safe then said, "We need this house for other guests. Don't worry you don't need to be in the hotel for long."

Although he sounded sincere, his reasoning did not comfort Behzad, but it worked for me. After all, Nasser had been our only friend for many months. I trusted him.

When we returned to the room to get our things, Behzad took my hand and looked in my eyes. His eyes were full of tears. He looked sadly at me for some moments before embracing me. He drew me tightly to his chest; his voice whispered in my ear, "Niki, I love you. I'm so sorry to put you through this situation."

This scared me. He sounded as though these were the last hours of our lives. *Why was he so convinced that they would kill us?* I wondered. *Why would they have waited so long to kill us if it was planned from beginning? Did Behzad know something that I did not know?*

He pushed me harder and harder against his chest. I was not sure if he was crying, but I was confused and shocked. The idea of being killed was so unreal to me, but it seemed to be a reality to Behzad. I remained still and quiet in his arms until he let go. He looked me in the eyes again, kissed me, and quietly said, "Let's get our stuff." On a slip of paper, he wrote, "Don't eat or drink anything, no matter who offers it."

In silence, we packed our few clothes and other items in a small bag and left.

We sat in the back seat of the car. Abbas drove and Nasser sat in the passenger's seat. Everything seemed normal. We drove in silence through the city. Behzad held my hand in his and looked out the window. I knew he was anxious. I interrupted the silence to ask Nasser how far we were from the hotel.

"It's not too far. We'll be there soon," he replied.

"Can we see you and Abbas while we are in the hotel?" I asked.

"I don't think so. In the hotel, you don't need us anymore," he said smiling. The answer made me uncomfortable and brought Behzad's suspicions closer to reality.

"It means that we can't see you anymore?" I asked, trying to get some information.

He turned to me, "I don't know. I hope we can see you before you leave."

I found something reassuring in his answer, but I did not know if it had a positive impact on Behzad. "I hope so. You're our friends and we have grown accustomed to seeing you every day. Try to come and see us if you can," I said sincerely. We had been like a family, quite an odd family, for months.

Abbas stopped the car in front of a hotel on a busy street. By entering that nice hotel, I was convinced that nothing bad would happen to us, but Behzad still seemed nervous.

Inside the lobby, Abbas went to the reception and soon came back with a key in hand. All three of us followed Abbas to the elevator and to the second floor. We continued to follow Abbas down a hall and waited as he opened the door to one of the rooms and all of us entered. Abbas handed the key to Behzad and shook hands with us before he walked away. Nasser stayed for a few minutes to tell us not leave the hotel until someone came for us. He wished us good luck and left.

"Welcome to our new jail!" I said laughingly to change Behzad's mood. Once again, Behzad put his finger to his lips as a reminder that the room might be wired.

*   *   *

It was about nine o'clock in the morning. Minutes earlier, Abbas and Nasser had left us. Now we stood in the middle of the hotel room. It felt as though we had been abandoned. I giggled and asked Behzad, who still held onto our bag, "Why don't you put the bag down?"

He put it on the dresser. He seemed to be waiting for something unexpected to happen. I did not know why he still was so afraid. I sat at the edge of the bed and asked him to sit beside me.

"No, let's go to the lobby," he said quietly. He seemed to feel safe as long as people were around. As we entered the lobby, we noticed there were few people. The receptionist, a young man, talked on the phone. It was not a busy hotel.

"I'm hungry, let's see if they still serve breakfast," I suggested.

A short hallway from the lobby led us to the hotel's small restaurant. Some hotel guests were having breakfast. A young couple with a cute little girl sat around a table in the middle of the restaurant. It was the first time since I had left home that I saw a family. I missed my niece and nephew and the warmth of a family life.

By then, it did not matter to me what would happen to us as long as things would change. I had no imagination or perspective for my own future. While having breakfast in silence, I thought about the events of the day and realized something. Unconsciously, I wanted what Behzad was afraid of would really happen. In fact, I was oddly disappointed to be in the hotel. I felt it would have been better if they had killed us. Behzad's tears and fears had no impact on me. I did not feel sorry for any of us, and I did not know why.

Though we sat in a quiet corner of the restaurant with no wire and no one close enough to hear us, I hoped that Behzad would not say a word. My wish did not come true. Behzad started talking in a very low voice, "Don't think that we are out of danger. We still don't know what plan they have for us. We are not safe in this room. The room is wired. Please be careful."

"Okay, I will. You're too worried. Take it easy," I replied.

"Niki, it is serious. Please take it seriously. Until we're out of here, anything can happen to us. Please Niki, be serious."

"I am serious. This situation is funny. Last week, they were so nice they wanted to give us a passport. Today you think they want to kill us. Isn't that ridiculous?" I asked mockingly. My mood had suddenly changed and my response to his concern had turned to contempt.

"I don't know what to think of it. Something is going on. Since we don't know what, it is wise to be careful," he whispered.

"Nothing is going on. They needed the house, as Nasser said, for other guests. You are paranoid. Oops! You see, you are not so careful at all. Have you checked under this table? There might be a wire." I mocked him again. I did not know why I was talking like that, neither did Behzad.

He put down the tea cup he was drinking and gave me a puzzled look. He took my hand and caressed it gently, "I know it's not been easy these past months. I feel guilty; and I'm sorry about it. I'm sorry I scare you, but ..."

I interrupted him impatiently and pulled my hand away from his. In a quiet, angry voice, I complained, "Will you please stop apologizing? Just stop! I'm not scared, you are. I'm just tired of being concerned about everything all the time. Wire, wire, wire, I'm sick of the word. Let them hear us. Let them kill us. Wouldn't it be better than this life?"

"Niki ..." he started to say, but I interrupted him again to ask him to leave it there. I was really angry and did not have the patience for more discussions. He respected my request. We sat in silence and played with our food to kill time.

I had been angry with him for the past week after the nice, old man's visit. I was angry with Behzad because I felt he was keeping me in the dark. I was not so naive that I hadn't figured out that if he had not agreed to their proposition, whatever it was, they never would have bothered with the burden of issuing us official Iraqi passports with false identities. I was furious about getting involved in something without having the least idea of what it was. I had my own passport. I did not need a phony identity on an Iraqi passport. The idea of being deceived had dramatically transformed me into an angry bitch in the past week.

*   *   *

It was August 29, the day of our anniversary. We had spent two more days in the hotel. Behzad seemed to have calmed down a bit or was trying to cover up his concerns. I had been trying to control my temper as well.

I opened my eyes to see Behzad staring at me. He rested his head on his hand and lay at my side. I could feel and see his love and passion for me in his eyes.

"Happy anniversary," he kissed me and said.

"Happy anniversary," I replied.

"I love you so much. You don't have any idea how much I love you," he said still staring directly in my eyes.

"No, I don't know. Tell me how much," I said playfully.

"More than my life! Nobody, nobody can ever love you as much as I do," he said softly. ."You asked me not to say I'm sorry, but I have to say that I never wanted this kind of life for you. After we get out of here, I promise you a life you deserve. I owe you my life. You are my whole life, believe me, Niki."

"I believe you. I love you too, and you don't owe me anything. Now let's have an anniversary breakfast. I'm always hungry. Before making any more promises, make sure that you can handle my appetite," I said to turn the romantic moment into a more humorous one.

It was about ten o'clock when we finished our breakfast. As we headed to the elevator to return to our room, the nice old man and his companions, the other Iraqi man and the translator, entered the lobby. I noticed a light of happiness in Behzad's eyes the moment he saw them. After greeting and shaking hands, the old man said that he had good news for us. They got into the elevator with us and followed us to our room. As we entered the room, the old man said to me, smiling, "Young lady, Nadia, the name you liked. You got it."

I smiled back at him. He waved the passports at us and said, "These are your passports and tickets. You'll leave us today."

"Today?" asked Behzad puzzled.

"Yes. You don't have much time to get ready. Your flight is this afternoon at one," he said and handed us the passports.

I was thrilled to hear that we were free to leave. At the time, I cared less about how. I looked over each page of the passport. On the first page, my photo was placed next to some imaginary person's information that was written in Arabic. As much as I understood from the Arabic texts were the name, Nadia Nader Jamal, born in Bagdad, date of birth some year and month in the Arabic calendar. The next page had Sweden's visa stamp. Other pages were empty. The passport, in my eyes, was my release writ; I enjoyed the feel of it in my hand.

"Give it back to me now. You'll have plenty of time on the plane to look at it more if you like," the old man chuckled and reached out to get the passports back.

I wanted so badly to ask him about my own Iranian passport, which they had kept, but I did not. I knew they would not give it back to me, and it was too late for it anyway.

"Get ready. At eleven o'clock, someone will pick you up," he said. Then he turned to Behzad, "Take care of this young lady."

"I certainly will," Behzad replied.

"By the way, happy anniversary," the old man paused to say as he was leaving.

That was a moment of happiness for both of us. We were going to be released from jail; my feeling was indescribable. Whatever awaited us was not my concern at that particular moment.

We had less than half an hour to get ready. We packed our stuff in the same small bag and went downstairs to the lobby. Then we sat and waited to be picked up. Some minutes before eleven, we were surprised to see Nasser and Abbas enter the lobby. I was truly happy to see them again so unexpectedly.

"You're here, good to see you," I tried hard not to reveal my surprise.

"We are happy to see you again too. We had to say good-bye," said Nasser.

Once again, we sat in the car in the company of our nice jailors. But this would be the last ride.

From the moment we arrived at the airport and got out of the car, Abbas and Nasser transformed into two dedicated security guards. They surrounded us tightly and moved unbelievably fast. We nearly ran through the terminal. At the entrance of the plane, a man came forward and gave passports and tickets to Abbas. The plane was empty of passengers. Abbas gave us the passports and boarding cards before directing us to our designated seats. Abbas and Nasser said good-bye, wished us a nice trip, and left the plane.

Chapter 14

Another Border

We had the airplane to ourselves for a bit. I needed that quiet hour on the plane to digest the fast, vital changes of our fate. Perhaps living in Iraq had taught me patience.

Our peace was interrupted when the flight attendants and other passengers boarded the plane. The captain announced the departure; the plane started to move. It took off and steadily flew over the sky. Feelings of happiness and sadness clashed simultaneously and gradually took over my heart. The happiness of getting away from Iraq faded away, bit by bit, as we traveled farther and farther away from my homeland. I was surrounded by strangers, and I was going to live among other strangers in yet another part of the world. I closed my eyes and tried to think positively. My only happy thought was that I would finally be able to call home and hear the voice of my loved ones.

Behzad's wish had been granted. The signs of fear and the worries on his face had been replaced by a lightness of satisfaction and glory. My struggle to push aside my suspicious thoughts about him seemed to be in vain. I needed some explanation from him. I could have brought it up while we were on the plane and could talk freely, but I did not. My tongue was tied; I preferred sitting in silence.

*   *   *

It was late in the afternoon on Friday, August 29, 1980, when we landed at Stockholm's airport. Going through passport control was much easier and faster than I thought it would be. Our only documents, which were the fabricated official Iraqi passports, did not make Sweden's immigration officials suspicious. I did not have any idea of what would happen if they had found us out.

But as ridiculous as it sounds, deep inside, I was hoping they would find out. Strangely enough, I was in a secret war with Behzad; it did not matter what happened to me as long as he was caught. I betrayed him by those wishes. But the fact was that I felt betrayed, even though I could not figure out how.

The evening was cool. We took a taxi and headed to a hotel located on a busy street.

I was so excited and impatient to get to a phone to call home that I nearly ran to the room. I asked the operator to give me a line to call Iran. My heart was beating fast, and my hands were shaking while I held the receiver. After couple of ring tones, I heard Ramin's voice. I almost shouted on the phone: "Ramin jan, it's me, Niki."

Not hearing a word from him, I repeated myself, "Ramin jan is that you? This is Niki."

"What do you want?" he asked coldly.

"How are you and the others? How is Mamman?"

"Everyone is fine," he said shortly and was quiet once again.

"Can I talk to Mamman?"

"She's not home."

"Where is she? Is she fine?"

"She's fine. She'll be home soon."

"Okay, I'll call in an hour. Tell her I'm fine and that I'm in Sweden."

"Okay, bye," he said in the same cold tone and hung up the phone.

I was stunned by his reaction. Motionless, I sat there with the receiver still against my ear.

"What happened?" Behzad asked.

"Nothing, my mamman was not home," I said almost inaudibly.

"Are you okay?" he asked. He sat beside me and took the receiver. "Call her later again. The phone is here; call how many times you wish. You are not okay, are you?"

"I'm fine. Ramin hung up the phone on me. He seemed angry. I'm sure the others are the same. I deserve to be treated like this, even worse than this."

"No you don't. You did not do anything wrong. Ramin is just a kid. Don't be upset. Let's go take a walk. You'll feel better. We're free, and it's our anniversary. Let's go out to find a nice restaurant to celebrate."

"I'm not in the mood for celebrating, at least not before I talk to my mamman, but we can go for a walk."

*   *   *

We returned to the room after taking a walk on the streets around the hotel. I called home again. This time I heard my mother's kind and excited voice: She kept asking if I was fine and safe. We talked for quite a long time, long enough for me to know that my running away had caused a lot of distress for my entire family, especially my mother. She had not been able to sleep at nights or control her tears. She was certain that she had lost me and would never see me again. As I understood, Mr. Arman had never told them about our visit. I knew how conservative he was. He did not want take a risk and put my family in danger in case Pasdaran would go after them. He might have thought it would be much safer if my family knew nothing about this escape.

* * *

We stayed in that hotel two more days. It was a good opportunity to talk freely and exchange our experiences and the episodes we had been exposed to in Iraq. We talked about Nasser, Abbas, and our visitors. We laughed at that stupid dot game we played to kill time. We also talked about the days when he was cynical, thinking the Iraqis had planned to kill us.

After all those conversations, I asked him to tell me about his meetings with the Iraqis. His response was more or less the same as he had written to me after each meeting with Iraqis. "They asked me to stay there and I said no."

Now we were in Sweden with a visa stamped in an Iraqi passport, which allowed us to stay in the country for three months. *What would the next step be?* I wondered. *What could we do after three months with our false identification?* Behzad seemed not to be concerned about anything. On the contrary, he was very optimistic and asked me not to worry. He was confident that he would find a way to get us a visa to stay.

* * *

It did not take long before he broke the news, which created a long, bitter argument between us.

"You know we have to go to Iraq's Embassy on Monday."

"What? Why?"

"We have to. In Iraq, they asked me to do that as soon as we got here."

"Why? Why do we have to go there?"

"I don't know why, they asked me to go there and I agreed. I didn't ask them why. I just wanted us to get out of there."

"Then we don't go to their embassy. We are here now; we don't have anything to do with them anymore."

"Don't forget, we have their passports and a visa for three months. We can't go around without any identity and visa. We need to know what they have to say."

"Do they have anything to say? Can they give our ID back to us?"

"I have no idea. We will go there to find out."

"Find out what? I'm sure you already know everything," I said sarcastically.

"Why do you say that?"

"Because I am sure that in those meetings in Iraq they told you exactly what they expected from you."

"I told you they just asked me to stay."

'They asked you to stay because they were in love with you! Now I understand their motive!"

"You're unfair. You know they needed me to stay to write articles, have a radio program, and work with other Iranians in Iraq to fight against the regime in Iran."

"Don't they have enough journalists to write for them? Are you that special and unique?"

"I'm not special or unique, but I am an Iranian journalist and know Iranians. My reports and writings would have more impact on the campaign."

"It's ridiculous; we were kept so long there just because they needed you, so desperately, for writing? Isn't it funny? If the Iraqis just came to talk you into staying, why couldn't I be present?"

"Because you are a woman."

"Is it what you want me to believe? Please stop this nonsense!"

"Don't you trust me, Niki? Do you think I'm hiding something from you?"

"I don't think, I *know* that you're hiding something. I'm sure you promised them something, otherwise they would not bother to do what they did for us."

"Now you're really hurting me. You are wrong. I did not promise them anything, I just tricked them."

"How did you trick them?"

"I convinced them that I could be more effective in Europe to actively fight the Islamic regime."

"Wow! What a trick! You are genius! How long did it take for you to come up with that idea?" I mocked him. Then I burst into anger, "Do you think you're talking to a donkey? If you even told this to a donkey, it would guffaw. Stop making up stories! Tell me the truth."

"I'm telling the truth."

"That's enough! Keep your secret for yourself and your Iraqi friends. I will not come with you to the embassy. Go by yourself," I said and left the room in extreme anger. I went to the lobby and sat in a corner, trying to cool down.

*   *   *

It was Monday morning. The first weekend in Stockholm was the least comfortable for me. Behzad tried to ease the friction between us, but I was still angry and bitter. "Niki, please let's go to the embassy today. I promise you; very soon I will find a way to get rid of them. We are not in a good situation. It's not the time for taking risks. I want you to trust me. I love you. I won't do anything to harm you. Please listen to me. We've come this far together. Please come just a bit longer with me," he pleaded as he sat on the edge of the bed, touching my hair and trying to convince me go with him.

I did not say a word. I had nothing to say either. I stood up and got ready for another chapter of my life. He was right. We had come so far together, there was no way I could separate myself from him now. We were not at the end of the journey yet.

Chapter 15

Frustration

An old elevator, which was kept in its original style, took us to the second floor of a nice, older brown building. The Iraq Embassy was similar to an ordinary office. It was nine o'clock in the morning, and we were the first visitors of the day.

As we entered the small waiting room, we were met with a picture of Saddam Hussein hanging on the wall. Not only did that remind me of Iraq, but the point of fact was that we still were in Iraq. The embassy of each country is the property of that country and once you are in its embassy, you are in that country.

A gray-haired, middle-aged man came to us. It seemed to me as though he had been waiting for us. With a pleasant smile, he shook our hands and greeted us warmly in broken Farsi. He introduced himself as Nosrat Kamal Abollah and asked Behzad to come into his office. I heard the words that I expected to hear, "Madam, you wait here."

I smiled and sat down on the leather sofa. *Oh, yes! As usual! I wait here, no problem at all,*" I nagged to myself as I watched them leave. After an hour of sitting and waiting, an old well-dressed Iraqi man offered me tea. The two men were the only personnel I saw in that office until a young, skinny man entered and walked straight into the other room. I understood the older man and the skinny, young man shared the office.

After a long while, Nosrat Kamal opened the office door and held it open for Behzad. Both men appeared to be satisfied and pleased with whatever they had discussed.

"Sorry to keep you waiting so long," Nosrat Kamal said compassionately to me in Farsi.

"No problem," I responded indifferently.

He smiled and turned to Behzad, "Now I'll ask Ahmed to take you to a temporary apartment."

"We have to check out of the hotel first," Behzad said as I gave him a puzzled look, not understanding what was going on.

"No problem, he can take you to your hotel first," Nosrat Kamal suggested and went to the office and called Ahmed, the young skinny man.

Ahmed came out and respectfully stood with folded arms in front of Nosrat

Kamal, who said something in Arabic then turned to us and said, "Ahmed will take you to the hotel. If you need anything just give me a call."

"Thank you, see you tomorrow," Behzad said.

I was speechless and did not know what I could say in that moment. The whole morning I had been trying to be calm and let myself go with the course of the wind, not against it, but what about now? I clearly heard my heart beating. I was exhausted. By just looking at my face, Behzad could see right through me. He knew me well. He tried to take my hand while we followed Ahmed to the parking lot, but I drew back from him in anger.

He whispered in my ear, "We'll talk about it later. Please be patient."

"I don't want to be patient. You go with him. I'll stay in the hotel," I growled in a low voice.

"Please Niki, let's talk later." He tried to keep me quiet so that Ahmed would not notice the clash between us.

In Ahmed's car, I remained quiet the entire way to the hotel. The real argument and my resistance to go to the apartment arose as soon as we entered the hotel room. Behzad tried to convince me that we did not have any choice at this time. "Look, I'm not happy about this either, but what can we do now? Trust me, I have not promised them anything. Why are you so paranoid? What do you think of me? What could they even have asked me for?"

"I don't know, but I know that there has to be something. Otherwise, they would not keep their talk with you so secretive."

"Please Niki, just trust me. I promise you that the first opportunity I have we'll go our way, but not now. Now we depend on them. Just think a minute. If the Swedish government doesn't let us stay here, what do we do then? Where can we go? Let's do what we have to do for now."

"I don't care anymore about what would happen to us. Everything is a mess. I feel as though I've been kept in darkness the whole time, and you're not helping me to understand what's going on. Why do they care about us and give us these services? What would you think if you were in my shoes?"

"You've not been kept in darkness. I know as much as you know. I'm not hiding anything from you. Why should I do that? Please, Niki, please trust me. It's not the time for an argument."

"Never is the right time. At least tell me what you and the guy in the embassy talked about."

"First, I told him why we escaped Iran. Then we talked about Khomeini and the revolution, nothing more."

"My God, you're a big liar! Did you ask him about the visa?"

"Yes, I did. He said we don't have to worry about it."

"What does it mean? It means that we'll be dependent on them our whole life!"

"I'll find a way, don't worry. For now we have to be careful."

"Being careful means to do what they want us to do? Okay, now we must obey them and let them decide where we live, what to eat, and breathe or not breathe!"

"It's temporary, be patient. The guy said that he was given orders to take care of us and arrange a place for our comfort, and it was his responsibility to …"

I interrupted him and scorned his attempt to convince me that Nosrat Kamal was doing us a favor. "Yes, you're right! What a nice guy! He sends us to a place that he can tap in order to keep a close watch on us."

"Whatever, we need them now, Niki. I'm not stupid; I know what I'm doing."

"I am sure you do. The problem is I don't know what I'm doing." I found no gain in arguing any more. I gave up. In that bizarre circumstance, the fact was that the final winner would be him. It was not a matter of being young and naive anymore. On the contrary, it was a matter of not having any other options.

He held my face in both hands and looked me in the eyes and said, "My crazy baby, you know you are my whole life." Then he kissed me.

I said nothing. Reluctantly, I slowly packed my stuff and left the room while he followed me.

After checking out of the hotel, we went back to the car where Ahmed waited for us.

*　　*　　*

The apartment was on a nice, narrow street with tall trees on both sides. The place was small and neat. I looked inside the closets as soon as Ahmed handed the key to the apartment to Behzad and left. They were full of men's clothes. There was some leftover food in the refrigerator. The apartment seemed to be someone's permanent residence. I believed it was Ahmed's apartment.

I decided to accept the situation for the time being and tried my best to be calm and not create a hell of my life. We were thousands of kilometers from Iraq, but nothing really had changed since we left that country. Once inside the apartment, we constantly censored our words and the topics of our conversation. The only difference was that now, once we were out of that apartment, we could talk freely. However, paper and pen still needed to be handy while we were inside.

*　　*　　*

The next morning, Ahmed arrived to take us to the embassy. I pretended that I had headache and stayed at the apartment.

It was noontime when Behzad returned. He seemed happy, and before I asked him about the meeting, he suggested we go out to eat. Once outside, he excitedly said, "I think I'm making progress with them."

"What do you mean?"

"I'll call Sami today and let him know that we are here. We'll see if we could stay with him for couple of days."

Sami was his older brother. He, his wife, and their baby girl lived in Lund—a small city in southern Sweden.

"That would be nice. So, we got *permission* to leave for couple of days. What a nice gesture on their part!" I said coldly.

"Show me some enthusiasm! It's just the beginning, Niki. I need some more time. It's a good thing that the guy trusted us to leave the city. I'll call Sami today, and we can go on Friday."

*　*　*

We walked to the train station, where Behzad called Sami from a pay phone as I stood by. What I could grasp of their conversation was that Sami did not believe Behzad was calling from Stockholm since Behzad kept insisting that he was not joking. Finally, Sami believed him and said he would pick us up at the train station in Lund on Friday.

As we walked toward the exit, a telephone service window caught my eyes. Because I did not want to call my mother from the apartment, I asked at the window if I could call Iran. The lady smiled and said that I was at the right place. I gave her my mother's number. She dialed the number and asked me to go inside a booth to talk.

This was the third time I had called home from Stockholm. My mother needed to know more about my situation, but she knew that it would be safer not to give information over the phone. We talked about general things as usual.

*　*　*

It was a rainy afternoon when we arrived in Lund and found Sami waiting for us at the train station. Sami was as tall as Behzad, but his skin was darker. I knew he was a couple of years older than Behzad and thought him to be in his early thirties, but his balding head made him appear much older. A pat on the shoulder was simply the utmost effort the two brothers made to show their emotion of seeing each other after so many years.

Sami was so surprised to see me that I wondered if I was unexpected news to him. He might have never known that Behzad was married. The look on his face and his comment after Behzad introduced me as his wife was a confirmation of my suspicions, "Behzad, you are full of surprises!" he said.

Sami shook my hand and greeted me warmly. Unlike Behzad's formal personality, Sami appeared to be more relaxed. He was brawny and handsome in his own way.

"What are you doing here? Have you lost your home address?' Sami joked as he walked ahead of us, leading us to his car.

"It's a long story," Behzad said.

"I'm sure it is," Sami said shortly and then turned to me, "Don't you have a jacket? It's cold and rainy outside."

"I'm fine, I like walking in the rain." I did not lie. I always enjoyed the rain.

Lund was an old, small town. The scent of the rain and the colorful red and orange leaves of the trees gave the streets a distinguished look. Autumn is my favorite season of the year. It makes me feel refreshed and relaxed, since nature reaches the peak of its maturity after the heat of the summer. Both the time and the place were perfect for me.

*   *   *

Sami was a medical doctor and lived in a small apartment with his wife Lena and their little daughter Felicia. Lena was blonde, thin, and tall with a sweet small face. Felicia was not an infant as Behzad had told me. The cute two-year-old had her mother's blonde hair and blue eyes, but there still was some resemblance between her and her father.

Sami was so cool and funny that I enjoyed spending time with him. After everything we had gone through, I really needed someone to make me laugh. In no time, I felt comfortable with him as we joked and made fun of each other.

Behzad gave him a summary of our adventure in Iran and Iraq and also told him about our fake identification. I complained about the current issues with the Embassy of Iraq, hoping Sami would have a solution.

"Oh, you guys are dangerous! Get out of here. I don't know you and you're not related to me whatsoever," he humorously said, aiming both of his index fingers toward the door asking us to leave.

"If I was you, and you came to my house with this story, I would have seriously kicked you out immediately," I remarked.

"Who said that I'm joking? I am serious. Get out!" he said in a funny gesture.

"Too late, sorry, we are your guests, your responsibility," I played his game, but soon I switched my tone from joking to serious. Desperately looking for a solution, I asked him,

"But seriously, Sami, what do you think we should do?"

"I don't know. It's a big mess," he said. "I can ask a friend of mine, who is familiar with immigration law. If you like, you can talk to him. He's a very good friend of mine."

"Not yet. It's not so critical right now. We have a visa for three months. I have to think about it," Behzad said.

"Let Sami asks him, Behzad. It doesn't do any harm to get the information," I said.

"Let's wait for a little while. We've not been here very long. We don't need to rush. Let me handle it, my dear. We will wait!" Behzad responded firmly. I was irritated, but kept it to myself and said nothing more.

Sami, however, criticized him. "You are really something, Behzad. How could you get yourself into such a mess? Why did you go to Iraq in the first place? Why not go to Turkey? Many people escape from Iran to Turkey. Turkey does not have any issues with Iran. You escaped from one danger to another one. You got out from a hole and threw yourself into a deeper one. You are crazy …"

Behzad interrupted him, "You've never been in my shoes to feel the danger so close to you that you would use whatever was handy to escape. So stop judging me." Behzad sounded irritated.

Sami ended the discussion by saying, "Whatever! Some people never change. Okay, who wants tea?"

Sami disappointed me by giving up on the discussion and changing the subject. However, it felt good to have someone on my side who wanted us out of the whole Iraq matter. I just hoped he would continue discussing the subject.

This short trip was exactly what I needed. And we did find the opportunity to discuss our issue with Sami a couple more times. We walked through the small city and to the Saturday market. We met some of Sami's Iranian friends who had come to the market, and as Sami joked about, to keep Saturday tradition alive.

We did not see a lot of Lena. She often stayed in her room or kept herself busy with Felicia. It was understandable since we could barely communicate with her.

*　　*　　*

Two days passed by in a blink. All too soon, we were on the train back to Stockholm. The honeymoon was over. We arrived in Stockholm late Sunday night; the next morning, Behzad returned to the embassy.

Although Behzad was caring and nice to me, due to our odd circumstances, I felt he had total control over my life. That unpleasant feeling had turned me into a nagging bitch, which I hated. I had lost a lot of weight. For some time, I weighed only 85 pounds. The anger had seized my soul and body. I did not want to give into rage, so I decided to control my anger and let myself flow with the events once again.

Days passed by with nothing to do. Every morning after breakfast, we rode the metro to different places just to kill time. I had no idea what we were waiting for; I tried not to care about it either. With my decision to remain passive and put my destiny into God's hand, I really felt free from the distress—at least for a short while.

*　　*　　*

It was late September 1980—less than a month since we left Iraq. One evening, we went to the train station so I could make my weekly call to my mother. Once there, I went to the telephone service window to ask for a line to call Iran. The assistant, a young lady, gave me a sympathetic look. In a compassionate voice, she said in English,

"I'm sorry about your country."

I did not understand what she meant. I smiled and asked, "What do you mean?"

"You don't know?" she sounded surprised.

"Don't know what?"

"Your country is at war."

"At war? How do you know that?"

"It's been all over the news since yesterday."

"War with whom?"

"Iraq."

"Iraq?"

"Yes, I'm sorry! All telephone lines are disconnected. There has been no communication with Iran since yesterday."

"Thank you," I managed to say. I was numb and could not easily digest the news.

"I'm so sorry," the lady offered her words of empathy as I slowly walked away from the window.

"Did you hear that?" I asked Behzad.

"Yes, I did. Let's go home and watch the news. I can't believe her," he said as he put his hand over my shoulder and squeezed me toward him.

"But if she's right … Newspapers! Let's go to buy one," I said as I spotted the newspaper stand.

The front page of all the daily newspapers had pictures of Khomeini and Saddam as well as maps of the two countries. We bought one newspaper in English and sat down on a bench in the middle of the station's main hall trying to understand the articles since our English was not the best. The reality was that a war had started and we did not have to be geniuses to figure it out. (Appendix G)

I felt a strange pain in my stomach and a sudden headache. Anxiety took over my entire body. It was a kind of fear that I had never felt before. Neither the darkness of the mountain on the night of our escape from Iran nor the moment when my horse lost its balance on the slippery narrow path could compare to this fear. I was scared to death then, but this fear was worse than the fear of the death. I felt something much deeper even though I was in a bright, large, hall surrounded by nice and peaceful people.

"Let's call Sami to hear what is really going on!" Behzad suggested and took my hand to pull me along to a telephone stand.

"Really? Mehrabad airport? The city too?" Behzad expressed his shock upon hearing the news that Sami gave him.

"The south? How bad is it?" Behzad's questions and his reactions to the news was more than enough for me to understand that the situation was serious and dangerous in Iran. The Iraqi forces had made a massive attack on Iran by invading the southwestern cities and air bombing the city of Tehran and its airport.

Horrible footage that I had seen of other wars replayed in my head. I visualized my city, my homeland burning, dead bodies all over the place, and my people covered with blood. I envisioned my mother's house in fire, but did not have the courage to look inside the house to see what had happened to my family.

I could not stand to visualize these terrifying images. I sat down and burst in tears. Behzad cut his call short and sat beside me on the floor as he tried to comfort me. People cast looks at us curiously as they passed by. I still was not able to say anything. I cried and listened to Behzad's calm, worried voice murmur in my ear,

"Okay, come now! Let's go. We'll come back later to see if maybe you can call home. Come now, we will go home and watch the news on television."

"Go home? Which home? The Iraqi's home?" I whispered so softly that Behzad could hardly hear it.

I stood up and let Behzad take my hand and lead me to what he called home. We rode the metro to the street where the apartment was. It was drizzling, and a cool wind spread the sprinkles around. I felt the moisture on my face.

It was getting dark. At the outer door of the building, I stopped and suddenly hurled my anger violently at Behzad,

"No, this is your home. I will never put a step inside it again. I'd rather stay here on the street."

"Niki jan, please. Why are you doing this?"

"Why am I doing what? Ha? Are you stupid? Or do you think that I'm stupid? They are killing our people. I'm sure you knew it. You knew they wanted to attack us. My God, how stupid I have been."

"Niki, don't say that. How could I have known about it? You're angry; you don't mean what you're accusing me of. Please calm down," he said softly and stepped forward to hug me. I pushed him away so hard that he almost lost his balance.

"Go away, don't touch me. I have had enough of you and those stupid Iraqis," I burst out and walked away.

"Wait Niki, don't. You're in shock. I am too." He followed me and tried to calm me down. "I know you're upset, so am I, but it's not the way to react ..."

Now we were walking side by side. The drizzle was turning to a heavy shower, and we went inside the metro station. I sat on the stairs and burst into tears again. He touched my wet hair and pushed my head to his chest and let me cry. The station was not busy; once in a while I heard the steps of passengers passing by. For a long while, we just sat there in silence.

Bezhad interrupted the silence to ask, "Do you want to go to a restaurant to eat something and talk?"

It was still raining, so we went to a restaurant close by. I asked for a cup of tea to get warm before ordering dinner. The confusion had made me crazy, uncertain, and suspicious. I didn't recognize who I had become. Across the table, the man I still loved sat and stared at me. I had crossed the border of our relationship a couple of times before, and each time, I regretted it. Indeed, no matter how badly my words would hurt him, he still had a soft and passionate temper toward me. This side of him made me angrier time after time, but I was always the one who ended up with a guilt trip. I seldom apologized, but it did not matter to him. He never expected me to say the words or ask forgiveness for what I had said even when there was no doubt that I had been unfair.

"Do you feel better now?" he asked, still staring at me.

"I'm fine," I responded.

"you are looking like a wet mouse",[17] he said making gentle fun of me.

I smiled and said nothing.

"We'll try to call again tomorrow morning. I'm sure that soon or later the phones will work. Maybe it is not as bad as they say. I'm a reporter; I know how the reporters exaggerate the news for the sake of the excitement. We don't know much yet. I understand you are upset and sensitive about this situation we are in now, but if we rush, we may make things worse."

"What do you mean? Don't you think things are already worse?"

"What do you want me to do?"

"Get rid of them. Let's move on with our own life."

"You know well that I'm working on it."

"No, I don't know. Tell me how."

"Just trust me."

This was the answer that made me lose my remaining patience.

"I'm sorry, I can't trust you anymore. That's it! I'll go to Lund and stay with Sami until I find a way. The worst that can happen is that I'll be sent back to Iran, which I hope they do. I am not going to play by your rules anymore. Do you get it?" I was really mad, but I tried to keep the level of my voice as low as possible in order to keep from making a scene in the restaurant. However, those at the nearby tables obviously could hear me. Some turned their heads to cast a curious look at us.

Behzad looked down and did not say a word for a long while. He had used this ploy before to let me know that I had hurt him badly.

We ate dinner in silence. I broke up the silence and said,

"I should have done you a big favor and stayed with the Kurds in Iran."

"Don't say that. I could not go through all of this without you. I'm not a bad person, Niki. You don't know how painful it is when you accuse me of being a liar and you can't trust me," he said in a very low, sad voice. He still did not look at me.

"I'm not sure about anything right now," I replied. "The only thing I want

---

17   **Wet mouse**, a humorous Persian expression for someone who is completely wet.

for now is to get away from these Iraqis. I don't want to know anything about your plan and when and how you want to release yourself from them. Just don't count me in. As I said, I'll go and stay with Sami for a while. I'll call him to ask if he can let me stay with them." I made an effort to keep my tone of voice soft, not demanding.

After another moment of silence, Behzad looked me in eyes and said, "Okay, we'll call him. It's late for you to go tonight. Let's call him tomorrow morning," he nearly whispered.

I did not feel any comfort or happiness in hearing this. It was as though he was trying to buy some time, and I had to spend another night in that apartment.

I had a strange feeling of an overwhelming, unknown guilt. *Did I feel I would betray my country by spending another night in a place that belonged to the enemy? Was my guilt trip due to my behavior toward Behzad?*

We returned to the apartment and turned on the television. In silence, we watched the news, but could not understand much of it. The report did show pictures and maps of Iran and Iraq. One map showed an Iraqi combat tank moving toward Iran. The pictures told us the entire story.

Horrible thoughts occupied my mind that night. All my struggles to get a straight answer to my questions from Behzad had led me to nowhere. I had tried all kind of tricks to get a clear idea of what was going on, but so far I was not successful. He was skillful at talking around the subject. He could talk a lot without saying anything. The more he explained, the more frustrated I became.

Behzad slept calmly on my side. I looked at him and wondered if I wanted to kiss him or kill him. It occurred I could do both at the same time. In fact, the only face I had seen of Behzad was a kind, caring, and loving one. He was actually a nice person, but I was always suspicious that something was going on behind my back. Not knowing what it was bothered me. I was in an annoying state of mind. *Was something wrong with me? Was I an attentive or obsessive person?* I really needed a friend, a stranger, it did not matter who, just someone I could talk to and make sure that I had not lost my mind.

*   *   *

I woke up to a sunny day. Behzad was in the kitchen making breakfast. I felt drowsy. I had slept for just a couple of hours the night before. I tried to close my eyes again to get some more sleep, but a severe headache did not allow it. I got up and looked at myself in the mirror. I looked terrible. My swollen eyes seemed to cover my entire face in the middle of a mass of long, black untidy hair. I did not care. I went to the kitchen to see if I could find some pills for my headache.

"Good morning, my dear. Are you okay?" Behzad asked. He seemed to have recovered from my nasty, hurtful accusations from the night before.

"I have a headache. Do you think there are any pills in here?"

"I'll look. Sit and have some breakfast."

He did not find any pills. I remained at the kitchen table waiting for the headache to go away by itself. Behzad stroked my hair as he handed me the tea cup and said, "Drink it. I'll go buy some pills."

"You don't need to go now. We can buy some later when we go out." I did not mention anything about going to the train station since it was a habit not to say much at home.

After breakfast, I packed my stuff and got ready to leave for Lund. Once we were outside on the street and walking to the metro station, Behzad stopped me.

"I've thought about what you said last night. I'm not happy about all of your accusations, but I can understand how you feel. I'll come with you. We'll stay with Sami for some time to figure out what alternatives we have."

"Really?"

"Yes. Isn't it what you want?"

"Of course it is. Thank you."

"I didn't want to tell you when we were inside."

"Yes, I understand, but can you just leave?"

"I don't know yet. I'll go back to the apartment and get my stuff. Wait for me in the metro hall."

It was really a nice surprise; however, I did not want to read too much into it. It could be a temporary change of mind to help me calm down. I went down to the metro hall and sat on a bench, waiting for him. My headache still bothered me. After fifteen minutes of waiting, I was worried about him. I imagined that the Iraqis could hurt him if he called to let them know that we were leaving. I regretted that I had not gone with him.

Some minutes later, I saw him approaching with his bag on his shoulder. As he came closer to me, I felt, despite what I had thought of him the night before, that I loved him. I wanted to jump up, run to him, kiss him, and tell him how sorry I was about the night before, but I did not.

At the train station, Behzad called Sami to let him know we were on the way to Lund. I walked over to the lady at the telephone service window and asked if the telephone lines to Iran were still disconnected. To my disappointment, the answer was yes.

Just before noon, we boarded the train to Lund. Once we found our seats and sat down, I asked Bezhad,

"What'll happen now? Will they come after us?"

"I'll call them and talk to them. We can't just leave. First of all, we have to think what to do next. Our visa is valid for two more months. We must be patient and careful."

"Now we can ask Sami's friend. Sami seemed to trust him," I suggested.

"Not now, maybe later. Let me think about it. Niki, I've promised you I will take care of it. Please be patient. I know what I'm doing, and I know how to deal with them."

"But this can be a good start. Sami said his friend knows the immigration laws."

"Niki, please. I asked you to leave it to me just a second ago. Didn't I?"

"Yes, you did, but I can't help being nosy. You know that."

"Please Niki, just don't push. Let me fix it."

*   *   *

It was dark by the time we arrived in Lund. We took a taxi to Sami's house. Lena opened the door and invited us in. We followed her to the kitchen. Felicia sat in her high chair, waiting to be fed.

We left our bags in a corner of the family room and waited for Sami to return from work. I felt like an intruder in Lena's life. She was nice enough to let us stay with them, but I had the impression that she was not happy about it.

"Can't we go to a hotel?" I asked Behzad.

"Why?"

"We can't stay with them for long."

"Who said that we would stay long here?"

"It doesn't matter long or short. It's better to go to a hotel."

"If you are worried about Lena, don't be. She's European; they have a different culture than we have. They're not as warm as we are toward guests. This is the way they are, but it does not mean she doesn't want us here."

"European or not, it seems we are not welcome!"

"If it makes you more comfortable, we will get a hotel, but not tonight. Sami would not like it."

When Sami opened the door and found us sitting there, he started joking and laughing, "See what kind of friends the Iraqis are? Didn't your mothers teach you anything about bad friends?"

"Don't tell me, tell your brother. All my friends are good unless I add you to the list of my friends," I joked in return.

Sami was a warm person and made me feel welcomed. He asked us to join him in the kitchen while he made dinner. Lena had finished feeding Felicia and left the kitchen to put her to bed.

Sami walked to the kitchen to make dinner. We talked about the war and its consequences. He filled us in with the news and what comments the analysts had about the war. When dinner was ready, Lena joined us. We struggled to make conversation in our limited English.

Until late that night, we talked to Sami about what options we had under the bizarre circumstances. Sami repeated his suggestion that we consult his friend. He strongly believed that we should cut all contacts with the Iraqis, despite any possible consequences.

*   *   *

After one week at Sami's house, we rented a student room from a friend of Sami's. It was a very small room, which was furnished with a full bed, a bookshelf, a small table, and two chairs. I was impressed at how a tiny bathroom with a shower and a small closet were built inside the small room. The kitchen was shared with ten students. Although the space was small, old, and ugly, it was beautiful to me. It was a pleasant feeling to enjoy some freedom and peace even if nothing was certain and predictable. Behzad, however, was still undecided.

The days passed. It had been two months since we arrived in Sweden, and the war had been going on for about one month. Contrary to what most of the war analysts believed, it did not appear that the war would be over soon. The news from that region was not so promising either. The war became more intense.

I called home as soon as communications were reestablished. Fortunately, despite the severe war condition and bombing of the cities, my family was fine and safe.

∗ ∗ ∗

Behzad finally agreed to consult with Sami's friend, Ala. The short, chubby, young man with small eyes and a smiling face came to Sami's home. Once the pleasantries were over, Behzad gave Ala a very short version of our story. When he reached the false identity part of the story at the time we entered Sweden, Ala grinned skeptically and shook his head for some moments. Then he asked, "Why? Why should they give you those documents?"

"I think it was the only way to get rid of us since we didn't have any passports," Behzad replied calmly.

"But still, it's weird," Ala stated as he shook his head again.

"These two guys are dangerous, Ala. We should keep our distance from them," Sami joked and we laughed. "Why are you laughing? I'm serious. I'm not going to be seen with you guys anywhere!" he continued in the same funny gist.

"Seriously, they might be considered dangerous. Iraq's government is not the government anyone should mess with. I suggest you go to the immigration office and tell them everything. They might protect you. It's your only choice. You have to cut loose from the Iraqis anyway," Ala suggested.

"But if they send us back?" Behzad asked.

"They won't. Iran is at war. Since you're escaping the Islamic regime, you have a very good reason to get political asylum," Ala said.

"What about the Iraqis? Will the Iraqis just sit back and do nothing when they tell the police about the false passes?" Sami asked very seriously this time.

"I don't know about that. But if you want to stay here legally, it's the only way. Otherwise, I don't have any idea what the Iraqis would do. I'm sure the Iraq Embassy can obtain some kind of visa for you to stay here, but it's up to you," Ala said.

"No way! I don't want them in our lives at all," I nearly shouted. I looked at Behzad to see his reaction, but he just ignored me and turned to Ala.

"Thank you, Ala. You have been very helpful. I must think about it before deciding to take any further steps."

We talked more about it that night with Ala and Sami. I was impatient for Behzad to agree with Ala's suggestion, but it didn't happen that night. I was disappointed, but I promised myself to be nice to him and give him the time he needed to think over.

*   *   *

Behzad made his mind up soon after and accepted Ala's advice. Sami agreed to take us to the immigration office and be our interpreter. As we left the house, Sami humorously said, "Do you ask me to sacrifice my life for you? I can see it now. If the Iraqis want to shoot you on the street while I'm walking with you, and they miss you, I'm the one who gets shot. I'm young and have a lot of dreams for my future. I'm not that crazy to be seen with you guys."

He was joking about it, but I took some of his words seriously and wondered what would really happen if we revealed the wrongdoing of the Iraqi government and its embassy. I felt uneasy about involving Sami in our bizarre situation.

"Sami, let us go by ourselves. You may be right. I don't want you to die young. I'm serious, don't come," I said and looked at Behzad to say the same.

"Niki is right. You don't need to come with us," Behzad said.

Sami laughed and said, "Today you're not so dangerous, not yet, so it's safe to be seen with you. But after today, I will put armor on every time I walk with you."

*   *   *

The immigration office was located in the local police station that was very close to Sami's house. We walked into the building together. A few people sat in the waiting room. In less than an hour, it was our turn. A tall, blond, and brawny officer asked us to come into his office.

Sami spoke to the officer in Swedish. After a short conversation, which we could not understand, the officer asked us to sit down. He looked at each of us then asked, "You are here to apply for political asylum. Is this true?"

"Yes," Behzad answered.

"Tell me why you want political asylum."

Behzad told him the same, short version of the story, which he had given Ala. The last part of the story was the most interesting part for the officer. He asked for our passports.

After looking thoroughly at them, page by page for some moments, he asked about our real names and other identity papers.

"Then you are not the people in these passports? You're saying that these passes are not forged and that the government of Iraq issued them to you. Is this true?"

"Yes, that's true," Behzad replied.

"Do you have any papers to prove who you really are?"

"No, we don't. Our papers were taken from us in Iraq," Behzad replied.

"We can't do anything today, anyway," the officer said and handed us some forms. "Fill out these application forms to request political asylum. You can make an appointment for an interview at the desk in the lobby."

As we got up to leave, Behzad asked if we could get the passports back.

"No, I'm sorry I have to keep them. Just come for the interview and bring the applications with you. By the way, ask for two separate appointments—one for each of you," he added.

Following his instructions, we made the appointments for a week later.

Sami believed that the whole process would take time even though the first step went smoothly. I was so relieved that the length of the waiting time did not matter to me. I felt like a criminal, who had confessed to her crime, and now, whatever would happen, I would accept as a punishment.

*   *   *

On the day of the interview, Sami accompanied us to the immigration office. Behzad's appointment was at ten o'clock and mine was at eleven. We arrived fifteen minutes early and sat in the waiting room. Over the prior week, we had talked and speculated about the interview. Sami joked about it, and Ala was optimistic. Behzad seemed concerned; I was pleased and positive. In fact, I had a very good week. My conscience was at peace for the first time since we entered the country.

This time, a different blond, tall, muscular officer appeared at the door and called for Behzad. Sami and Behzad got up and followed the man into the office. An hour later, Behzad's interview was over. As soon as he stepped out of the office, the officer called me in.

A baby-faced, powerfully built man sat behind a plain desk. The office was small and simple, not like the offices in the big houses I had been in Iraq. Sami and I sat across from the officer.

The officer sat at the edge of the desk and handed me a photo album.

"Look at the pictures in this album and show me which of those faces you recognize," he said.

I looked through each page carefully. There were pictures of men, most with Middle Eastern faces. On the last page, I pointed to a picture and said,

"This man is Nosrat Kamal Abdollah. He is the man I saw in the Iraq Embassy."

"Thank you, we think it's enough."

That was it! My interview took less than fifteen minutes. Somehow I was disappointed. I had expected them to take me more seriously and ask me more detailed questions or, at the very least, let me finish my version of the journey. Instead, I was treated the same way as I had been treated by Iraqis. Even though I was in Europe, the male officers were not interested in hearing what had happened to me in my own words.

*   *   *

So far, it seemed that everything was going smoothly. Now we had nothing to do but to wait. During this time, we enrolled in school to learn the Swedish language. With Sami's help, we applied for financial aid from immigration services, which would pay most of the expenses for immigrants, like us, who waited for the government's decision. We rented a small and fully furnished apartment from an old couple, who had decided to divorce. The apartment was located in a nice area of the city with a beautiful view.

We were not the only ones who had escaped the Islamic regime. Many new Iranian immigrants joined the waiting crowd every day. The Iranian community became the largest minority in the city.

*   *   *

We made a life for ourselves in Sweden as we awaited the government's decision.

The war continued at home. The regime took advantage of its citizens with the ongoing war. Those who so recently had protested the unpopular regime now fought for their country against the external enemy. The war allowed the Islamic regime to establish itself.

We followed the news and participated in political gatherings and vigorous discussions, which took place every Saturday at the city's plaza.

I regularly called home to talk to my family to make sure that the war had not affected them. As I was told, it had not.

Later on, I learned that my brother, Ramin was sent to the war front during his military service. He was injured and got hospitalized for quite some time.

I also found out that some other young relatives were killed in the war; and some others were executed because of opposing the system.

Chapter 16

Hunger Strike

After some months waiting for the final decision of our immigration status in Sweden, I started thinking about having a baby. I was twenty-four years old and ready to be a mother. I missed my family and needed a family of my own. Besides, ours had become a loving and devoted marriage. Finally, I brought it up to Bezhad. Happily, he embraced me, lifted me up in the air, and sang: "My little baby will have a baby ..."

Soon after, I found out I was pregnant. Since then all my attention and dreams focused on our upcoming baby. The period of the pregnancy gave me a spiritual peace and was the most relaxing time of my life. Everything that had happened seemed so remote. I did not let the past ruin my inner peace.

*　　*　　*

My baby girl, Mitra, was born on a beautiful summer morning in 1981. She lightened my life and remains my "Sunshine." The moment I felt her warm, soft, tiny torso resting on my chest, my world changed, as did my perspective on life. I was not that crazy young woman anymore; I was a mother. From that moment on, the word "I" would be replaced by "we" and refer to me and my daughter. It was an unbelievably wonderful feeling. Behzad was happy and excited as well. Mitra was not his first child, but he acted as though she was. I was overjoyed to see him as the perfect father.

Mitra was a great joy to both of us. Our small family, in that small city, was my entire world. Despite my worries and anxiousness about my family and the war in Iran, I still felt happiness. I liked having friends around, so our social life expanded. Sami and his family were my favorite people. I had learned to speak Swedish and could communicate with Lena. I found her to be a very warm person. Sami always made me laugh. Felicia was a cheerful little girl, but I had to watch her all the time. The moment I looked the other way, she would try to harm Mitra.

*　　*　　*

It was more than a year since we had applied for political asylum. Still, there had been no response from the immigration authority or the public attorney assigned to our case.

We had finished the school of Swedish language. However, since we did not have work permits or even an ID, there was not much to do. I was busy with my newborn baby, so the situation was not as hard on me as it was on Behzad. He started pushing the attorney to be more active and requested a "fast track" for the case. He made many visits to the attorney's office and talked to him, but the response was always, "You have to wait. This takes time."

Fed up with waiting, Behzad wrote a letter requesting a decision for our case. He sent it by registered mail to the immigration office and a copy to our public attorney. The response to his request was the same—we had to wait. Apparently, this was not a satisfying response.

He sent another letter to the immigration office and the attorney to inform them that he would go on a hunger strike until the immigration office reached its final decision. He also warned the authorities that he would go to the media in case it became necessary.

This time, he received a call from the attorney, trying to talk him into changing his mind, but Behzad was determined to keep his pledge. He sent another registered letter to immigration, but this time he included a deadline date. On the given date, since no official decision was sent to him, he refused to eat and sent another letter to the authorities to notify them of his hunger strike. Every morning, he went to the post office to send the letters by registered mail.

Days passed with no reaction or response from the immigration office. His attorney called Behzad and asked him to break his strike.

As the days passed, Behzad became weaker. After a week, he did not have enough energy to go to the post office; I did it for him. I watched him get weaker. The color of his face turned yellowish. The daily changes of his condition scared me, but he had confidence and tried to give me courage,

"I know what I'm doing. They can't ignore me. One of these days, they have to do something. I promise you that I won't die; I'm just weak, but not hungry. It was hard to control my hunger on the first two days—but not anymore."

At the beginning of the second week, the attorney called and happily gave the news that the processing of our case had started and a decision would be made soon.

"I won't break my strike until we officially receive the final decision," Behzad determinedly told the attorney in a very tired, weak voice.

The attorney's promise did not work; Behzad continued his hunger strike. I was not as strong as he was to witness him melting away. He could hardly walk. Sami was very concerned as well. He asked him in his funny way to quit, "Don't count on me to take care of your wife and child if you die. That's enough, you're dying. Is it worth it? When the authorities say the process has started, it means that 90 percent of the job is already done. So get up and eat something."

Despite our pleas, Behzad refused to quit.

His firmness and the confidence about the outcome worked for him. On the twelfth day of his strike, the attorney called, this time with really good news. We were approved for political asylum and a permanent residency.

Behzad's courage and success meant a lot to me. He was my hero, and I felt much more affection and love for him. I had everything—a beautiful baby, an affectionate husband, and a good life. I put my efforts into keeping our home warm and pleasant. Behzad did the same. Mitra was growing into a sweet, talkative, little girl and made our life more joyful.

Unfortunately, the permanent residency that included work permission did not help Behzad find a decent job. I was home taking care of my baby and was happy, but I needed a job too. We enrolled Mitra in day care; she enjoyed being there from the first day. She soon became accustomed to her caregivers, and I started looking for a job.

I found a job as a janitor in a hospital. I was the only immigrant on my team. Even though it was not my favorite job, I was happy about it. It would help us to make our own income and not be dependent on social welfare. With no job opportunities in sight, Behzad started working as janitor in the hospital too.

*   *   *

In 1983, we had been in Sweden for three years. Mitra was two years old. I had taken some economics classes in college and had worked as janitor, and later on, as a care giver in a healthcare center. Behzad held different service jobs as well.

In that year, Shahram was on a business trip to London. It was a good opportunity to see him. All three of us made a trip to London. When Shahram embraced me warmly, a sense of peace filled my spirit and tears ran down my face. I felt a release.

We had one week to talk about the past three years. He updated us on the war situation in Iran and how badly it had affected peoples' lives. I had a lot to tell him, but I did not find even a short moment to be alone with him. Behzad never left me alone. Shahram had not approved of Behzad from the beginning and did not find him trustworthy and honest. Indeed, by then, out of necessity, he had accepted him as a family member.

It was not until years later that Shahram told me, "I never trusted that guy. You had Mitra and seemed to be happy, but it was something about him that bothered me and made me uncomfortable. I wanted to talk to you to make sure that you were happy, but he never let us talk. He was around the whole time. Even when we walked on the streets, he intentionally walked between us. That made me more suspicious."

Our one week together passed too quickly. It was hard to say good-bye not knowing when I would see him again. But the time we had lighted my spirit of hope. It was a reassurance that he would remain my brother and my protector throughout my life, no matter what. It was a huge relief to me.

*   *   *

My mother came to Sweden shortly after we returned from England. She had experienced a long, difficult period of distress, first, because of my runaway and later because of Ramin being in the front line in the war against Saddam. She really needed a break.

She stayed with us for six months. Having her in the house made our place a warmer and more loving home. Behzad tried and cared a lot to keep my mother happy. Mitra, a happy three-year-old, became attached to her. Mitra talked sweetly in Farsi and Swedish. She liked singing and dancing. Each day, after coming home from day care, she would try to teach my mother what she had learned that day.

As much as I was curious to know what had happened after we escaped, my mother was unwilling to talk about those tough days. But I insisted. Reluctantly, she spoke about that period when I was missing.

She had been despondent during that time and thought she had lost me forever. She had called my work and my friends. No one knew of our whereabouts. During the same period, they read in the newspaper about a bus accident on the road between Tehran and Mashhad, in which a young couple was killed. Desperately, they called the police and hospitals until they found out that the couple was not us.

After two weeks, Pasdaran came looking for us, asking for us. Obviously, she had no idea, and Mr. Arman had not told her anything. Eventually, the Pasdaran were convinced that my family did not know and had not heard anything from us or about us. They stopped contacting my family.

When I asked her whether Pasdaran told her the reason they were looking for us, she hesitated for a moment, searching for the right words, before responding,

"You know, one can't really trust Pasdaran. They charge people for crimes with no evidence. So, I could not believe them when they accused Behzad of frauds. They were, indeed, after Behzad and told me that you were innocent. They never actually mentioned the newspaper, but they claimed that Behzad was a charlatan and many lawsuits had been filed against him."

My jaw clenched. I felt a sudden anxiety and did not know what to say. I had been trying not to think of Behzad as a bad person, as a liar, or as what that Pasdar had said to my mother, "a charlatan." I had convinced myself that Behzad was a good man. Indeed, I was fooling myself. But by this time, I had succeeded in trusting him. I regretted asking my mother that question.

"Of course, they would say so. Their intention was to trick you into telling them where we were," I said to my mother, hoping that it was the truth.

I did not talk about that subject with her again. I needed the past to remain in the past. Thinking about it only gave me anxiety.

*   *   *

Shortly after my mother left, Behzad's family started to immigrate to Sweden. They had lived in Abadan, a city in the south of Iran at the border of Iraq, which had been the main front of the war. The entire city had been constantly bombed by the Iraqi army and suffered tremendous damage. Some of its inhabitants survived the attacks by escaping to other cities. Other Iranians escaped the country through Poland and East Germany. Once in Sweden almost everyone would receive humanitarian asylum due to the ongoing war.

Behzad's family was lucky to get away unharmed. They had left Abadan and went to Tehran. Later, they decided to immigrate to Sweden. In less than a month, Behzad's siblings and mother came to Sweden through Poland. I found them nice people and, in no time, they became like a family to me. Sami and Behzad had five sisters. I liked all of his family, especially his mother, who was a nice, caring lady. Mitra and I were now a part of that big family as well. Our life in that small city changed in a good way when Behzad's family settled in Lund, and we enjoyed a very close and pleasant relationship with each other.

As much as I enjoyed Behzad's family and was happy that Mitra would have so many relatives close to her, Behzad did not seem to like it. I never understood why. His family was wonderful. Our gatherings were almost always full of laughter, singing, and simply entertaining. However, Behzad seldom joined us.

Chapter 17

Hypocrisy and Religion Converting

Due to the stream of Iranian immigrants to Sweden, and in particular to the southern cities of Sweden, the Iranian community in Lund was increasing. Nearly all of the Iranians knew each other. To me it was good fortune to have contact with a large number of people. Since Behzad's big family had come to the city, I could not complain about being lonely.

However, deep inside, I was not happy about myself and my occupation. I was educated and needed to have a more professional job, but it was nearly impossible to find any in that small city. So I thought about going back to school.

I made the decision to apply for medical school. To do that, I needed both my high school and college diplomas from Iran, which Shahram sent to me. My application was accepted, and I was admitted to the medical school to become a doctor. Because of this admission, I was eligible for a student loan and did not need to work anymore.

I enthusiastically started my education. At the time, four-year-old Mitra was still going to day care. I managed to split my time between my family and my school work. However, the classes were not easy and required much studying. I spent a lot of time in the lab and participating in a study team.

Behzad considered the idea of publishing a newspaper for emigrants. We discussed names for it, the topics and news that would be interesting for the readers, the number of pages, and so on. He seemed very serious about it, and I encouraged him. Everything seemed to be coming together for us.

One day when we were talking about his idea, he said that he was thinking of changing his name to a Swedish name. His reason was to make it easier for him to work with Swedes. He believed that it was a huge advantage to have a Swedish name as a publisher instead of a Persian name that many could not pronounce.

A proud Iranian, I hated the idea and told him so. However, he was free to do so, given one condition. Under any circumstances, he was not to involve me or Mitra in his business.

"Both your name and your newspaper are yours, but I don't want to see your Swedish name anywhere in this house. Put it just on your paper." I couldn't have made it any clearer.

He changed his name officially to Peter Samson, but he never made any effort toward publishing the newspaper. It seemed he just wanted to have a new identity. Shortly after, he decided to go back to school. Since I was still upset about the name issue, I never asked him why he had changed his plan.

In the meantime, I successfully finished my first term of school and started my second term. Behzad claimed that he intended to become a chiropractor and applied to a good chiropractic school in Stockholm. He believed there would be plenty of jobs for chiropractors, and two years study was worth it.

"We can move to Stockholm. You always wanted to live in a big city, now you can transfer to Stockholm University. We can enroll Mitra in a day care there," he suggested.

He was right. I liked living in a big city. I had lived in Tehran most of my life. I agreed to the plan, and he prepared to attend college.

*   *   *

One evening, after dinner, I was preparing Mitra for bed when two Christian missionaries, a man and a woman, came to our door. This was not unusual. However, each time one of us opened the door, we would say, "No thanks." This time, Behzad opened the door and invited them in.

"Why did you do that? Are you in the mood to talk to them now? Send them away," I told him in Farsi.

"Let's see what they have to say," he replied calmly as he led them to the family room.

I said no more and went to Mitra, who impatiently called for me. Indeed, it seemed to me to be simple, innocent curiosity on Behzad's part.

Mitra already had her book ready to read to me. She liked the same story, which I had read to her over and over. Now that she had memorized the whole book, she pretended to read the book to me.

After Mitra fall asleep, I joined Behzad. Both of the two, young Swedes were blond and attractive. They talked about Jesus and discussed the Bible. I found the subject boring and wished them to leave, but Behzad seemed very interested and passionate about the subject. He would bring up a new question for more discussion.

They left after about an hour. Before leaving, they gave Behzad a Bible and some other books. They also promised to find a Bible in Farsi for him. The Behzad I knew was not religious at all. So after the missionaries left, I made fun of his enthusiasm and the questions he had asked them. Evidently, he was not that serious about their conversation as he laughed at my comments.

The missionaries came back a couple of days later and brought a Bible in Farsi for Behzad as they had promised him. They returned a few other times before he was admitted to the college of chiropractic and left for Stockholm and the college.

Because I was in the middle of the second term of school, Mitra and I stayed in Lund. The plan was for Behzad to find a place to rent for us, and a day care for Mitra. It was not difficult for me to transfer to the University of Stockholm.

Everything went as planned. He rented an apartment and found a day care nearby for Mitra. He came home to Lund every weekend and called every day. He never came home empty-handed. He always had something for Mitra and me. He seemed happy and enjoyed the school.

During the first few weeks of his schooling, I had my suspicions whether he really attended the school. Whenever I asked him about the school, he refused to talk about it. His response was that the school was like any other school and then changed the subject of conversation.

*   *   *

One weekend, during one of his visits to us, I woke up early in the morning to find him sitting at the edge of the bed and staring at the wall in front of him.

"What's the matter? Are you okay? Have you seen a ghost?" I asked teasingly.

He turned to me and in a soft quiet voice said, "Niki, I have a strange feeling."

"You're not well?" I asked concerned.

"No, no, it's hard to explain. I'm a changed man," he replied and held both of my hands. He stared at me and continued, "I had a strange dream. Why should he choose me?"

"Who chose you? A dream is dream. Tell me, I'm an expert in interpreting dreams," I said.

"It's not a joke, Niki. It was not really a dream. I saw Jesus, here, staring at me. He told me I was a Christian," Behzad said in a mystifying way in attempt to make it to seem divine and supernatural.

"Is that all? You should have invited Jesus to stay for breakfast!" I mocked him and left the room. I told myself that he had a new scenario prepared for me. I would wait to see the rest of the play.

I did not have a long wait. A week later, when he came home for the weekend, he had the surprising news I had expected.

*   *   *

It was Friday evening, and Behzad had come home for weekend. As usual, he had some gifts for us. Mitra, who was excited and happy that her father was home, ran to him and pulled his hand to make him go with her to play. He lifted her up and embraced her and then went to her room to play. Hearing them talking and laughing was wonderful. While I felt happy and lucky to have such a nice family, a bizarre feeling still bothered me. I wanted so badly to push away that unwelcomed feeling, but it was stronger than the power of my wish.

We had dinner in a warm and happy atmosphere. Mitra wanted our full attention. We sang her songs together; she stopped us to correct the portion of the song we had not sung correctly. After dinner, Behzad gave her a bath and helped her get ready for bed. She wanted both of us to tuck her in, but she wanted me to read to her.

*   *   *

"Niki, I have something to tell you," Behzad said in a serious manner as soon as I left Mitra's room and closed the door behind me.

"What's that?" I asked.

"Let's sit down."

We went to the family room. I sat across from him waiting for him to speak.

"I'm a Christian," he said softly without looking at me.

"Okay, you're Christian and ...?" I asked and waited for more of an explanation.

"I've converted to Christianity," he stated and looked up at me to see my reaction.

"You and Christianity?" I grinned and asked doubtfully.

He did not say anything. I asked more questions, "Don't you want to say more? Why so sudden?"

"I've read the Bible and other books about Christianity. Niki, believe me if I say that it is exactly what I need. It made me think about Jesus and his sacrifice. I've found the truth about God, about life. I saw Jesus in front of me, do you remember? It was last week. Jesus asked me to be a Christian," he explained.

"Jesus didn't know you when he asked you," I mocked him.

"I knew that! I knew that you would never believe me. Niki, I'm a changed man. I'm a better human being now. What's wrong with that?"

"Nothing is wrong with it. I could buy it from anyone else but not from you."

"I need you to have faith in me. It was not a quick decision. I've been thinking about it for a while, but I was not able to decide. Last week, Jesus helped me to decide. Niki, believe me, I saw him."

"You want me to believe you! Tell me when was the last time you mentioned God's name in front of me? I know you are preparing some swindles, but your games do not fool me anymore. Now, tell me what your plan is and who you want to deceive," I said calmly.

"I'm sorry that you think of me like this," he said quietly as he covered his face with his hands. He stayed in the same position for a while.

"Please, don't play games with me. Tell me what your agenda is, I'm sure you have one. First you changed your name, and now you have become a phony Christian. I'm sorry to say, but I can't buy it; even if the whole world does."

"People change, Niki. Didn't your own brother Shahrooz change?"

"I told you, I agree that people change, but least of all, you. By the way, Shahrooz has never deceived people. My problem is you, not Shahrooz."

"What problem? I'm a Christian and a better person. How can this be a problem?"

"Okay, okay. Congratulations! I hope and pray to God that I am wrong and you are right. Just keep your religion to yourself and keep Mitra and me out of it."

"I promise you, this would not be a problem for you. It would make our life together much better."

I thought this would be a good time to confront him about his study, which I had been suspicious about. "Do you really go to school or are you busy with Bible study?"

"I was going to school, but I'm not now. I'm working in a church," he said indifferently and tried to get past it rapidly.

"Wow! You work in a church! Getting closer to Jesus! How come I never thought about it? So you've already succeeded to fool the priests. Such an intelligent one! Why didn't you tell me sooner? I would be even more proud of you," I jeered at the edge of bursting into anger.

"It's not true. I'm not fooling anybody," he said innocently.

"Aren't you? You have lured everybody. You had planned to leave the country and therefore you used everyone including those Kurdish leaders. Your plan was perfect, you were genius to fool them and even the Iraqis to help you to escape and give you a passport. You knew very well that you would never get any passport from Iranian authorities, because you were a wanted charlatan and if you were caught, you would have been in jail. You are a criminal. You played with me for months. You are the master of all liars. Do you want me to remind you how many more people you have deceived? You are a liar, a thief!" I was really mad. I wanted to say more, but stopped there.

He said nothing and looked down. After some moments of silence, he lifted his head and looked me in the eyes. His eyes were full of tears. Those tears were not unfamiliar to me. I stared at those tearful eyes and said, "Save these ridiculous tears for those who don't know you."

He looked away from me and turned to the other side of the room. In the same innocent tone of voice, he said, "I'm a changed man. Jesus is in my life now. He forgives me and helps me to be a better person."

I had nothing more to say. I was exhausted and had enough surprises for one night. I left the room. That was the last time we talked about it for weeks. I had no idea how to deal with the situation. The only way was to keep things cool and wait to see what would happen next.

Luckily, I had Mitra to keep my mind off Behzad. School and studying filled most of my time. The last thing I needed was another hurricane in my life. This time it was not just me. Mitra was the one who would be hurt the most.

*   *   *

Weeks passed as usual. I was getting closer to the end of the term and studied hard to prepare for the final exams. One morning, as I studied at home, the mailman dropped the mail through the slot of the door. I picked the mail up and went through it. One piece caught my attention, and my heart started pounding fast. It was a letter addressed to Mitra Samson from the Municipal Registration Office.

I sensed that I was about to face another surprising problem. I opened the envelope. It was a letter of confirmation of changing Mitra's last name to Samson. I was furious and could not control my anger. I was already fed up with Behzad's unexpected and bizarre actions, which I tried to ignore. But I was not going to ignore this. With the letter still in my hand, I burst into tears and slid down against the door until I was sitting on the floor. I had no energy to move; I just sat there for a long time.

Finally, I pushed myself to get up and control my anger. I called Behzad pretending everything was fine. Then I nonchalantly mentioned the letter, "A letter came in the mail today addressed to Mitra. It says that her last name has been changed to Samson. Isn't that strange? It has to be a mistake, isn't it?"

"I'm sure it is. You know these offices; they make mistakes all the time. Don't worry, I will call them and fix it," he calmly replied.

"But it's a big mistake. They can't just change her name without our permission," I said, struggling to appear calm.

"Because my last name is changed, maybe Mitra's automatically is changed too, but don't worry, I'll fix it. How is Mitra? Is she home?" he asked quickly to change the subject. I played his game too. As calmly as I could, I made casual conversation with him.

After that conversation, I called the Municipal Registration Office and asked about the letter. They explained that it was not a mistake; it was requested by the parents in writing.

How could my signature be on that paper? I wondered. It was impossible. I had no doubt that Behzad had forged my signature. I asked for a copy of that request to be sent to me. Afterward, I searched for an attorney in the phone book. I found one and made an appointment for the next week.

As soon as I calmed down, I called Behzad again and said, "It was no mistake. It was my mistake to trust you."

"What do you mean? It must be a mistake. I promise …"

"Don't say that word anymore. You are such a jerk! I'm sick of you and your lies," I shouted at him and hung the phone up on him. He called many times, but I did not answer the phone. I was so frustrated that I did not want to hear the same lying denials.

By then, it was clear to me that he was engaged in something. But I could not figure out what "that something" could be. So many drastic changes in a so short period of time did not make any sense.

So many thoughts ran through my mind. *Is it possible that he never broke off his involvement with the Iraqis? Has he fooled not only me, but even the Swedish authority, by applying for political asylum and revealing our fake identities? Did he have the consent of the Iraq Embassy, and it was part of his plan? Is he an Iraqi secret agent? Is that the reason he moved to Stockholm? But why is he working in a church? Was converting to Christianity a trick to get himself to the church? Am I paranoid or is he just a sick man?*

These questions and others circulated in my head. I had tried to ignore those suspicions to make it possible for the three of us to live a normal life. Now what? It was impossible for me to remain in denial and play the game with him. I was fed up!

*   *   *

The next morning, I took Mitra to day care and returned home. As I was getting ready to study for an exam, I heard Behzad open the door.

"Niki, *azizam*—my dear—where are you? Why didn't you answer the phone? I was so worried," he called to me as soon as he put his foot inside. I did not answer him. I was not happy to see him, and I didn't want to hear his voice.

When he leaned down to kiss me, I pushed him back and took my books and swiftly left the house. He came after me, begging me to come back home to talk. He still insisted that the name issue was just a misunderstanding and he would fix it.

I did not have enough strength or patience to deal with his lies anymore. I took a bus to the school and went to the library to study. As it had been the day before, it was a completely vain attempt to concentrate. The books were open in front of me, but I could not concentrate. I packed my books to leave the library, but I did not want to go home.

It was a cold, sunny day in October. I decided to pick up Mitra from day care to spend a nice day with her. We could go to downtown, have lunch, and see a movie. Mitra was the only one who could give me a sense of comfort and peace. While I was with her, I was a kid again. I could see the world through her eyes. The smallest insect or a green leaf on the snowy and icy ground was interesting. We would sing, talk, and laugh at anything. I was her playmate, and she was my hope in life. I needed her the most. I left the library and took the bus to the day care to pick her up. But she was not there; Behzad had already picked her up.

I thought of talking to a friend of mine, but since I had not mentioned to anyone about my private life and problems, I decided that it was not such a good idea. Living with Behzad had turned me into an inward and private person. Although I had lots of friends, some closer than others, I could not be open with any of them as real friends would do. I had somehow become like Behzad when it came to friendships even though I was not secretive as he was. Suddenly, I felt empty and alone for the first time in my life.

I left the day care and wandered aimlessly around the area. My thick boots and gloves were not enough to keep my fingers warm. I walked downtown and stopped at a coffee shop. I ordered a cup of hot tea and sat in a corner. I don't know how long I sat there, but it was getting dark outside. I had no choice but to go home.

*   *   *

I opened the door and heard Mitra's and Behzad's voices in the kitchen. I went straight to the bedroom to change and heard Behzad talking loudly to Mitra so that I could hear, "Mamman is home. Do you want to help me set the table for her? She must be hungry." Then he called me to join them, "Niki jan, we've been waiting for you. Come and see what we've made for you."

I went to the kitchen after I changed. Food was already on the table. Ignoring Behzad, I went to Mitra and hugged her.

"What about me? I want a hug too," Behzad said in a childish voice. He was trying to lighten the tension by pretending everything was the same as had been before. I said nothing to him but asked Mitra about her day. She excitedly told me about the nice day she and her father had together.

We sat down to dinner like a happy family, except I did not feel any happiness. For Mitra, and perhaps for Behzad, that evening was like other evenings. Mitra was excited about playing hide and seek with her father earlier. She told me how she found Baba behind the sofa. Behzad interrupted her to add some funny comments to make us to laugh. Mitra did not feel the tense atmosphere, and I tried to act as normal as possible. That night, I didn't talk to Behzad and tried hard to control myself and stay calm.

The next morning, Mitra, as usual, woke up early and climbed into bed on my side. I embraced her and held her tightly. She fell sleep again. I stayed awake looking at her and thinking. Peacefully resting on my arms, she was so tiny and innocent. *What impact would a divorce have on her life?* The thought of a broken family for her had never crossed my mind. I doubted my decision to seek a divorce. I blamed myself for being selfish, and then I would remember how Behzad had deceived me. He was a good father, but I had completely lost my trust in him. I knew he loved me, but it was not good enough for me anymore.

"Mamman, wake up." With her small hand, Mitra gently stroked my face. I woke up to a smile that invited me to begin a new day. I got up, kissed her, and looked at my watch. It was late. "Sorry dear, you must be very hungry," I said, feeling guilty.

"No, Baba and I had breakfast," she said in her sweet Farsi and then asked, "Can I go to *Dagis* now?"

I smiled at her use of the Swedish word for day care. "Do you want to go to Dagis? Okay, then let me change, and we'll go," I said.

"I help you," she said and ran to get me some clothes to change into. She liked to help me dress and brush my hair. It was the highlight of her morning, and I let her to do that.

In the kitchen, Behzad sat at the table while he read the daily newspaper. He put the paper away as we entered the kitchen. "Good morning, ladies. How are my girls doing today?'

"She's not your girl, I am! She's Mamman" Mitra laughed and corrected him.

"Really? Is she your mamman? How should I know that?"

"She is. You know she is," she said and laughed again.

"Now I remember. You're right, you are my girl and she's your mamman."

I enjoyed watching their conversation. Mitra was so sweet and happy. That was the way a morning should start. I wished time would stop there or that we could travel back in time a couple of months.

Behzad took her to day care, and I got ready to go to the library. Contrary to the day before, I felt calm, so I was hoping to get some work done for my upcoming exams. By the time I was ready to leave, the mail had been delivered. I picked it up and found an envelope addressed to me from the Municipal Registration Office. Hastily, I opened it to find a copy of an application to request a change of name. I expected to see a forged signature of mine under the paper, but it was my signature. I had signed it. This was unbelievable! I checked it over and over. I looked at it under a light, in case he had expertly copied it. With no doubt, it was my signature.

*   *   *

"How? How did you get my signature? Tell me!" I threw the paper at his face and shouted at him, demanding a response the moment he opened the door and put his foot inside.

"Calm down, my dear, please calm down," he said coolly, trying to calm me down.

"Liar, crook! I don't want to see your face anymore. Just get out and never come back."

"Niki jan, please! I can fix it, I can fix it. I promise," he said and came to me to quiet me.

"Go to hell! Leave me alone! Get out!" I pounded on his chest repeatedly with my fists. I had lost it completely. I was hysterical.

He took my hands in his to stop me and said,

"I can't see you like this. You are my whole life. Don't do this to yourself."

His coolness and those words put me into such a rage that I forcefully released my hands from his and ran to the bathroom. I locked the door and burst into hysterical tears. In my anger and rage, I cried for a long while.

When I stepped out of the bathroom, I was surprised to see Behzad sitting by the door. He stood up, but said nothing. I ignored him and took my books and left the house.

*   *   *

Behzad stayed with us for couple of days. I did not talk to him, but he acted normal as though nothing had happened. He did not miss any opportunity to tell me how much he loved me. Mitra was happy to have her father at home.

Finally, I figured out how he had my signature on the application. We used to do our tax returns together. Since my handwriting was not so good, he would make a copy of the return that we both would sign. I remembered that, about a month earlier, we prepared the tax return and he had it ready to sign.

One morning, when I was late for school and had to rush out, he asked me to sign the return before leaving. He knew that I did not have time, at the time, to check the papers. He had the forms turned over page by page for me to sign, which I did. He had inserted the application for change of name in between the forms for me to sign, which I did without noticing it.

*   *   *

A few days after Behzad went back to Stockholm, I had my appointment with the attorney. By then, I had managed to tone down my anger. Behzad's presence exasperated me; his absence was a real relief.

I was determined to apply for a divorce, which I did. Thomas, the middle-aged attorney, informed me about the law regarding divorce cases. He said that I could apply, but it would not be processed until six months from that date. This was a "reconsideration period" for couples with children and was set by law.

As I left Thomas's office, I felt surprisingly free and relieved. I was not in high spirits; but by some means, I was pleased. I went home and called Behzad to let him know about it. The news came as a shock to him. He remained silent on the line for minutes. Then he repeated over and over that I must be joking and that I was not serious about it.

*   *   *

During this reconsideration period, Behzad came home every weekend. He tried his best to convince me to change my mind about the divorce. He talked for hours explaining why he changed Mitra's name. He claimed it was for her sake. He believed she would be better off with a Swedish name instead of a foreign one. He argued that it would do her good when she started school. He admitted that he knew I would never consent to changing her name. He felt he had no other choice than to do it himself. He wanted me to forgive him and give him a chance to correct it. He asked me not to split our family up, if only for Mitra's sake.

Those words did not ease me. Our life together was over for me. I could not handle more lies and false promises.

Chapter 18

Price to Pay

At the peak of my conflict with Behzad, Ramin decided to go abroad for his higher education. He had completed his two years of mandatory military service. During one and one-half of those years, he fought at the front of the war with Iraq, in which he was injured and hospitalized for some time.

Following his plan, he sent me a copy of his high school diploma in order to apply for admission to any Swedish university. Thereafter, he could apply for a student visa.

As the war in Iran continued, it was difficult to get any kind of visa and nearly impossible for a young Iranian. I took a chance and was able to get a letter of admission for Ramin in the medical field from the same university I was attending. With the admission letter in his hand, he applied for a student visa from the Embassy of Sweden in Tehran.

As he waited for the response from the Swedish Embassy to his request, an unfortunate incident occurred that made my family decide to send him to the United States. The United States had not (still has not) an embassy in Iran due to the hostage crisis. So, Ramin had to go to Turkey to apply for a U.S. visa from the American Embassy in order to leave Iran as soon as possible. While Ramin waited in Turkey for the visa from the American Embassy, a student visa was issued for him by the Swedish Embassy. He returned to Iran to get ready to join us in Sweden.

At a time when it was nearly impossible for any young Iranian to obtain a visa, Ramin had obtained one with no hassle. At that time, usually the only way for Iranians to enter any European country was through illegal means. To me, it seemed that God was at Ramin's side. In a matter of days he flew to Sweden.

* * *

Mitra and I waited impatiently for Ramin at the airport. I did not recognize him until he waved to us. To my surprise, his thick, black hair was shaved. It had been about five years since I had seen him. He was just a teenager then. Now, at twenty-one, he was a young man.

Ramin passed through the crowd and walked straight to us. He was not sure which of us he should hug first. He lifted up Mitra. I hugged him as I touched his bald head and asked, "What happened to your hair? Have you missed me so badly that you lost all your hair?" He just laughed.

Seeing my happiness, Mitra jumped up and down in excitement. Since I had talked a lot about Ramin to Mitra, she impatiently had been waiting for *daei* Ramin—Uncle Ramin—to come and play with her. She insisted on sitting by Ramin in the back seat of the car.

I was very curious about his shaven head. Ramin had always taken great care in his appearance, shaving his hair off was not his style. I insisted that he tell me about it. At first, he tried to pass it off by making jokes about his own baldness, but my stubbornness won out.

"Sister, don't mess with me. I've been a cell mate with criminals. I'm not the same nice guy anymore," he said jokingly.

"Seriously? You're kidding; you've not been in jail, have you?" I grinned and asked, stunned.

"I'm not kidding. Let's talk about it later."

*   *   *

Mitra was already asleep, snuggled up next to Ramin, and we had a long way to drive. It was a good time to hear what had happened to him. "Okay, Daddash joon—dear brother—tell me now. I'm dying of curiosity," I insisted.

"It looks like you won't let it go! Okay, I tell you. But you should know that these types of incidents are now a part of the daily life in Iran. It happens all the time and can happen to anyone; this time it happened to me and my friends. Having fun in Iran is a crime. Pasdaran and other militant groups of the regime watch you to make sure your life is miserable," he explained before he began his story.

Indeed, I could already guess what he were going to tell me, since I had heard that many nasty and inhuman episodes at the hands of the revolutionary guards and other paramilitary groups occurred on a daily basis.

"One of my friends had a birthday party over a month ago," Ramin began telling the story. "Some of his relatives and friends including me were invited to the party. It was like a family gathering. Music, dance, drinks, and having fun makes it a real good party. As you know, all of these are illegal in Iran since the Islamic regime. To be extra cautious we kept the volume of the music low. Even though alcoholic drinks are banned in Iran, it's easy to buy them. They are smuggled into the country. Some people even make alcohol at home."

"Anyhow, in the middle of the party, all of the sudden the sound of shattering windows, and loud thump on the door was heard. In no time some armed Pasdars stormed in. Everybody was stunned and terrified. With the rifles aimed at us, they cursed and called us names. They searched the house and ordered us to go with them."

"It was winter time and the weather was freezing cold. We were transported to an unknown location; there we were ordered to stand with face toward the wall in the yard. We were left in the same standing position until 3 PM next day. Then we were taken inside the building. They separated men and women. They shaved our hair and took pictures before sending each of us to solitary confinement, with no charge."

"The cell was cold and dark. I was in the cell for two more days. There was no bed to sleep on except the bare floor. Not even a toilet to pee. Some bread and water was pushed inside through a small opening."

"Two days later I was released from the cell and taken for interrogation. I was beaten and practically tortured in order to confess that I belonged to the organization of Mujahidin Khalgh. At that time, I figured out that they thought they uncovered a secret political meeting in my friend's house."

"After interrogation, we were transferred to a multiple cell with other criminal inmates. The inmates treated us badly, since they were told that we were member of Mujahidin. But soon they understood we were not and changed their attitude against us."

"We were kept in the jail for five more days. On sixth day we were ordered to appear in the court. The court house was located a couple of blocks from the detention center.

In jail uniform and wearing hand cuffs and foot chains, we walked to the court house through the streets. Since the Mujahidin organization supported the Iraqi invasion and officially collaborated with the enemy, the common people in the street, thinking that we were Mujahidin members, spat at us and called us traitors."

"We came to the courthouse. We appeared in front of a mullah whom to our surprise functioned as the judge, prosecutor and defense attorney! In other words 'all in one.' Can you imagine a courtroom occupied by about twenty prisoners, standing in cuffs, waiting, and having their fate in the hands of a mullah, who was not aware about our cases or charges? And no solid evidence whatsoever?" Ramin wondered, before continuing his unfortunate story, "The mullah looked scornfully at us and listened to the opening statement from one of the Pasdar. The charges as we heard officially for the first time were 'conspiracy against the Islamic Republic per Mujahedin organization's instruction, having illegal political meetings, drinking alcohol and having party with the opposite sex'.

Our appearance in the court was very short. The mullah sent us back to jail to wait, and stated contemptibly, "You've had enough time to enjoy the life, now it's time for you to suffer and pay back."

"We walked back to the jail again. Five days later we were taken back to the court for hearing. Apparently, they could not find anything to support political activities against the regime, not even any connection with the Mujahidin. However, they found enough evidence for drinking alcohol and partying with opposite sex. In less than fifteen minutes the court session was over. Each of us was sentenced to two weeks in jail and forty-five lashes." Ramin stopped speaking here for a moment.

"What a story! It's just unbelievable! What happened next? Did you still have to go to the jail? You already served the jail time, didn't you?" I asked.

"Yes, we already spent ten days in the jail, but we had to stay some more days to complete the jail time," he responded and then continued, "We were taken to a large room in the basement. There were couple of benches and on each side a bearded guard waited for us. One by one we were pushed to the bench. We had to lay down on it and the guard whipped us.

"The most tragic of the whole episode for all of us was my friend Kia's case. His wife had a heart problem. She handed over a doctor certificate to the judge. The judge ignored it and she got the same punishment as the others. So when it was her turn, her husband, Kia, was taken to the room to watch his wife's whipping. Kia was devastated. He screamed and cursed. In response he got harsher whipping. His wife had to be transported to the hospital.

"To make a long story short, after whipping, we were taken back to the cells to wrap up our jail time."

I was stunned at such barbaric acts and thought that the wounds and pain of the lashes on those youngsters would go away by the time, but the scars on their soul would surely chase them forever.

"What did happen to Kia and his wife?" I asked Ramin curiously.

"His wife recovered after spending some time in the hospital. Now both are fine, but they are trying to get away from the country as soon as possible," Ramin explained.

"Savage bastards!" I said. I felt hatred toward those cruel men and women. "Do you still have the scars on your back?" I asked.

"Yes, but it's getting better," he answered.

"Did they give any medicine to heal the wounds after that?" I asked.

"Are you kidding me? They would have enjoyed pouring salt on the wounds to see us suffer more," he said.

"Was this incident the reason that Shahram and Mamman sent you to Turkey?" I asked.

"Yes," Ramin confirmed.

*   *   *

Ramin also shared another inhuman incident which quite often occurred to the women in Iran after the revolution.

Using violence to enforce hijab rule was part of the new Islamic regime's policy.

Therefore organized gangs were assigned to terrorize the women. Assaulting, stabbing, use of acid, and razors to deform the women's face; and many other barbarian tackles were exercised to make sure that terror would succeed;

unfortunately these sadistic acts worked well.

One on the victims was Shadin, Ramin's then girlfriend and later on my sister in-law. Years later she told me in her own words about what she went through when she was just eighteen years old and was walking home with her friend Melody: "We were just a couple of blocks away from home, when two bearded men approached us. One of them in a very offending language asked us why we did not wear proper hijab. I got upset by this question and told him it was not his business. He said, 'Oh, Yes, it is my business, you whore' and pushed me hard so that I fell on the ground. The other guy took out brass knuckles and punched on my face and kicked me. I fainted and did not feel anything until I woke up in a taxi. Melody told me later that the guys jumped to a waiting car and left the scene. Luckily a taxi driver had seen the incident and came to help. He drove me to the nearest hospital.

"I was in terrible, unbearable pain in my face and right arm. Because of ongoing Iran-Iraq war, all hospital rooms and even the hallways were occupied with the wounded army soldiers from the war front. So, I was not admitted to that hospital. The taxi driver drove me to another hospital. I was rejected from that hospital too, because of facility limitation.[18]

"The taxi driver took me again to another hospital, where my father ran barefoot the entire way to, when he heard the news.

In that hospital we were told that they would accept patients who personally themselves or anyone in the family had donated blood for the wounded soldiers. My father desperately called some family and relatives to finally find a cousin who used to donate blood. I got admitted after my cousin came to the hospital to show his membership and also donated blood.

"Anyhow, with all these, finally a doctor checked me up and said that I needed to have an urgent surgery, but the hospital surgeon was not available. He gave me some pills for pain and sent me home.

"I was terribly in pain, but my father was worse than me. He was so desperate that he was willing to do anything to get a surgeon to do the surgery on me and make my pain go away, but it was no way. We went home. I was miserable. My jawbone was broken and my teeth were stuck in my upper jaw. I threw out the food and the blood through my nose, because the passage through my mouth was closed due to the injury.

"My brother kept calling his friends to find a surgeon to do the surgery on me. He found one and we went to a hospital, there the surgeon, Dr. Parto worked. Now it was middle of the night. Dr. Parto came to me and kissed my forehead and said, "My dear, what did they do to you? Don't worry, I fix it. You'll be fine."

"He did fix it as he had promised. He did the surgery. I was hospitalized for a week. I was not able to eat any food about six months. I was fed intravenously

18 Economic sanction due to American hostages' crisis at that time was another reason for the hospitals not being equipped with necessary equipment.

the first weeks and later I could eat soup by straw."

"Did you ever report the incident to the police?" I asked Shadin.

"My father did. The police said: 'It's an Islamic country and you and your daughter have to obey the Islamic rules if you don't want something like this to happen to you again' and then hung up on my father," Shadin said and continued to tell me about the surgeon Dr. Parto.

"You can't believe what happened to Dr. Parto. Do you know anything about Ghatlhaie Zangirehee—the chained murders? Shadin asked me.

"Yes I know," I responded.

"I loved Dr. Parto for what he did for me, so I used to go to his office every time I visited Iran. Some years ago I was in Iran and decided to visit him. I found out that he was stabbed to dead in his own home. It is said that the gang killed him."

"Why would the gang kill him?" I asked.

"He was a socialist and the way he murdered was exactly the same pattern that this gang does the job," Shadin responded.

It was hard for me to believe how cruel and shameless my own countrymen could be. *Are they really my civilized countrymen? Where were they before? If they existed before, they had to be damn good actors to play a good guy's role for quite long time.* Once question after another ran through my head. *Does religion make a person simple minded or is religion used by some malicious individuals as a tool to satisfy their own sick minds?*

Chapter 19

In the Throes of Collapse

"Please Niki, don't do this. I love you. I love Mitra. Please don't take it from me. I'll do whatever you ask me to do, just don't break up this family. Think how it would hurt Mitra," Behzad pleaded each time he came home and asked us to go to Stockholm with him.

"Okay, do you want me stay in this marriage? That's fine. I will, but not before you change Mitra's last name to her original one," I told him as he blamed me for tearing the family apart.

"Oh, Niki, please, it's our life, our marriage we're talking about. It's not a contract. We must save our marriage first, with no preconditions. Please don't make me do something as a condition. I've promised you, and I do again, that I will change her name—but not as a condition."

"You're right, this is a precondition, but I'm sorry to tell you that it is the only way."

We had similar discussions numerous times with no result. In the beginning, I was resolute with my decision. However, I later came up with another solution and presented it to Behzad. "Forget about my previous condition. I will get the form to request the name change, and both of us will sign it. As soon as she gets her last name back, *together* we will apply for changing her last name again to your new one, whatever it is. I think this is a simple solution."

"It sounds wonderful, thank you Niki. You and Mitra are everything to me. You're my life. I promise to keep both of you happy," he agreed and went on with more promises.

In fact, I was not so happy. I knew he would have new surprises at any time. In addition, I still was not sure what he was doing and what his agenda was regarding the church and Christianity. Why he had obtained a new identity, a new religion, and moved to Stockholm was a mystery to me. Nevertheless, I still loved him and needed to give my marriage another chance. I wanted a perfect life for Mitra. She was a happy, innocent little girl who loved her father. She was only four years old; it would break my heart to take a normal family life from her.

Moreover, I was tired of living in a small city. Now I had the opportunity to live in a big city and continue my education in a well-known university.

Ramin could attend the university there as well; he had no objection to living in Stockholm.

∗   ∗   ∗

It was late May. I had finished my second term of school and would continue at the university in Stockholm. Ramin had finished the language course and was admitted to the same university. Behzad had prepared everything for moving, but he still had not signed the form, which I had signed weeks earlier.

I had left the form on his desk and expected him to sign it before we moved. I reminded him a few times. Each time, he said that he would sign, which he never did. Ignoring my proposal made me resolute in not withdrawing my request for divorce. I knew he was expecting me to do my part first, but I had taken the first step by moving to Stockholm. Now I waited for him to do his part. Indeed, it was quite clear to me that he was confident that he could manipulate me as long as he wanted and that I would be the one to give up.

∗   ∗   ∗

In the beginning of summer, we moved to Stockholm. The church, which he worked for, paid for the relocation costs. The apartment he had rented was small but nice. It was located in a quiet area, some distance from the city.

Shortly after we settled down, Mitra started going to day care, which was not far from home. She quickly adapted to the new environment and liked the place. Ramin continued going to school to improve his Swedish. I found a temporary summer job as a caregiver at a retirement center. Behzad had gained a position within the church and was highly respected and popular among the church workers and priests.

I tried to care less about his agenda and what he was doing. It was an unambiguous fact to me that he was taking advantage of them. In some instances, he tried to persuade me that he was a genuine Christian, but I definitely could not buy it. "You can fool the entire world, but you can't fool me anymore."

Despite all the uncertainty, we had a pleasant summer as a family. Ramin, with Behzad's help, had already applied for a residency permit and moved to a student room.

In addition to preaching in the church and officiating at ceremonies, Behzad worked as a teacher in the community school. He taught the Swedish language and computer classes. Moreover, he arranged weekend camping trips and activities that were fun for everyone. Mitra and I enjoyed participating in those activities with Ramin and his friends.

Behzad planned free, short trips for Iranians to different cities. These trips were sponsored by the church in order to recruit more Iranians to convert to Christianity. In addition to activities and entertainment, Behzad also preached.

On those trips, I saw a different side of Behzad and abilities that I never knew he possessed. He was a good speaker and entertainer. He translated some gospels of the Bible to Farsi and put them in a form of a musical poem for everyone to sing. The church was very pleased with his work.

*   *   *

In the fall, Ramin and I started school and studied full time, which required many hours in the school and library along with some training.

My relationship with Behzad was good; he was still acting as a caring husband to me. Not a single day passed that he did not say how much he loved me. However, neither of us mentioned anything about our unresolved dispute.

I still had the form and expected him to sign it. Time was running out and the six months of the divorce reconsideration period was getting closer to the end. The six months passed and Thomas, my attorney, called to ask if he could continue the divorce process. My answer was, "Yes." Three months later, Behzad and I received separate letters, informing us of the court date. This gave us two more months to play the game with one another, which we did. Both of us pretended that nothing was going to happen soon. However, he brought up the issue time after time, asking me to change my mind. Each time, we had the same short conversation.

"Niki, don't do this to us. Think about Mitra."

"Do you have any solution for it?" I asked to remind him to sign the form.

"I will sign the form, but not just now. The foundation of our marriage has to be love, not a stupid form."

"I want a marriage, which is based on love and trust. You've broken the trust and you have to fix it."

"Please Niki, don't be so stubborn. You'll regret this."

*   *   *

We were getting closer to the date of the hearing for finalizing the divorce, which would take place in the city of Lund, where the divorce was filed. One day before the appointment date, Mitra, Behzad, and I took the train to Lund.

Oddly, we had fun together on the way to Lund. We played and sang with Mitra. We had lunch in the train's restaurant, making fun of each other, laughing, and having a good time like a happy family going on vacation.

I did not feel anxious or worried at all; Behzad seemed to feel the same. I knew that whatever happened in Lund would lead to my liberation and peace of mind. The sense of uncertainty regarding Behzad's real personality and his bizarre secretive agenda that had bothered me for quite a long time had to end. It would come the next day, and this chapter of my life would be closed.

*   *   *

In the evening, we arrived in Lund and took a taxi to Behzad's mother. She was living with Jila, one of her daughters. Our arrival was not expected, so seeing us at her door surprised her. I loved her humble and tender character. I used to call her Maadar jan—dear mother.

She embraced us gladly and invited us in. She was happy to have us there and called all her children, who lived just some blocks from each other in the same area, and asked them to join us. I really had missed them all. We used to see each other nearly every day, and I had enjoyed their company.

Since they were not aware of what was going on between Behzad and me, they were curious to know the reason for the unexpected trip. I left it to Behzad to tell them. Not willing to give the real reason, Behzad just said that we had missed them and that we needed to get away for couple of days. Obviously, it was not a convincing reason. Sami humorously said, "Do you expect me to believe you? Next time, when you miss us, just send a round trip ticket to us!"

*   *   *

The next day, I woke up to a sunny but cold morning. Mitra slept at my side like an angel. Behzad was not in the room. I heard Jila and him in the kitchen.

I got up and dressed for court. I still was calm and collected. Felicia, Sami's little girl, who had slept over, came into the room and ask for Mitra. I let her wake Mitra up, and we joined the others for breakfast.

In the kitchen, Jila and Maadar jan set the breakfast table. Jila was a humorous, young woman. She and Sami had similar personalities. Behzad and Lena, who had come to pick up Felicia, sat at the table in silence. I kissed Maadar jan's cheek and said good morning to everyone.

Throughout the morning, Behzad tried not to look at me or talk to me. The night before, we had pretended everything was fine and avoided talking about the day to come. Now we were about to get divorced in a matter of hours. Both of us were very good actors.

It was time for us to leave for the court appointment. I asked Lena if Mitra could go to her house and play with Felicia for a couple of hours. I saw the look of curiosity on everyone's faces, but none of them tried to pry.

When I went to the room to get my purse, Behzad came after me. He took my purse from me and stood still for several minutes looking at me, saying nothing.

"We'll be late, we have to go now. Give me my purse," I said.

"Niki, don't do this to us," he said softly, but sadly.

"Why? I didn't see any signature on the form," I said.

"You'll be sorry, Niki. I don't have more to say to you. But I want you to know that you'll be sorry," he said firmly. Before I could say anything in response, he handed me my purse and rushed out of the room.

*   *   *

I took a bus to the courthouse. Thomas, the attorney, was already there. As I sat by Thomas going through some paperwork, Behzad and his lawyer entered the lobby. Behzad rushed pass us so fast that his lawyer nearly had to run to get alongside him. As they walked into the courtroom, we followed them.

It was the first time I had ever been inside a court. Unlike courtrooms that I had seen in American movies, this was just an ordinary room furnished with a conference table and some chairs. Thomas and I sat down at the table across from Behzad and his young, chubby attorney. Soon after, the judge and the court secretary entered the room.

The judge had dark skin and brown, thick hair. His bony, long face appeared to be that of a strict person, but his kind, brown eyes implied the opposite. The secretary, a middle-aged, thin woman with a fair face and short blonde hair sat next to the judge. She had paper and pen handy, waiting for the judge to start the hearing.

Behzad's face was stiff, and he avoided my eyes. He looked sad, and I, in an idiotic moment, felt guilty for his sadness. However, I was determined to go through the process in order to gain some peace of mind once and forever.

It might have not been fair to Mitra, not even to Behzad, but I was too exhausted. *I do not have any strength left to face more lies and surprises after the fact,* I thought to myself in the silence of the courtroom.

The judge started the process. Thomas, my attorney, briefly informed the court of my request to be granted a divorce. Behzad's attorney acknowledged my request and added that his client was not willing to agree to a divorce. The attorney added that his client was aware that he had no choice other than to accept the court's verdict.

The judge asked me if I had taken enough time to reconsider my decision. My response was, "Yes, I did."

Without any more discussion, he declared his ruling granting the divorce and mentioned that the official documents would be mailed to us later. It was bizarre that in a matter of minutes everything was over. It was a short and hassle-free process—at least I thought it was.

Real life was so different than the movies. The court, the judge, the ruling, and the whole situation were so contrary to my expectations. My feeling at the time was an odd combination of disappointment and relief. *That was it? Now we were not married anymore? Should we go home and figure out where to go from there?* I thought to myself.

I looked at Behzad to see his reaction. He still refused to look at me.

"Are we done?" I whispered to Thomas,

"No, custody of Mitra is next," he whispered back.

He had told me before that the hearing for custody of Mitra and the divorce would be at the same time. I had requested custody, and Thomas had assured me it would not be a problem. He told me that in most cases mothers usually got custody. In rare cases, in which mothers were abusive or by any reason not suitable, fathers gained custody. In my case, there was no chance that Behzad would get custody of Mitra.

After going through some papers with the secretary and giving her some instructions, the judge asked to start the process of the custody case for Mitra. First, he asked Behzad to explain why it would be better for Mitra to stay with him.

Behzad cleared his throat, sat bolt straight, and did not look at me. His facial expression had turned him into a stranger. As he started talking, I understood that my impression was right. The person facing me was not my loving and caring husband; this man was a cruel liar.

"Niki is an unstable person. She's aggressive and not capable of taking care of anybody. She hits Mitra and abuses her physically and verbally. In general, she's not a good mother …"

I was stunned, heavily shocked. I was not sure it was real or a nightmare. I looked desperately around, seeking help from Thomas, from the judge, from anyone. But no one stopped him, and he enjoyed picturing me as a psycho and a dangerous mother.

"Behzad, Behzad, why are you lying?" I asked Behzad then turned to the judge and implored, "He's lying, please, don't believe him."

"Keep quiet," the judge told me firmly.

"But, he's lying."

"One more word, I'll ask you to leave. Understand?"

I kept quiet and looked at Thomas to help me out. He whispered to me to stay calm and that I would have time to speak.

Behzad, who seemed to enjoy the scene, continued, "Once, she was aggressive and hit Mitra so badly that if I was not home she could have killed her own daughter. Since then, I'm frightened of leaving Mitra alone with her. She's also very irresponsible and doesn't care about anyone but herself; she's getting worse since she started going to school again. I love Mitra. She's my whole world; I would sacrifice my life for her."

As he continued to talk, I could not control my tears. I thought that my life was over. I had lost Mitra. If the judge believed Behzad, I would not even get a right to see my child.

When it was my turn to speak, the judge asked me to give him a reason why Mitra would be better off with me. I had not prepared myself for such a fight. I had never imagined getting into such a desperate situation that I would have to reveal who the real Behzad was. The irony about it was that I was not sure if I knew who the real Behzad was. I had thought the only positive side of him was his role as husband and father, but now that side had been destroyed in front of my eyes. I had to admit that I did not know the man.

"He's a fake. He is manipulative and can fool anyone. He had changed his identity couple of times in Iran; and he did it again here in Sweden and converted to Christianity to fool the church. He's not an honest person. Everything he said about me is a lie. I have never hit or abused Mitra. He said I am an irresponsible mother; I'm not. He is the irresponsible one with two other children with two different women in Iran. He calls them his biological kids, yet he does not know where they are and what they're doing …"

Behzad hastily interrupted me to say, "Those kids are dead. They were killed when Saddam dropped bombs over the city they were living in."

"Oh my God, you really are something! How can you say such a big lie?" I erupted, shocked that he would say such a thing.

The judge warned us to keep quiet, and then asked me to keep talking.

"He's lying. He does not even know where they are. He left his second wife the day after his son's birth while she still was in the maternity ward. He has never seen his son since."

"It's not true!" Behzad said quietly.

"It is!" I responded.

The judge silenced us. Looking at me, he said, "Talk to me." Then he turned to Behzad and said sharply, "And you keep quiet." With the room silent, the judge again turned to me and asked, "Do you have more to add?"

"I love Mitra and would never harm her. Anyone who knows me can confirm that. I've never abused her, and I'm not aggressive. He just makes these lies up," I said as my last defense.

"I've heard enough. You'll get my ruling soon," the judge said and left the room followed by the secretary.

I was not able to stay in that room for another minute and rushed out. Thomas did not have a chance to talk to me. I needed to get home to Mitra. I thought I had lost her. I wanted to be with her, to feel her, before they would take her away from me. I was running and my face was soaked in uncontrollable tears.

"Niki, azizam, wait, wait," I heard Behzad calling me from a distance.

"Go to hell!" I ran faster as I heard his steps behind me.

"Please, Niki jan, azizam, wait."

"Leave me alone, go away."

"I won't. I love you Niki, please wait."

"I hate you, leave me alone."

At the bus stop, I slowed down to catch a bus, and he caught up with me. As I got onto the bus, he followed me and sat beside me. I could not stop crying. The bus driver and the few passengers tried not to look at us, but I could feel the tension.

"Please, Niki jan, don't cry," Behzad pleaded.

"Get away from me, please," I murmured and nearly begged him, but he would not leave me alone.

One of my friends, Parisa, lived in that area. To get rid of him, I got off the bus near her house and ran as fast as I could. He ran after me. I reached Parisa's house and rang the bell nonstop; she opened the door. I rushed into her house and tried to shut the door on Behzad, but he pushed himself in. Parisa was stunned. She had no idea what was going on.

"What's wrong? What's happened?" Parisa asked.

"I hate him. Parisa jan, please throw him out," I begged Parisa. Then I turned to Behzad and shouted, "Go away, I don't want to see you, go away, and get lost!" I picked up an ashtray from the table and threw it at him. Fortunately for both of us, he dodged and the ashtray hit the wall.

"Parisa, please throw him out from your home. I can't stand him. Parisa, I beg you, throw him out," I sobbed.

"What is wrong with you guys?" she wanted to know.

Neither of us answered her. She patted my hair and tried to comfort me as she politely asked him to leave. "Behzad jan, leave her alone for now. I don't know what happened between you two, but she needs to be alone now."

"I won't leave without her," he stubbornly insisted.

"Okay, you won't go? Then I'll go," I said and walked to the door.

"Stay, both of you, Sit down and talk like adults," Parisa said in an effort to make peace between us.

"I don't have anything to say. He took Mitra away from me. I hate him," I said and left. Not giving up, Behzad followed me. I took a bus to Sami's and tried to ignore him. I controlled my tears and succeeded in calming myself down. I reached Sami's home with Behzad tailing behind. He was quiet. He had not said a word the whole way.

Mitra and Felicia were playing outside in the playground with the neighbors' kids. I did not bother their play. I just sat on a bench and watched them. Behzad sat by me.

It was cold, but sunny. I watched Mitra in her blue, thick jacket and reddish, ribbed, woolen hat. She was swinging, competing with Felicia and trying to swing higher and higher, neither seemed to care about the cold.

Cold and tired, I went inside the house. Lena sat at the table in the kitchen sewing. She was not curious about our business. I needed to cry more. I needed a friend to comfort me. I decided to go back to Parisa.

I thanked Lena for watching Mitra for me and told her that I needed to visit a friend for couple of hours then Mitra and I would return to Stockholm later in the evening. Behzad stood by the window, turned to me, and said in Farsi,

"We have tickets for tomorrow, not tonight."

"You can stay. Mitra and I are leaving tonight," I said reluctantly.

"The three of us will go tomorrow," he responded firmly.

"Mitra and I will go tonight," I repeated.

"The three of us go tomorrow or Mitra stays and goes with me tomorrow." He made his point.

I was too worn out to argue with him and said nothing. I turned to Lena who stopped her sewing machine to hear me. "Lena, I am going to see my friend. I will be back soon," I said and left the house.

I had hoped that he had given up following me, but he had not. He followed me again. Why? Did he enjoy torturing me or he was trying to play a concerned partner? It did not matter to me anymore, and I did not have enough strength left to fight him again. I turned back into the house. Lena looked at me. I answered her unasked question, "I changed my mind, and I won't go to see my friend."

It was lunch time. Lena put the sewing machine away and asked me to call the girls in to eat. I called the kids many times, but they did not come in. I went to the playground to get them to come in and eat. I watched them running to the house. I wanted to stay there, just sitting on the swing to let the time pass by. I moved like a robot. I had been deceived and was going to lose my baby. It was too painful. The wound had made me numb.

"Mamman, come inside," Mitra's sweet childish voice jolted me. I went back inside.

The food was on the table and everyone was ready to eat. The kids were loud and happy. They were eager to eat and return to the playground. I sat with them, but I was not good company. I could not stand to be around Behzad, so I excused myself from the table. My head pounded.

*   *   *

After lunch, we left Lena's and Felicia came with us to be with Mitra. We went back to Maadar jan's house. She could easily tell that something was wrong. Concerned, she asked us if everything was fine. I said it was not; Behzad said nothing. He lifted Mitra up and took Felicia's hand to go to the playground.

This gave me an opportunity to tell Maadar jan and Jila what had happened. I was surprised to learn that the news did not shock them. They had thought our behavior had been peculiar since the day we appeared unannounced at their house. However, hearing what Behzad had done in court upset and angered them.

Both women tried to console me by promising that nobody could take Mitra away from me, and they would not let it happen. Jila said that if it did happen, she personally would be my witness to back me up. Maadar jan said the same, but she also tried talk me into reconsidering and giving Behzad another chance.

She pointed to her own wedding ring on her finger and said, "My daughter, do you see this ring? Despite all the suffering, this will be in my finger as long as I breathe. The ring is sacred. From the moment one wears this ring and swears to keep, it becomes sacred."

I found it odd how deeply she felt about marriage. I did not know much about her husband and nobody talked about him. I only knew that he was in Iran and none of his eight children wished for him to be around.

After venting my frustration by talking to them, I went to the bedroom to get some rest and try to get rid of my headache. I closed the door behind me and sat on the floor. I remembered what was said in the very same room earlier in the morning. Behzad had warned me that I would regret the choice I had made to proceed with the divorce. Now it was clear as daylight that he would use whatever, even Mitra, to destroy me, but I could not let him use Mitra as a tool for the job. I had to fight back.

Crazy or not, I started talking to myself to find the courage to fight him. I promised myself that I wouldn't let anyone take my baby away from me. I vowed that I would never let him have the pleasure of seeing my tears ever again. I got up and took a long shower. Refreshed, I looked at myself in the mirror, demanded that the figure in the mirror stop pitying herself, and assured her that Mitra would stay with her.

Talking to the mirror bolstered me, and I forgot about the headache. I put on some warm clothes. On my way outside, I noticed Behzad resting on the sofa in the living room. I did not look at his direction, but I knew that he was watching me to make sure I would not leave the house by myself. I didn't know why he was so obsessed about it, but I didn't care at the time. I opened the outer glass door of the living room, which directly opened to the playground. So he could, with no trouble, watch me and the kids.

"Mamman, look, I've made a sandy house," Mitra shouted happily as she saw me coming. I joined her and Felicia in the sand box. We made funny figures with the sand and laughed at them. We moved over to the swing set and swung higher and higher.

It was getting colder and the sun was already down. The kids went inside, but I stayed outside and continued to swing. The movements in the air kept me from negative thoughts, which would ruin any confidence and hope I had earlier given to the figure in the mirror.

However, I could not swing forever. I had to put my foot on the ground and face the reality of the situation. In a matter of hours, my life had dramatically changed. I reminded myself that I had thought about the reality of divorce and felt ready to deal with its challenges. However, I had never thought about the possibility of losing Mitra.

From that point on, it would be an absolutely dreadful challenge for me to face and deal with the unpredictable personality of the man I saw earlier that morning in court.

*   *   *

Sami came to take Felicia home. As he entered the house, he sensed tension in the air. "What is wrong? Can anybody tell me what's really going on?" he shouted.

It was like I had prayed for that question. I needed him to know too. I wanted people on my side.

"We got divorced today," I was quick to say. Behzad rushed out of the room.

"What? Divorce? Are you serious?" Sami was truly shocked.

I told him the whole story and the story of the day in the court. He shook his head and for the first time since I had known him, he looked serious. As I told him about the lies Behzad had said to the judge in order to picture me as a wild and abusive mother, my tears started again.

"Don't worry; nobody can take Mitra from you. I personally promise you it will not happen." Sami said; and to change the sad atmosphere, he humorously said, "Don't worry. I'll gather a huge squad of witnesses to testify that you are a good mother."

*   *   *

The next morning, I woke up and found Mitra sleeping on my arm. Carefully, trying not to wake her up, I released my arm and got up. It was very early and everyone in the house seemed to be asleep. I had asked Jila the night before to get another room for Behzad for the night.

I looked at myself in the mirror, I looked worse than ever. My puffy, red eyes were a sign of an awful and restless night. The mirror did not lie. I had held Mitra in my arms and cried through most of the night. I imagined the terrifying possibility of not having her with me; it was an unbearable torture.

As difficult as it was, I survived the night. Now was the first day of my new life. We had to go back to Stockholm in a few hours. *What will be next?* I started questioning myself. *Where can Mitra and I live? Behzad will never leave the house and I cannot stay there anymore. Why didn't I think of that before?* It was too late to blame myself. I had to find a place soon. However, we needed somewhere to live until I found a place of my own. Ramin lived in a small student room so that was out of the question. In addition, he had asked me not to involve him in our problems. Behzad was his friend, and he did not want to take sides. Negin, a good friend of mine, was my only option. I would ask if Mitra and I could live with her for a while. She, as well, did not know anything about my divorce. The news would come as surprise to everyone who knew us.

Chapter 20

Struggle

The return trip to Stockholm seemed endless. Ironically, as Mitra and I kept each other company, Behzad attempted to make me jealous. So that when Mitra and I were in the train's restaurant, he entered with a beautiful Swedish girl. Mitra happily said, "Mamman look, Baba is coming."

"Yes, azizam, but he is busy; we should not bother him now. Okay?" I told her to keep her seat and not run to him.

During the entire trip to Stockholm, Behzad and the girl kept each other company. He was desperately and ridiculously trying to make the point that if not me, there would be other young, beautiful girls available for him.

* * *

It was late at night when we arrived in Stockholm. We took a taxi home.

"Azizam, are you tired? Do you want me to make you some tea?" Behzad asked as soon as we got home. It was absurd that he still pretended to be my caring husband. I said nothing and walked away to get Mitra ready for bed. I did not care to get ready myself for bed; I just rested on the sofa.

"Niki jan, come to the bed, why stay on the sofa? Please Niki, come to bed," he continued to pretend nothing had happened.

Was everything just a big joke to him or was he too dumb to understand that nothing would be the same anymore? I chose to ignore him. He finally gave up and lay down on the other sofa.

* * *

In the morning, as I opened my eyes to the familiar surroundings of my home, I remembered this was not my home anymore. Behzad was already awake, sitting on the sofa, looking at me. "Good morning," he said.

I did not respond. I got up and went to Mitra. She was asleep. I took a bag and filled it with some of her favorite toys and books. Behzad watched me and asked me not to do that. But I wanted to get out of there as soon as possible. I had to wake Mitra up. She was the one who usually woke up early in the mornings but not that morning. I woke her up and told her that we would go to Negin's.

"Does Baba come with us too?" she asked.

"No, just you and me," I answered.

"Nobody goes anywhere," Behzad said and lifted Mitra up and kissed her.

I took some clothes for Mitra. "Put her down," I said quietly.

He kissed her again and put her down.

I helped Mitra dress. With my purse over my shoulder, I carried the bag of Mitra's toys and books in one hand and took Mitra's hand in the other. I was ready to leave.

We walked toward the door, but Behzad rushed to stand between us and the door. "Niki, this is your home. It's our home. Please don't break this family apart."

"It's too late, move back."

"No. I won't let you destroy what we have."

"Get back, don't make a scene, she's watching."

Mitra held my hand and watched us in silence. She was five years old, and it was the first time she witnessed a harsh conversation between us. Since the day in court, she sensed that something was wrong. She was already confused, but I could not understand how that bizarre situation affected her.

"Do you want to go? Go, but you should know that the moment you leave this house, there will be no place for you here anymore," he warned me and stepped away.

I did not say a word. As I opened the door, he demanded, "Give me the key. You don't need it anymore."

I opened my purse, took out the key, threw it at him, and shut the door behind us on the way out.

*   *   *

We walked the couple of blocks to Negin's house. Mitra was quiet. She didn't ask why we didn't eat breakfast before leaving or why her baba did not want us to leave. She never asked why she had to come with me to Negin's and not to day care.

She held my hand and walked with me. I didn't know what she was thinking or if she was sad and scared. I didn't know what was circulating in her little head. I wished I knew.

"We will go to Negin's and ask her to make you a tasty breakfast. Then I will take you to day care. How does that sound?" I foolishly tried to give her a pleasant picture of an ugly situation to please her.

"Okay," she replied and remained quiet.

Now I could tell that she was angry with me. She loved her father, and I had not brought him with us. She wanted to stay home to make her baba happy.

Should I tell her that "home" was gone forever? Should I tell her that she had stupid parents? What kind of future could I describe for her to make her happy again?

Did I have anything positive and hopeful to tell her about? How should I handle this mess?

I stopped, put the bag down and sat in front of her. She looked at me innocently. I hugged her, but still did not know what to tell her. "Are you still sleepy?"

She shook her head.

"I know you're hungry. Do you want to have breakfast in dagis—day care?"

She nodded.

"Okay, we will go to Negin's first, and then we'll go to dagis. In the evening, when I come to pick you up, we can go and get some godies—candies." I felt stupid, trading a family for some candies, but it made her momentarily happy.

"Lördagsgodies—Saturday candies?" she asked sweetly. She was allowed to eat candy on Saturdays.

"Yes sweetie, Lördagsgodies."

*   *   *

Still in her pajamas, Negin opened the door to us. She was a pretty, slim, single woman about my age. We met each other on the first trip that Behzad had arranged for Iranians.

"Hi, do you want two uninvited guests?" I asked.

"Come in. So early in the morning? Has something happened?" she asked.

"Sorry, did I wake you up?"

"No problem, I had to get up soon anyway. Why are you here?"

"Behzad and I have some problems, I'll tell you later. Can we stay with you for awhile?"

"Of course you can. Let's go to the kitchen. Have you had breakfast?"

"No, but Mitra wants to have breakfast at dagis today," I replied, looking at Mitra to assure her that I had not forgotten.

"How are you, Mitra jan? Did your mamman wake you up early too? Do you want some orange juice?" she asked Mitra. Without waiting for an answer, Negin poured a glass of orange juice and handed it to Mitra.

Mitra sat on my lap while she drank her juice. Negin was curious to know how serious our conflict was. To give her a clue, since I preferred not to talk about it in front of Mitra, I just told her that it was serious and over between us. She was stunned and asked me why I had not told her sooner. Sooner or later, what difference would it have made? Nobody could heal the broken trust.

I took Mitra to day care. She was happy that she would have breakfast with the other kids. She kissed me good-bye and ran to them. Her teachers were busy with the kids at the breakfast table. I waited to speak to the teachers; I thought it would be best if they knew about the situation. They could keep an eye on her for awhile to make sure that she handled the new situation well. As I waited, I watched Mitra; she was happy and talkative as usual. I felt somewhat relieved.

I talked to one of the teachers and told her of the change in Mitra's situation. Hearing about parents getting divorced was not new or shocking to them. Many kids lived with one parent. She promised me she would watch over Mitra and let me know how she was handling her new life.

*   *   *

Negin told me that Mitra and I could stay with her until we found a place to live. She, like many others, had a good image of Behzad; it was hard for her to believe otherwise. She suggested that his behavior in the court was a desperate attempt to make me give up my decision for divorce even if it was not a smart move on his part.

"You don't know him, Negin. Please don't try to justify his deception."

"No, I'm not justifying anything. I think both of you are stubborn, but he took it too far. I know he loves you, but men are big kids. They think they are smart, but sometimes their behavior is immature. This time, Behzad chose a childish way to keep you."

"Don't lecture me, please, not now. He's not like other men. He is smart and knows what he's doing. He's the father of my daughter, and I don't want to put him down. But you are my friend, and you should know that he is a fake. His entire life has been based on lies and deception. I was dumb enough to think that he would be different with me. Right now, the last thing I need is for you to try to simplify this situation. I don't care about anything right now, but Mitra. I'm scared Negin. I don't know what I'd do if they took Mitra from me ..." I burst into tears again. Negin hugged me and tried to console me that it would never happen, which I could not believe.

*   *   *

Negin gave me the key to her apartment and left for work. If it had been a normal day, I would have gone to school—but it was not. I had to make some plans. My mind raced. *What should I do now? Why did I overlook the fact that this day would come? Why hadn't I prepared for this day? Where and how I could find a place for Mitra and myself in such a short time?*

I blamed my negligence in not being prepared for this day. I panicked at the thought that my only income was my student loan, which would be enough for a couple of months. However, this was not the time to blame myself and absolutely not the time to panic. I had to move quickly. Finding a place to live was my first priority.

Not wasting any time, I went to the Department of the Residential Services for Students to rent a student apartment. However, I was told that no apartments would be available until summer, which was too late for me.

I went to the library and looked through the daily newspapers, searching for an apartment to rent. I found a few in the neighborhood. I returned to Negin's house to call the rental apartments. Unfortunately, I could not afford the monthly rents. My thoughts began to collide. *What could I do? What a mess! I had to find a job. What about my school?*

I was about two months away from finishing my third semester and one week away from losing custody of Mitra. I had no money and no place to live. Behzad on the other hand worked in the church and was highly respected. How could I prove that I was capable of taking care of Mitra? I would definitely lose her to Behzad. I was in a confused, messy situation and panicked once again. Such a state of instability would ensure that I had no chance to get custody of Mitra.

I looked at the image in the mirror. She was a mess too. I cried and cried, asking God for help. Then I looked at my reflection and grumbled aloud, *This is not the time to feel sorry for myself. I need to act wisely.* I realized that I needed to take a break from school, find a job, and get a place to live with Mitra. I would fight to keep her. That was a promise I made to myself.

It was Friday afternoon and Negin would be home soon. I had to pick up Mitra. I could not do much until Monday. I searched inside the kitchen cabinets to find something to make for dinner. I put some music on and started cooking, singing along with the music. It was good therapy.

It was time to get Mitra and take her to the candy shop to fulfill the promise I had made that morning.

After playing in every playground as we walked to Negin's, I had to talk her into going to Negin's, but it was hard to make her comfortable with the changes.

*   *   *

The weekend passed peacefully. Negin asked me not to worry and offered her place until we found an apartment of our own. Mitra spent some hours with Behzad, who tried to behave civilized. I sent Negin to get some of my and Mitra's clothes from Behzad.

I told Ramin what had happened. He was so loyal to Behzad that he told me, for a second time, that he did not want to be involved. I understood him, but I was a bit disappointed. However, I had a feeling that he blamed me since he had total trust in Behzad. It was bizarre to me that Behzad had succeeded in fooling everyone, including my own brother.

*   *   *

It was Monday and the beginning of the first week of my and Mitra's new life. This was the day when I would positively and energetically take the steps to fix my life for the path ahead.

The night before, after those restless and sleepless nights, I finally had a good sleep. It was bliss to open my eyes to a sunny and promising day and have Mitra sleeping sweetly by my side. She held one of her favorite stuffed animals against her chest and had grouped some others around her on the bed. I watched her for a while. My beautiful little girl deserved a good life. The selfishness of her parents had already taken her away from her home. I felt a sudden twitch in my heart, but before the negative thoughts could take over again, I jumped up, kissed Mitra, and rushed to get ready for the day.

My first task for the day was searching for a job. After taking Mitra to the day care, I took a bus to the District Employment Center. Inside, there were a few people ahead of me, waiting. I took a number and joined them.

When my number was called, I approached the desk. An elderly lady asked me to sit. Obviously, she knew why I was there. I needed a job. Still, she just looked at me, waiting. I told her that I was in an urgent situation and willing to take any kind of job. I told her that I was a medical student and had some experience working in hospitals.

After a search on the computer, she gave me a name and number to call for an interview for a temporary position as a caretaker in an adult center. Then she asked me if I knew any computer software, which I did not.

I told her that I had Bachelor of Science in Finance and had a couple of years of experience in my country, Iran. Upon hearing that, she recommended that I take some classes in computer and accounting in the occupational center. I agreed that it was a wise recommendation, and she registered me for those classes, which would start in a couple of months.

After all, it was my lucky day, a promising day. I was eager to get home to call about the job. Yet, searching for an apartment was my other priority, so I rushed to the library to look for ads for rental apartments. I found a few.

*   *   *

The long, productive week passed. I was interviewed and got a temporary job in the adult center. I would start the job on Monday. I took a one semester break from school. The hunt to find a rental apartment had not been successful yet. I called Thomas, my attorney, every day to check if the judge had made a decision, but still there was no ruling.

Mitra was not happy that we weren't going home. She called her father every day. Every time the doorbell rang, she expected he would be at the door, so she jumped and ran to open it. Disappointed that he was not at the door, she became edgy. It was hard to see her hurting. I tried to keep her busy and Negin helped me with that. Behzad was nice enough not to bother me during the week. Mitra spent the weekend with him.

*   *   *

The week after, I started working full time. Mitra had to stay longer in day care, which she did not object to. Luckily, she liked the place, which made me feel less guilty about it.

In the middle of week, I received unbelievable news. While on break at work, I had called Thomas. I heard the excitement in his voice,

"Hi Niki, good news!"

I felt a sudden heat filling my body and couldn't respond.

"Are you there, Niki?" he asked when he did not hear me saying anything.

"Mitra is mine?" I asked in a trembling voice.

"Yes, the judge ruled in your favor," he said, and I heard him chuckle.

"Thank you. Thomas. Thank you," I said again in excitement and relief.

"I'll send you the official document soon," he said.

"What happened, Thomas? After all the bad things Behzad told about me, why did the judge rule in my favor?" I asked.

"People are smarter than Behzad thinks. By the way, this judge is very smart and is good at reading people," Thomas said.

"I love this judge; please thank him on my behalf if you see him. And I thank you a thousand times …" I was so excited that I just rambled on.

*   *   *

A couple of days later, I received the official divorce and the custody documents. That was it. Life had been good to me, and I appreciated it. Mitra and I were on our own.

Now I was even more desperate for a place to rent. I had already applied for a student apartment and my name was on the waiting list, but I knew it would take a long time before I would get one. I did not have time to wait.

However, even with all good things that had happened, it was difficult to sleep through the night. I woke up several times in the middle of the night, thinking. One of these nights, I thought about Kjell. He was one of the church members who truly believed in Behzad and had become a good friend to him. I had met him and his wife on one of the many trips that Behzad used to arrange. Kjell was the dean of the University of Theology. Some of the students' apartments in my area belonged to that university. I decided to ask him for help in getting an apartment. It was a great idea, though I was not sure that he would help.

Having made the decision to take a chance, I went to his office the next morning. He was a very nice and friendly, middle-aged man. He embraced me warmly and expressed his regret on hearing the news about the divorce. He did not pry; however, he said that he had never seen Behzad so miserable. I was still angry with Behzad and didn't care how he was feeling. Over the last two weeks, after I had received custody of Mitra, he had stopped coming by Negin's to see Mitra. Mitra missed her father and called him every day. Perhaps he needed some time to get used to the idea of having lost the fight for custody.

Kjell did not hesitate a moment before saying that he would absolutely help me to find a place to rent. My God, I was so happy, so lucky. Life was going well for me.

Kjell kept his promise. In less than a week, Mitra and I moved into a small, partially furnished two-bedroom apartment in a nice student area. The rent was reasonable and affordable. A refrigerator, two full beds, a dining table and chairs, and some kitchen items were included. I borrowed sheets from Negin for the first night in the apartment.

Mitra was excited about her new room, which had one wide window facing the street. Nevertheless, she was not convinced that her father would not be living with us anymore. She asked me where Baba would sleep.

*   *   *

The day after we moved in, I called Behzad to talk about moving out the rest of my clothes, other personal belongings, and some furniture.

"Niki, whatever is in this house, belongs to you. This is your and Mitra's home. Come back here. Stop doing this to us," he said calmly.

"Keep your home to yourself. I just want my things," I said.

"Nothing will leave this house. Come back home."

Upset, and disappointed in him, I hung up the phone on him. It was hard enough to ask him for something, even though it was my right.

Thomas, my lawyer, had warned me this might happen and had proposed to let the court decide how to split the belongings, but I never imagined that it would come to this.

Now that Behzad made it clear to me that I would not get anything from him, I decided to take legal action. Thomas was in Lund and could not help me with this, but he referred me to Lars, a lawyer in Stockholm. With the help of Lars, I filed a claim against Behzad. The legal process would take a long time. But in the meantime, I needed money to buy some necessary items for our apartment in order to make it a home.

My brother-in-law, Hamid, was like a brother to me. He was a businessman and frequently made business trips to Europe. Once in a while, he visited us in Sweden. I felt comfortable asking him to lend me some money. He quickly transferred money into my bank account.

I furnished Mitra's room with a small bed, new bed linens, a nice little desk and chair, pink curtains, and some pictures on the wall. I also furnished the family room with a television and an orange and green striped couch. Even though we still needed more furnishings, I was very happy with what we had.

Once we settled down, Behzad started calling and asking me to go back to him. At first, as soon as I heard his voice, I hung up the phone. Later, when I felt some inner peace, instead of cutting him off, I listened to what he had to say. He always told me how miserable his life was without Mitra and me; he said he would do anything to get us back. He repeated the same things over and over. I started to feel sorry for him, but my feelings for him had changed enormously. I could not imagine being able to love him anymore, and I told him that every time he called.

Having been unsuccessful in convincing me over the phone, he changed his strategy. This time, he used Mitra. On most weekends, he picked up Mitra and spent time with her. However, he stopped doing that even though he called Mitra and told her that he would be there soon. Mitra would get ready and wait for him, but he never showed up. She called him repeatedly; he would not pick up the phone. It was unbearable to see her waiting impatiently, but there was nothing I could do. She paced back and forth, waiting for him outside in the cold. My attempts to keep her busy by playing with her or suggesting places we could go did not keep her from waiting for her baba. His behavior was erratic. Sometimes he never showed up. At other times, he showed up unannounced. I called him many times and begged him to stop hurting Mitra, but he always blamed me for tearing apart the family and stated that the responsibility was mine.

After a while, he started to come for Mitra, but he taunted me by not bringing her home on time. Often, he was hours late. This was his way to control me, which usually succeeded. It was difficult for me to schedule any plans for myself. This kept me at home, waiting for him to pick Mitra up or waiting for him to bring her back home.

The short period of peace, if one could call it peace, was over. I expected another fight, the fight over splitting our belongings. This would entail another court session. Lars, my new lawyer, was confident that it would be a straightforward case and that Behzad would have to give me my share.

*   *   *

Ramin tried not to let the disputes affect his friendship with Behzad. Although he was busy with school and his own circle of friends, he was loyal to Behzad and made time to spend with him.

Ramin had some cash with him when he came to Sweden. Behzad deposited the money in his own bank account for him. Fortunately, Ramin could get student loans and let the money accrue interest in Behzad's account.

One Saturday, Behzad picked up Mitra for the weekend. Ramin was out of town with some friends on the same weekend. After I kissed Mitra good-bye and they were leaving, Behzad casually turned back, as though he had forgotten something.

"I nearly forgot to give you this. This is Ramin's money. You see him more than I do. Give it to him," he said and handed me a check.

"Why me? Give it to him yourself," I replied and gave the check back to him.

"I don't know when I will see him. I'm closing my account, and I want to give him his money as soon as possible. Just give it to him."

I took the check and looked at it. The check was in my name. "Why is it in my name?" I asked.

"Is it? Let's see," he said and took the check back. "You're right. I don't know what I was thinking when I was writing it. What difference does it make? You sign the back of the check and give it to him," he said and gave the check back to me.

"It makes a difference. Write another check in Ramin's name," I said and handed the check back again to him.

He took the check and asked me for a pen. I went inside to get a pen. When I returned, he was searching his pockets. "I don't have my check book. I must have left it at home. Just sign it and give it to him. I know you won't cheat him with his money."

I hesitated for a moment but decided there wasn't a reason why I shouldn't take the check. So I did.

When Ramin returned, I gave him the check. He was stunned that Behzad would suddenly give him back the money.

"I never asked him for my money. Did he say why?" Ramin asked.

"He said he was closing that account. It doesn't matter why, just be happy that he gave you your money back."

"Why do you say so? Please, don't try Niki!" Ramin protested.

"Don't try what? I just said be happy to get your money back," I responded

"You know what I mean," he said.

Ramin got his money back, and we both forgot about it.

*   *   *

Some months passed, and it was time for the court hearing. The courthouse and the courtroom looked similar to those in Lund. The difference was that only five people were in the courtroom this time: the judge, his secretary, me, Lars, and Behzad, who was there without an attorney.

The hearing began with Lars reading my case to the judge, who then turned his attention to Behzad to hear his side of the case. Unlike the previous hearing, he was not as uptight and seemed relaxed. He looked at me this time, but I could not tell what those looks meant.

His side of story was very simple and straightforward. He claimed that he had given me money to put the financial disputes behind us. He had undeniable evidence for his claim, which was the copy of the check he had written in my name.

All my attempts to convince the judge that the check issued in my name was not actually mine but was intended for my brother were in vain.

This deception did not impact me as hard as his lies at the first hearing in Lund.

Indeed, the blame was fully on me this time. I was angry at my own stupidity. I was the one who had promised me not to get entrapped by him again. I had disappointed myself. I was angry at myself rather than at him.

Consequently, I lost my case and got nothing because I had let him easily fool me. Behzad lost his friendship with Ramin. Angered that Behzad had taken advantage of his friendship and trust, Ramin severed his relationship with him forever.

*   *   *

The turbulent months of my life had added up to a year. While I continued to struggle with Behzad, I also tried to put my life together and make a peaceful life for Mitra and myself. Mitra seemed to be the same happy, little girl, who wanted my attention all the time. She had adapted to the changes in our life though I sometimes felt that she missed her father very much. I became less restrictive regarding keeping an exact schedule and tried to be more flexible to allow Mitra to spend more time with her father. Behzad seemed to be happy about it too, but it was still not enough for him to stop bothering me. He never missed an opportunity to make things difficult for me.

*   *   *

For some time, I had thought about revealing the real Behzad to the church people, who cherished and respected him as a loyal and true Christian. In order to put my plan into reality and take a counteraction or revenge, I invited Anders the priest of the church, Kjell the dean of the University of Theology, and a few others of Behzad's church friends and coworkers to meet with me.

They all were very nice people; I had met them many times while I had lived with Behzad. They were true believers. But from my viewpoint, they either could not see through Behzad or fooled themselves as I did for years. Behzad was smart, but he was not so smart that the judge in Lund could not see through his false character. Therefore, it was hard to believe that these nice people were so naive to miss any signs of that sham.

Kjell and his petite, pretty, red-haired wife, and Anders the priest, a middle-aged, white-haired man with a serious sharp look arrived first. Eve and her husband Tony joined us shortly after. Eve was a happy, older woman. Unlike her slender, tall husband, she was rather short and chubby.

I served them coffee and cakes as we talked casually about the normal daily life and the weather. Although they never asked why I requested this gathering, I could read the curiosity on their faces. Finally, I changed the subject by telling some true stories about Behzad's dishonesty, his past, and his present. I also warned them that he was using Christianity and, in particular, the church for his own interest, and that he would end up deceiving them. I advised them to be cautious and not to be misled by his false charisma.

After I finished speaking, no one spoke for some moments. The priest finally broke the silence,

"I'm sorry to hear this. Thank you for telling us, Niki. It's unfortunate to hear that he's done so much harm, particularly that he now is a Christian."

Although the others expressed their disappointment, they were very cautious not to judge him by what they had just heard. Before they left, the priest said that they would talk to him. Then he kindly asked me to count on him if I needed anything.

"Thank you," I responded, "but the only thing I need is a normal, peaceful life for Mitra and me. When you talk to him, ask him to let us have that."

*   *   *

Long after that meeting, I ran into Eve on the street. She told me that after the meeting at my house, they confronted Behzad. They told him about the meeting at my house and asked if the accusations were true. Apparently, he listened to them calmly and without saying a word he left. He did not show up at the church for days, which made the priest and other church members feel guilty. They decided to approach him to ask for his forgiveness for not having faith in him as a good Christian and to ask him to come back to the church.

*   *   *

Chapter 21

⟋⟍

The Intruder

I took some computer classes and started working at a company as an accountant's assistant. There I met Erik, who worked in the communication department. We started dating. Cheerful and funny, he was three years older than me. Tall and well built, he had a soft, full, brown beard. His silky and light brown hair set off his bright blue eyes. He was full of energy and could cheer me and Mitra up. He made me laugh, and he loved Mitra. He took the time to play with her as though he were a five-year-old boy. Mitra not only enjoyed spending time with him, but sometimes she would call and talk to him. Indeed, he was the one that both Mitra and I needed in that period of turmoil.

During the same year, Shahram and his family made a trip to Italy. I planned to take a trip with Mitra and join them, but I needed my and Mitra's passports, which Behzad still had in his possession. I asked for these and other personal documents. To my surprise, he gave them to me without causing any problems. This allowed us to take the trip and enjoy two wonderful weeks with Shahram and his family.

A couple of weeks after our return from Italy, I had to leave very early in the morning to take the train to go for a job interview. I did not feel comfortable waking Mitra up so early in the morning, and I did not have enough time to take her to day care. I asked Behzad if he could come early in the morning to allow Mitra to get up at her usual time and then take her to day care.

That day, he came early in the morning. I gave him the key to the apartment to lock the door and asked him to drop the key in the mail slot when they left the house. When I came back home in the evening, the key was there and everything was in order.

One evening, about a week later, I got home and found the place a mess. All of the cabinets and drawers were wide open. My papers and documents were strewn across the floor. The glass door in the family room that led to the playground was open. Nothing seemed to be missing in the house. I looked through the documents on the floor; the only missing documents were the passports and my birth certificate. I did not need to think twice to come to a conclusion about who the intruder was.

I called the police. Two officers showed up. I told them about the incident and who I thought the intruder was. I told them about the key. Certainly, he had the entire day to make a copy of the key before dropping it in the mail slot.

The police checked the door in the living room. According to the officers, there were signs of some damage on the lock of the glass door, but there was no sign of force to break the lock. After writing up the report, the officers asked me to come to the police station the morning after to complete the report, which I did. It was not a big and important case for the police to investigate further. They might have questioned Behzad about it, and he might very well have denied any accusation.

Once again, I was on my own, facing another ordeal with Behzad. For the sake of Mitra, I had tried to look forward and make peace with him. Why did he need to do such nonsense? I was really tired of his games. I had tried many ways to deal with him. My last attempt to play cool had worked for a short time. I knew it was impossible to cut him completely from my life since he was Mitra's father and she loved him. I had no choice but to find a stable ground for compromise; I certainly had failed to find one.

I knew that he enjoyed seeing me frustrated and worked to find ways to keep me annoyed. One way to avoid any further friction was to stop talking to him. It seemed to work quite well. But one night, there was a knock at the door. When I opened it, no one was there. However, some of my books, which I had left in his house, were stacked in front of the door. I brought them inside and found all the documents he had taken from me placed in between the books.

*   *   *

Chapter 22

_~M~_

Key to Heaven's Gate

In 1986, the ongoing, bloody Iran-Iraq War entered its sixth year. Thousands of Pasdars and civilians had been killed. Ayatollah Khomeini decreed the war as a jihad, a holy war. He stated that all Muslims in the country, of all ages, were obligated to go to war to fight the enemy of Islam. His proclamation was a smart way to draw massive religious volunteers in addition to the regular army soldiers into the front lines. However, the decree also made it possible for religious governmental organizations such as Islamic Jihad to use this as an unofficial right to recruit the boys.

Members of the Islamic Jihad made regular visits to the schools, seeking volunteers to draw into the front line. They preached about the excitement of fighting and also conveyed a magnificent image of heaven. They promised the boys, usually ages twelve and up, that if they were killed in this holy war, they would go to heaven as martyrs. The Islamic Jihad agents inspired the children by offering a necklace with a key hanging on its chain. The volunteers wore the key to the heaven's gate around their necks. There were rumors that these keys were made in Taiwan, China, and Korea!

Enrolled voluntarily, these children did not need their parents' consent. Since the children did not have any regular training, they were sent to the front lines to clean up the minefields for the regular army. This matter became a parent's most horrible nightmare. Parents sent their sons to school in the morning not knowing if they would return home. To keep their children safe, some parents preferred to send their sons abroad during the war—legally or illegally.

A close friend of my family in Iran had a twelve-year-old son, Nima. The family worried sick that he might be recruited. The boy's father, Massy, contacted me to find out whether there was a way to get his son out of the country to live with me for a while. I promised him I'd do my best and get back to him soon.

Fortunately, a friend of mine, Maryam, was passionate about helping Iranians with political and humanistic crises. A hyper, tiny woman, Maryam was some years older than me. She had already assisted some Iranian families to get into Sweden. I asked for her help. She told me to call a woman named Leila and gave me the number.

When I called, I was greeted by a loud, piercing woman's voice announcing that she was Leila. I told her about Nima and my reason for calling. She confidently claimed that she could arrange a safe way to get the young boy to Sweden in exchange for a rather large amount of money.

I called Massy and told him about the deal. He was so desperate to save his son that he did not hesitate to accept the deal. I made a verbal contract with Leila of 50 percent of the money up front; the balance would be paid after the boy safely arrived in Sweden. From then on, my contact person was Maryam. This made it more convenient for me to get information and details.

"Nima has to get to a European country such as Germany. When he gets there, I'll tell you what to do next. But the thing is that someone has to accompany him from Germany," Maryam said.

About a month later, Massy and Nima arrived in Germany. He sent me money to pay Leila to set up the next phase of the plan. I volunteered to be Nima's companion from Germany to Sweden.

It was summer, and I was working at the time. I took two weeks of vacation. Mitra and I took a train to Frankfurt to meet up with Massy and Nima. It had been about ten years since I had last seen Massy and his family. Nima was just a baby then, now he was a skinny, tall boy. His bright green eyes reminded me of his mother, Sepi.

Massy had not changed much over those ten years. Short, but powerfully built, he was a nice man with a chubby face. He already had a room for me and Mitra in the hotel where he and Nima had temporarily been living. The plan was that at the end of the week, I would call Maryam to get instructions on how to proceed. This gave us a week to have a real vacation. It was also a very good opportunity for Nima to become familiar with me and Mitra. During the few days we spent together in Frankfurt, I found him to be a curious and smart boy. An adult could have a real conversation with him even though he still was a playful kid.

On Saturday, I called Maryam to get the instructions, which she gave me in detail: "Lufthansa has a flight to Stockholm on Wednesday at 5:00 PM. Buy tickets for that flight for the three of you. Make sure that none of you have any baggage to check in. You should have only carry-on. Nima is to have his passport only—no other documents at all. Then you and Mitra check in and get your boarding cards. At 4:15, a guy by the name of Omid will meet you there. Don't look for him. He'll find you. Just be there at 4:15 and wait for him. From there, Omid will tell you what to do," she explained.

It sounded straightforward. We still had a couple of more days to enjoy in Frankfurt. Massy bought the tickets for the flight that Maryam had specified.

*   *   *

Wednesday arrived. Nima was restless and excited. Neither Massy nor I knew what would happen. We had put our trust and fate in Maryam, who was very confident every time I spoke to her. In any case, Massy and Sepi were determined to take a chance and do whatever was needed to send their son to a safe place.

We arrived at the airport at 2:00 PM. Massy was eager to get us there early. Since we had time to kill, we had lunch in a restaurant. Around 4:00 PM, I checked Mitra and myself in and got our boarding passes. We walked back to Massy and Nima to say good-bye to Massy and left him.

At 4:15 PM, Nima, Mitra, and I waited for Omid. A couple of minutes later, a young, short guy in a very neat and stylish outfit walked up to us. He had an attractive, small face and shiny black hair.

"Hi, Miss Niki. I'm Omid," he said.

"Hi," I responded.

"Come, we go sit there," he said and walked toward a bench a few steps away. We followed him and sat.

"Now, remember exactly what I tell you to do. First, you go with the kids and stand in the line. But when it's your turn, you go to that second window," he said quietly and nodded his head toward the window. "Do you know which one I mean? The second window. Do you see that blond guy sitting behind it?"

"Yes, I see him," I said.

"If he's busy with others, you wait until he's free. Then you and the kids go to him. Don't say anything, show him your boarding cards and then just pass him," Omid instructed.

"Okay, I got it," I said.

"Do you have Nima's passport?" he asked.

"Yes, I do," I responded.

"Give it to me," he said.

I opened my purse and gave him the passport.

"When you get to the gate, go to the bathroom and tear Nima's ticket up and flush it in the toilet. Be 100 percent sure that it is completely gone. Not the smallest piece of it should be left," Omid emphasized to me. "Does Nima have any other documents with him?"

"No, nothing, per Maryam's instruction," I responded.

"That's good! Okay, now listen this is very important. When you arrive in Sweden, you tell the airport police that you don't know where Nima has come from, and the only thing that you know is that his father had asked you to meet him at the gate. Don't mention anything about Nima being in Germany. Remember, you must tell them that you met Nima at the gate and that you don't know how he got there. Nima will be sent back to Germany if you mention anything, that's why you must be very careful," he repeated to make sure I understood the importance.

"Yes, I understand," I said.

"Make sure that Nima does not mention anything about Germany. They usually don't ask children, but still make sure that he understands this," Omid said. As he was getting up, he said, "Now you can go and stand in line."

I thanked him. With the children, I walked over to join the line to get to the gate.

Omid walked with us to the line to ensure that the officer at the second window saw us. The officer quickly looked at us and immediately turned his eyes away. Making sure that the officer noticed us, Omid stepped away and stood a couple of steps away from the line.

Since most of the passengers already had passed the checkpoint to the gate, the line was not long. Three windows were still open for service. Fortunately, when we reached the head of the line, the second window was free. We approached the window. A hefty, middle-aged officer with fair skin and blond hair drew his hand toward me for the boarding cards. I gave him mine and Mitra's. He looked at them and with no words returned them to me. I took the cards and the children and I left just as Omid had told me to do.

That step went well. It was about fifteen minutes before departure, and the plane was boarding. I took the kids with me to the bathroom and followed Omid's instructions. I tore Nima's ticket in small pieces and flushed it down the toilet. Then we joined the short line to board.

We took our seats. Shortly after the plane departed, I began to relax, but Nima was still uneasy and twitchy, he was eager to know what would happen. Obviously, I had no straight answers to his questions.

After landing at the Stockholm airport, passengers got ready to disembark the plane. Suddenly, we heard the flight attendant's voice, via intercom, asking everyone to remain seated. I panicked and assumed that it pertained to Nima's illegal entrance into the country. The passengers looked stunned. A few minutes later, two police officers entered the passenger cabin and walked straight to our seats. I was asked to stay with the children as the rest of the passengers were allowed to leave. I was terrified that Nima would be deported to Frankfurt on the same plane.

"Aunty Niki, what do we do now? Do we go to jail?" Nima was agitated and scared, asking me in Farsi.

"No dear, we don't go to jail. Just relax," I said to calm him.

When the last passenger left the plane, the officers walked back to us. One of them pointed at Mitra and Nima and asked me, "Whose kids are these?"

"She's mine, and he's the son of a friend of mine," I responded.

"Passports and tickets," the officer requested.

I gave him my passport and ticket and also Mitra's.

"What about him? Where is his passport and ticket?" the officer asked.

"I don't know. I don't know if he has any," I said.

"What do you mean? How did he get onto this plane?" he asked firmly.

"I don't know," I responded.

"You do know. Was he in Frankfurt?" he asked in the same tone.

"I don't know. I met him at the boarding gate. I don't know how he got there," I explained.

"He happened to be there at the exact time you were there! Is this what you want us to believe?" he asked.

"No, I knew he was there. His father asked me to meet him there and take him with me," I lied again.

"Where was his father?" the officer asked.

"I don't know. He called me," I answered.

"Was he in Frankfurt with his father?" he asked.

"I don't know. He didn't tell me," I responded.

"You're lying," he said.

"I don't know what you want me to say. I met him at the gate," I kept up with my story.

After a brief conversation with his colleague, the officer demanded "Come with us!" and stepped back to let us get up and leave the plane.

"Can I get my carry-on?" I asked him

He took my carry-on and gave it to me.

The three of us exited the plane followed by the officers. They escorted us to a room and told us to wait there. Indeed, I had expected a harsher encounter and a cruel confrontation from the officers, but contrary to their appearance, they had been soft-mannered.

We waited in that room for about an hour. The kids were tired and restless. Mitra fell asleep in my arms. Nima could not sit still. He walked around impatiently. He was very nervous and asked me over and over what was happening. I tried to ease his fears by telling him that everything would be fine and we would go home soon.

Finally, a police officer asked me to go with him. He told the children to remain there and assured me that they would be fine; he would look after them. I followed the officer to a small office in the same section of the airport. A female officer sat at the only desk in the office, and a male officer sat on a chair by her side.

The woman pointed to a chair in front of her desk and asked me to sit. She was a middle-aged, pretty blonde officer. The male officer was much older. The bone structure of his face with a small, sharp nose and piercing, blue eyes gave him the look of a substantial tough guy.

"You have a boy with you. You know that he illegally entered the country. What do you have to say," the female officer asked firmly.

"He is my friend's son. His father asked me to meet him at the gate and take him with me. His parents were very worried about him if he remained in Iran."

"Then you know that he is illegally here; we have to send him back. Tell us where he was before you met him at the gate as you claim."

"Please don't send him back. He would be sent to the war and be killed. Please don't do that. He's only a kid."

"What did you do in Germany?" she asked, ignoring my plea.

"Nima's father asked me to be there to take Nima with me. He did not want him to be alone. He needed me to accompany him."

"Then Nima and his father were with you in Germany?"

"No, it was just me and my daughter. His father had given me the time and flight number; I got tickets for myself and my daughter on the same flight. He told me to meet Nima at the gate, which I did," I lied again.

"You're a good liar. Do you know that lying to the police is a crime?"

"I know that, but I'm not lying."

"Why did you take him with you when you knew that it was an illegal action?"

"I was going back home anyway. I had been told to meet him at the gate. How should I know it was legal or not?"

"You better tell us the truth; in any case he has to be returned. Who helped him to the gate?"

"How do I know? He was there by himself when I met him."

"You do know that I can deport him right now?"

"Yes, I know you can, but please don't do that. He's a smart kid; it's not fair to send him back. He would be sent to the war and be killed. I'm sure you know how many kids are sent every day to clean the mine fields in Iran. Please let him stay."

"I can't let him stay. For now, take the kids and go home. But tomorrow morning, take the boy to the immigration office. They will decide if he can stay or not," she said in the same firm tone.

I could not believe my ears. That was it! At that moment, and by that nice officer, Nima's life and future was saved. Speechless, I sat put. It was as though I was waiting for confirmation, waiting for someone to tell me that I was awake and not dreaming. The officer provided me with that confirmation. "You can go now!" she said.

The male officer smiled at me. Now he did not seem as tough as I thought he was. Although he had not said a word the whole time, he had silently listened to our conversation.

"Thank you so, so much! You just saved a boy's life. Thank you, thank you …" I was so excited and grateful that words were just spouting from my mouth. I went to the children to give the good news to Nima.

"What happened, Aunty Niki? Do they send me to jail?" Nima shouted the moment I entered the room.

"No dear, why jail? You can stay with me and Mitra until your mamman and baba come."

*   *   *

The next day, I took Mitra and Nima with me to the Immigration Services Office. I was not worried about the rest of the process. Nima's case was not new for the government of Sweden. They, as well as other European's governments, were aware of the hazardous situation of the children in Iran. Therefore, those kids who were lucky enough to get into the country would be given humanitarian asylum.

At the Immigration Services Office, I completed the application to request humanitarian asylum for Nima and filed it. From that point on, we knew that it was a done deal. Sooner or later, he would receive permission to remain legally in the country. Nima lived with me and Mitra for about a year before his parents succeeded in obtaining a permit to join him.

Chapter 23

❦

Kidnapping

The conflicts between Behzad and I seemed to be endless. He started bugging me about Mitra's custody. He wanted me to agree to a joint custody. Tired of the constant arguments and his persistence about the custody, I finally agreed. The joint custody seemed to work. The tension and hostility between us eased, if not completely ceased.

*　　*　　*

By 1987, my life had gradually become relatively stable. Mitra was six years old and it was time for me to get back to school again. Mitra, school, and my friends filled my life, which I enjoyed. Also I enjoyed spending time with Erik, but I was not ready for a serious relationship. However, a peaceful, enjoyable life was the last thing Behzad wished for me to have. He was determined to make my life miserable. Unfortunately, his way to do that was through Mitra.

His wish for a joint custody of Mitra had been fulfilled, but his period of satisfaction was short. He started using the same old tricks to torture me by making Mitra unhappy. Once again, he would not show up for Mitra, who would wait for him for hours. At other times, he unexpectedly showed up at the door.

The tensions between us evolved into frustrations and fights. In response to my request that he stop taking his selfishness out on Mitra, he calmly said, "You're the one who's selfish. You are the one who took a normal family life away from her, not me; if you care about Mitra, then come back home."

*　　*　　*

That year, I broke up with Erik and returned to school. In the same year, Ramin's longtime girlfriend, Shadin, came to Sweden for a visit. They married, and I got a good friend. As Ramin and I went to the same school, we had some mutual friends. I had a rich social life. Interestingly, Behzad had changed once again. He spent more time with Mitra and volunteered to help me when I needed it.

It seemed that my life was finally in balance. The peace and harmony of a normal life put me in a comfort zone. I even considered giving Behzad another chance. Behzad, who never had given up on me, was happy and hopeful; he tried his best to be patient with me and be there for Mitra and me.

I tried to look forward and leave the past behind. I had convinced myself to forgive him for his dishonesty and the nasty face of his character that he had revealed to me over the past two years—but it was not easy to forget. I was nervous and undecided. I was unsure about my feelings for him. I needed him to be around as a good father to Mitra and a friend to me. However, I could not imagine living with him once again. Hence I decided it was not worth it to go through another ordeal.

Having reached my final decision, I told him that we would be better off to remain friends for Mitra's sake. He made no response and left. I didn't hear from him for some time, and my attempts to talk to him were in vain. He would not answer the phone.

Some weeks later, at the local shopping center, I bumped into him as he walked hand in hand with a tall, pretty, blonde woman. Although he was not my husband anymore, and despite the fact that I had rejected him many times, jealousy filled my spirit. I walked up to them and told the young woman, "Let go of my husband." She said nothing and walked away. Behzad was stunned and tried to explain to me that she was just a friend.

I did not know why I was so angry and reacted so foolishly. I turned away and walked home. I felt ashamed and stupid. I did not want him; so why did I care? Did that mean I still loved him? Or was I so self-confident and selfish that I just needed him to be around to tell me how much he loved me and would never give up on me? I believed the latter question was the closest to the truth.

He called me that same evening. I apologized for my stupid reaction and told him that he did not need to explain anything to me and wished him good luck. Indeed, he sounded like he had not expected that response. However, it was a confirmation of my final decision, which disappointed him. Selfishly, I enjoyed it.

*   *   *

While I enjoyed a period of peace, Behzad's attitude changed once again as he made his own plans for my life. That game started one summer evening when I sat in the family room with one of my friends, who had a son about Mitra's age. We talked and watched the kids through the glass door while they played in the playground.

At one point, the boy was playing with the other kids and Mitra was not there. The area we lived in was very safe and the playground was enclosed by the neighboring houses. I stepped outside to look around, but Mitra was nowhere to be found. I asked the boy where Mitra was. He said that she went with her father.

Behzad lived just a couple of blocks away from me. I called him and asked if Mitra was with him, he said that she was and hung up the phone on me. I called back to ask the reason for his sudden meaningless action, but he did not pick up the phone.

This came as a hard shock to me. He was free to come and get Mitra whenever he wanted to. There were no visiting restrictions or any objections from my side; I could not find any reason for him to, indeed, "kidnap" her. I was frightened; he most certainly had an agenda again.

From my point of view, I had done everything to ease the tensions between us. I tried to make a peace with him, but no attempt seemed to be enough. As soon as my life started to get back on track, he would find a way to hold me back. Sadly, he succeeded every single time. The agreement for a joint custody had satisfied him for a very short period of time. I had nothing else to offer him. *What would happen now? Was that stupid action of his another trick to infuriate me once again or was it something else?*

At first, I tried to keep my temper under control, but after calling him many times and getting no response, I went to his place. The building was gated and locked. I had no choice other than to wander around the building. *Would he take her someplace where I would never see her again?*

I went back and forth between my home to call him and the closed gate of his building. It was getting late, but I did not want to go home without Mitra. I knew that Behzad would never have done this if he had not had cruel intentions. I was frightened. I called Erik, whom I had recently started seeing again. He stayed with me the entire night in front of Behzad's building.

Early in the morning, as soon as the first person left the building, Erik and I entered the building. I went to Behzad's unit and rang the bell. There was no answer. I knocked at the door and called to Mitra through the door—still no answer. Convinced that Behzad was not there, I decided I needed to file a report that Mitra had been kidnapped by her father. The response I received from the police was that they could not do anything since he had joint custody, which meant this was not a case of kidnapping.

This was the worst scenario. No one could help me. I cursed myself for trusting him on such an important issue. I sat on the bench outside the police station and cried helplessly. Desperate, I went back to Behzad's and waited outside the closed gate and then back to my place and called all mutual friends, but no one knew anything.

Days passed. Most of the time, I sat behind his building. I called his family in Lund to find out if they had any information, but I received no answers. I was living in hell. During those sleepless nights, I lay on Mitra's bed and cried endlessly. No sympathetic words eased my pain. I was scared to death of the thought that Behzad had taken her somewhere out of the country and that I would never hear anything from her again. After days of waiting, I returned to the police once again, but received the same response.

On an early morning several days later, I sat on the bench by the gate. When I saw Behzad coming out of the house, I ran to him, "Behzad, where is Mitra?"

Silence! He did not say a word. He did not even look at me. He passed by me hastily.

"Please, Behzad. Just tell me where she is. Wait, please wait. Why do you do this? Please, tell me," I begged as I ran after him.

He ignored me totally and quickly passed ahead of me and sped away.

I knew he enjoyed seeing me run after him and beg. It reaffirmed his power over me; unfortunately, the only means to carry this out was Mitra. I did not care about anything at the time; I would do anything to get Mitra back.

I chased him to the street, prayerfully wanting him to tell me that Mitra was all right. Unable to control my tears, I pleaded, "Just tell me how she's doing and when I can see her. Please tell me. Please Behzad, wait ..." Remaining rigid in his stance and with a severe look in his eyes, he reminded me of that stranger I first met in the divorce court a couple of years earlier.

He hailed a taxi and left; I was totally crushed but hopeful. I walked back to the bench. The neighbors had seen me for days around the house. I could tell that they were suspicious, but they were nice enough not to confront me. Some would pass by with a hasty hello. I cared little about my surroundings.

A couple of more days passed with no news about Mitra. During this time, I called Sami and the others in Lund every single day. Finally, one day his sister Jila answered the phone. I asked her if she knew where Mitra could be.

"What? Don't you know where she is?" Jila nearly screamed.

"No, Behzad kidnapped her and I haven't seen or heard of her since."

"That son of the gun! Why did he do that? Is he sadistic or what?" Jila sounded really mad. "Don't worry, she's fine. I saw her last week."

"Last week? Where?" I asked excitedly.

"In Småland, a province in southen Sweden. It was Behzad's wedding. We just got back today. The wedding was last Saturday. Do you mean that he just took Mitra and did not tell you anything?" Jila continued to talk and ask questions, but I could not hear her anymore. I had heard what I needed to hear—Mitra was fine and in the country.

"Do you know when she'll be back?" I asked.

"No, but you know what? I'll call Behzad right now and yell at him. Don't worry, I will ask him to let Mitra call you. She'll be back soon. Don't worry," she said to comfort me. I could hear in her voice that she felt guilty for Behzad's deed even though she was not the guilty party.

"I am so relieved, Jila jan. Thank you so much. You gave me the best news."

"Behzad has always been an unpredictable and crazy guy. Didn't you know he was getting married?" Jila asked.

"I knew he had a girlfriend, but when could we talk like two normal adults to each other? How could I know that he was getting married? Now that he's married, I hope he minds his own life and lets me live mine," I said.

That day, Mitra called. It was the first time I had heard her voice in two weeks. Jila had kept her word to make sure that Mitra would call me. Hearing Mitra's voice was enough for me to forget about my days of misery. She told me about her father's wedding to Ingrid and that she missed me.

"I miss you too, I wanted to call you, but I didn't have your number. Why didn't you call me?"

"Baba said we would call you later, but he said that I could call you now."

"Okay! Tell me, when do you come back home? I miss you so much!"

"Baba said soon."

After ending the call, I sat with the receiver in my hand, thanking God for the good ending. The misery was over, but it left a hurtful scar in my soul. Once again, Behzad had used Mitra to put me on my knees and knock me down. It was the longest period of time Mitra and I had been away from each other. He knew it would hurt me, and he enjoyed it. But had he ever thought about Mitra?

A sudden rush of anger spread through me. Behzad was my worst enemy; I was locked in a one-sided war. He had used the most unethical method to defeat me. I could not let him use Mitra, the most valuable part of my life, to further fight against me. But I didn't know how to keep that from occurring. However, Mitra came back home some days later. It was enough for me for the time being.

Chapter 24

$\sim \mathcal{M} \sim$

The Ceremony of Baptism

With the New Year, 1988, everything seemed to have calmed down. Mitra was seven and started school. I continued my classes. Erik and I broke up again. Behzad did not bother me as much as he had before. Ingrid, his wife, was nice and a very religious Christian. I noticed that she really loved Mitra like her own; Mitra loved her too. Ingrid worked at a day care and was very good with children. Indeed, having Ingrid in Mitra's life was a blessing or so I thought at the time. Being part of a normal family life had been my dearest wish for Mitra and had seemed unreachable. Ingrid brought a sense of family life to Mitra and soothed my guilt somewhat. In addition to her motherly kindness toward Mitra, she seemed sincere. Gradually, Mitra spent more time with Ingrid and her father; she seemed happy.

After having passed through the stormy years, my life seemed to be perfect. I studied hard and started dating.

Despite my busy schedule and problem-free life, I was not happy. I felt restless; nothing and no one eased my distress. I could not stay in any relationship for long. Erik reentered my life from time to time, but I still was not ready for a serious relationship. We repeatedly ended our relationship peacefully.

Once, while I was studying at home, I experienced a sudden anxiety attack. I felt as though the mental pressures on me, which had added up over the years, had become too much for me to keep inside anymore. My entire body began to shake; my heart beat loudly and fast as if something heavy was pushing on my chest. My throat was blocked; I could hardly breathe. I called Negin, who took me to the hospital. I was kept for some hours under medication and observation.

That incident was followed by weeks of sadness, depression, and anxiety. Fortunately, medication helped me to recover. Though the trauma was an unpleasant experience, it saved me. It led to a revitalization that gave me a new life and energy. I returned to my own skin. I regained my happiness and began to enjoy my life. I was refreshed.

I concentrated on my studies and took school more seriously. Behzad seemed not to have any more reasons to bother me. However, he would remind me at times that the family life I had taken away from Mitra had been given back to her by his marriage. He acted as though he had sacrificed his life for Mitra and that I was the source of all our problems.

*   *   *

During this period of time, Behzad asked my permission for Mitra to be baptized. My impression was that by allowing a baptism, we were choosing a religion for Mitra. I was not quite sure if it was a good idea.

I was born a Muslim, my religion was chosen for me the moment I opened my eyes to this world. As a child, I performed the necessary rituals that my mother had taught me and asked me to do. As I grew up, I began to have doubt about my beliefs. Now, at this point in my life, if I had to classify myself, it would be theistic.

All of Mitra's friends and most of the students in her school were Christians. I was aware that it was very difficult for children to be different from their peers. With her black hair and brown eyes, Mitra was already different. Did I want to add to it? I also hoped that she would find her belief later in life as I did. So, I gave my consent to Behzad.

Early on the morning of the ceremony, I received a call from Behzad asking me not to participate in the ceremony.

"Why not?" I asked him, surprised.

"This ceremony is just for Christians. You're not Christian. So you shouldn't come," he said.

"Do you think I'm stupid or what? What's your real reason behind this? Mitra is my daughter, no one can tell me what to do or not to do when it comes to her. Do you understand? You should tell this to that church of yours and to those Christians who don't want me to be there. Tell this to Jesus himself too!" I said and slammed down the phone.

I tried not to let Behzad ruin my morning. I was confident that there was an intention behind this. Perhaps he wanted the church to believe that I was against Mitra being baptized and that I was angry about it. My speculation was later confirmed by a member of the church, who had talked about it with Behzad prior to the ceremony.

I ignored his request. My mother was in Sweden at the time and accompanied me. The church was crowded. Other children and adults were to be baptized also. Mitra sat by Ingrid and Behzad in the first row. As she saw me and my mother, she stood up to come to us. I shook my head to indicate she should stay put.

Our pew was several rows behind Mitra's. My mother had brought her camera and took pictures of every single movement. I admired this amazing woman. An easy-going person, she accepted change and respected others beliefs and ideas. For most faithful Muslims, it is difficult to watch members of their families convert to another religion, but my mother's approval shone on her happy face.

The priest who performed the ceremony was Anders, whom I had invited to my home years earlier to reveal some truths about Behzad. He baptized several children and adults before calling for Mitra. Followed by Ingrid and Behzad, Mitra walked to the priest and stood by him. A strange feeling took over me. *This is my daughter and the ceremony is for her. Why should I sit and watch?* I felt I had to participate directly in the ceremony. I joined them and stood by the priest. The ceremony began. The priest took Behzad's and Ingrid's hands to put on Mitra's head to read prayers. I did not care what the ritual was; I put my hand on her head as well and let them finish the ceremony.

My good feelings of the morning were later replaced by anger and disappointment. I felt betrayed by the people of the church and Anders in particular. *How could he simply ignore me?* I thought. *Do God and Jesus care whether I was a Christian or not? Wasn't it enough that I was her mother? How could my daughter be blessed by the hands of a charlatan and other strangers but not mine?*

The ceremony was over and people left, but I did not move. My mother asked me why I was waiting. I did not have an answer. I saw that Anders was ready to leave. I went to him. Choking back my anger and holding out my hands, I said, "These hands have taken care of and protected Mitra since she was born. How could you ignore me? I trusted you and your church, but clearly it was a big mistake."

The priest listened, but he did not look at me. He did not say a word. I had nothing more to add either. I was hurt and scared. *Were they taking my daughter from me in the name of God and Jesus?*

I left the priest and found Mitra outside the church with her father. I asked her to come home with me. She took my hand, but Behzad asked her to stay since they had arranged a party for her. Mitra was confused. We had put her on the spot, and it was not fair. I told her to stay for the party and come to me later. I kissed her and left with my mother.

I went home and cried to wash the bad feelings away. My mother was wise to let me be by myself to cry out my pain. I was not sure what irritated me most. *Was it Behzad's call in the morning asking me not to participate? Was it because I watched Mitra stand by some strangers, who had not believed me and disappointed me? Was it the fear of losing Mitra to strangers? Or was it my selfishness because I was ignored and kept in the background?* I was confident that it was not jealousy as I had no feelings whatsoever for Behzad and I liked Ingrid. In fact, I had more respect for her than for Behzad.

Chapter 25

Destiny

It was 1989; four years of instability and agitation were behind me. I was in very good spirits. It was the most normal and least dramatic period of my life since Behzad had entered into it.

My friends and I frequented an Iranian club restaurant on Saturday nights. On one particular night, the restaurant was not very busy. I was there with Ramin and Shadin and a group of friends. Across from our table and on the other side of the restaurant, a group of young men and women sat together. When the dance music started, they headed to the dance floor. A tall, handsome young man with thick and rather long, black hair caught my eye. He noticed me. I was confident that he would approach me. Relaxed, I continued to talk and have fun with my group of friends.

Later, I walked toward the restrooms, knowing that he would follow me. He did just that and said hello. Before we had the opportunity to introduce ourselves, my group of friends stood up to leave. I had to say good-bye to him and join my friends. That had been a casual, fun night for me. But I was too busy with school and could not hang out with my friends as much as I did before. I forgot about the dark-haired guy.

On another Saturday night one year later, a famous Iranian singer was scheduled to perform in the same club restaurant. My friends and I made plans to see the performance. The club was overcrowded. While dancing with my friends, I spotted the same guy dancing with the same girl he had danced with the year before. He saw me too, but I ignored him, suspecting that he had a girlfriend.

After some dancing, we sat down to take a break. Suddenly, I felt a tap on my shoulder. I turned my head and saw the guy standing behind me.

"I won't let another year pass," he murmured in my ear.

"What?" I asked.

"It's too noisy in here. Can we talk outside?" he asked louder.

We met at the same place where we had begun a short conversation a year earlier. We started over, introducing ourselves and exchanging phone numbers. He said that he had returned to the restaurant several times hoping to see me again. He made a good impression on me, but I did not take him seriously because he was with the same girl.

"Wasn't he the same guy from last year?" my friend asked as soon as I made my way back to our table.

"Yes, he is, but I think he has a girlfriend. We'll see," I shrugged and said.

The next morning the ringing of the phone woke me up. It was Kami. His call made me happy, but I still had concerns about the girl. I did not want to get involved in a relationship when there was another woman in the picture. My first question was about her. He assured me that they were just friends. That was nice to hear. We talked a while and a relationship began. Kami changed me. He brought back my lost trust in honesty and morals. He made me believe in love again. I was madly in love with him. He did not express his feelings and love, but I felt his passion for me. I trusted him enough to open my life story to him, which I had never told a soul. He was my love, my friend, my companion, and my comfort. I was able to be myself. His calmness and honesty brought out the happy person I had once been and not the angry bitch that Behzad had made me over the years.

*   *   *

Kami and I continued a long-distance relationship for about five years. He lived and worked in a city near Stockholm, but we spent most of the weekends together. He did not like living in Sweden and was trying to move to the United States. However, I had never thought of leaving Sweden since Mitra was my priority. Our paths for the future were not destined to cross.

Fortunately, Behzad did not bother me as much as he had in the past. The storm had cooled down. I took another break from school and started working again. After finding some comfort in my life, I wanted to enjoy it as long as it lasted; I needed more free time to spend with Kami.

Mitra attended school and was very active. Basketball and friends filled her life. She practically lived with her father and Ingrid; although she would sometimes come to me directly after school and on weekends. Ingrid, Behzad, and I never missed any of her basketball games or school programs. Mitra would find us sitting on benches some rows away from each other as she played basketball. Her smile, and the look of satisfaction on her face at seeing us, would stay in my mind forever.

As she grew into her teens, I noticed she was undergoing some changes. Mitra was no longer the same happy and talkative little girl. She, who used to try to be the center of attention, was now shy. She stopped speaking Farsi; my attempts to make her speak to me in Farsi were in vain. I considered it as a phase of becoming a teenager. Moreover, I noticed that she was more comfortable with her Swedish friends and was not shy about socializing in Swedish. I decided to stop persisting that she speak Farsi and socialize with Iranians.

Unfortunately, as much as I tried to make Mitra and Kami establish a good, close relationship, it did not happen. When I first met Kami, Mitra was a happy and talkative seven-year-old child. She connected to people easily but needed my attention all the time. Kami had never been around kids, so he treated Mitra like an adult. The coldness between them bothered me and made me tense and uncomfortable. However, my solution was to keep them away from each other as I was not sure what the future held for me and Kami.

*   *   *

Years passed, and I never returned to the medical school. I continued working as an accountant for various companies. From time to time, some of my family members visited.

*   *   *

In 1994, I was still in a long-distance relationship with Kami. He had already applied for a green card; sooner or later, he would leave for the United States. I loved him, but I could not see any common future for us. I decided to take some distance from him to make the separation less painful. We talked about it and decided to end our relationship.

As much as I tried to keep myself busy to let time ease the difficult separation did not help. It was not easy for Kami either. Finally, the time he would leave for the United States arrived, and he told me that he would leave very soon. He wanted me to think about going with him. Indirectly, he had just proposed to me, and it came as a surprise. I had never thought about leaving Sweden.

As much as I loved Kami and moving to another country would be exciting, I could not live far away from Mitra. Even though she practically lived with her father and had a stable family life, I was her mother and was always available to her. I could not just leave. I had never been far away from her and had never thought about it either. She was twelve at the time; I was not sure I had the courage to be away from her. It was not fair to her either. I was torn. I wanted Kami in Sweden, but that was impossible. He had made his decision to leave Sweden long before we met. In general, he never liked the climate of Sweden, particularly its cold and long winters, so he was determined to leave the country. He had been waiting for his green card more than five years. The reality was that in order to have a future with Kami, I would have to go with him. I had to be thoroughly confident about my decision. I decided to bring up my dilemma to Mitra and ask her opinion.

Once I was driving her to a basketball camp, I told her that Kami had asked me to marry him and move to the United States to start a new life together. I told her how important it was for me to know her opinion and feelings about it.

"If you want to marry him then do so," she said casually.

"But if I do, then I have to leave Sweden," I explained.

"It's up to you if you want to go or not," she said coldly.

"But I really want to know how you feel about it. It's very important for me to know before I make a decision," I insisted to get a straightforward answer.

"Obviously, I won't be happy if you leave," she said.

"That's why I need to know exactly what you think and feel about it."

"You'll be living there forever?" she asked.

"I don't know if forever, but at least for a long while," I responded, and in order to not be pushing her for a quick answer I added, "You don't have to say anything right now darling, think about it, we can discuss it later if you like."

"You know, Mamman, I made up my mind, I don't need time to think over. I think it is a good idea that you'll go to the United States I think it is a better country. I can come and stay with you during Christmas and in the summer. If you had wanted to move to a country other than the United States, it would be much more difficult for me to visit you. But America is a place I'd like to come and see," she said, giving me her honest opinion.

"You mean that it would be okay for you if I go?" I asked surprised.

"Yes, why not? I am going to miss you, but we still can see each other," she replied.

"Of course we can. I wish I had talked to you sooner instead of thinking and worrying. You are a smart girl," I said.

"Mamman, if I had said no, what would you have done?" she asked innocently.

"If you were not so important to me, I would not have asked you," I answered.

"That means that you would not marry Kami?" she asked me to get a straightforward answer.

"No, I would not. If my marriage would make you sad, I would be sad too. Kami would not be happy to have a gloomy wife. It would not be fair to anybody," I assured her.

"Are you happy now?" she asked.

"Of course, I'm happy," I answered.

We talked about it the whole way to the camp. She was realistic and smart for her age. I was relieved, though it was difficult to think of being away from her. I comforted myself knowing that we would spend Christmas and summers together. Now there was nothing to prevent me from marrying Kami and leaving Sweden.

From then on, everything happened quickly. I was happy and excited. Kami was the best thing that could happen to me. He was my true love and a trusty, wise, and confident man. Of course, we had disagreements during the five years we had known each other. We also broke up a few times, none of which lasted for long. We talked, discussed our issues, and moved on. In contrast to my shortsightedness and lack of perseverance, Kami was patient, and he took every aspect of a matter into consideration to make the final decision.

However, I still had my doubts, not about him but about myself. Despite the sweet conversation I had with Mitra, my happiness and excitement faded the moment I thought about being so far away from her. I was not sure that I could stay away from her for long.

Since I always lived for the present and did not worry about the future, this time I did the same. Although I never had any sense of belonging to any particular religion, I strongly believed in God. He led me to experience the ups and downs of life, but he never left my side or disappointed me. He always helped me when I desperately needed him. This time, I put my trust in him as well and decided to go wherever life would lead me.

*   *   *

My mother, Shahram, Souri, and Kami's parents came to Stockholm for the wedding. The happiness was tinged with sadness. Mitra, who knew soon or later I would be leaving, was sad. I could read it on her face. It was heartbreaking to see my beautiful, innocent baby so unhappy. Kami's mother was not particularly happy either. I was not sure if she even liked me. She was quiet and sad; everyone felt her disappointment and sadness. I understood she would have preferred that her son's wife carried no baggage from the past. Whose mother would not? However, Kami's father was happy and charming. Kindhearted and nice, I loved him the moment I met him. He paid attention to Mitra like a caring grandparent.

Our wedding which was an unforgettable event of my life took place on a pleasant summer day.

*   *   *   *

Our life in Stockholm as a married couple lasted less than six months before Kami left for the United States to find a job and arrange for a place to live. A month later, I made the trip to Los Angeles. This was my first visit to the United States, and I stayed for three weeks.

Kami's brother and sister had lived in Los Angeles with their families for many years. I met their friends and relatives, who also lived in LA. Everyone left a very good impression on me. I enjoyed my time with Kami. It was like a honeymoon for us.

With all its traffic jams and lengthy freeways, LA was not quite the city I would want to live in. Everything was so spread out that going places took hours. Everyone was dependent on a car. I liked riding buses and metros rather than being stuck on the freeways and surrounded by cars.

Is this the place where I have to live for the rest of my life? I wondered. The answer was "*Yes.*" I soon became used to the city because I loved Kami. Still, I longed for Mitra. I loved spending time with Kami and it was hard to leave him to go back to Stockholm, but I felt I needed to go back to Mitra. Confusion occupied my mind once again. *Would I be able to live so far from my baby?*

Chapter 26

Migration and Uncertainties

Shortly after I returned to Stockholm, Kami succeeded in getting a job in LA. Now I needed to get ready to leave for good. I started selling the furniture and other household items.

The most painful part of moving was giving up my apartment. The last day at my apartment, before returning the key, I became so emotional that I sat on the bare floor and cried. This place had been Mitra's and my home for many years.

I had cried harder the day I moved the last piece of furniture from Mitra's room. Memories of those last ten years passed before my eyes and tugged at my heart as tears fell down my cheeks. I removed the stickers that Mitra had stuck all over the door to her room. I removed the piece of paper I had put on the wall to measure and mark her height on a weekly basis. Sometimes she had insisted that I measure her height every day. To make her happy, I would mark a bit higher on the paper to make her believe that she was growing tall.

One day earlier, Mitra was in this house with me. She did not cry, but the sadness in her eyes reflected the pain she felt. "Mamman, I wish everything could change to the way it used to be," she said so innocently and her words stuck in my mind for a long while.

*　　*　　*

But nothing was more painful and heartbreaking than the moment I had to say good-bye to Mitra. Her tears ripped at my heart and blocked my throat. I was trying to comfort both of us by promising her that she would be with me for the summer, which was couple of months away. I questioned the decisions I had made. *Am I a selfish and careless mother? Should I just call off all the plans and stay close to her?* However, I had to give it a try.

Once I was on the plane, I shed tears to release my doubts and wash away the uncertainty and sadness from my spirit. I had to start the new chapter of my life with optimistic thoughts and determination. I owed it to Kami and myself.

*　　*　　*

My new life started in a nice, small apartment with love, passion, and hope. My first step was to apply for the U.S. residency or the so-called green card. We had hired a counselor, David, to assist me in the process. He informed us that the average processing time was at least five years. He also added that during the waiting period I did not have many legal rights such as acquiring work permission in order to legally work in the United States. I was not eligible to apply for a driver's license according to a new law that became effective in the year that I arrived. The worst part was that I could not leave the county. If I did, I could not reenter the United States until my green card was issued.

The first couple of months in LA everything was still new to me. I started going to school to learn English. I liked our simple life and loved Kami. But for some strange reason, I did not feel his love anymore. He did not pay much attention to me and I did not know why. I speculated that since he had always lived as a single person, this transition might take time for him to adjust.

*   *   *

Mitra came to stay with us for two months that summer. She liked LA very much, and I took her to many places. Unfortunately, there was still a cold interaction between her and Kami. It made me uncomfortable when all three of us were together. Still that did not prevent me from spending pleasurable time with Mitra.

Mitra's return to Stockholm after two months left another scar on my already hurting heart. I was restless and depressed. I tried very hard not to reveal my sadness to Kami and not let my state of mind impact our marriage. It helped to some extent, but it was not hard for him to read my mind.

Without a proper residency status, I felt passive and worthless. This harsh reality was beyond my comprehension of life in LA. Now I could not even leave the country. I felt so lonely. *What am I doing in America? I don't even like living in LA. Kami would be better off if I left. Should I just pack and leave or try to give my marriage a chance?*

I was there because I loved Kami, but something was missing. I wondered if he really did love me any more or if he already regretted our marriage. Perhaps he felt he didn't have all my heart and my mind for himself anymore, as in fact half of me was left in Sweden with Mitra.

*   *   *

Some years later, when we were talking about the past, Kami acknowledged that he questioned our marriage too. He had asked himself whether it was wise and practical to marry a woman with a child and split them by moving to another country and cause more emotional damage. But he overcame the doubt by time, and as he put it, "Love always prevails!"

*   *   *

The smart way was not to give up in such a short time. I needed to do something to break the ice between us. I realized that the problems were mine. I had to stop pitying myself. My problems were not Kami's fault. He had not expected that the process time to obtain the green card would take years. Moreover, my distress over being away from Mitra was not his problem either. It had been my decision to immigrate to the United States with him. Now it was up to me to smash the wall of gloom and my apathetic vision on life.

The first step was to look for a job—any kind of job. Since I did not have a work permit, a job with a regular salary was out of question. So I started looking for accounting jobs in some Iranian companies. Those jobs did not pay well, but I was happy to have something to do.

Ultimately, I became accustomed to life in LA. I still missed Mitra terribly. Sometimes, I secretly cried hysterically to ease my longing for her. My attempts not to let my sadness have any effect on Kami and our life worked in some degree. Our relationship became better and we grew closer. I felt his love again.

Kami got a better job and higher position. We moved to a bigger apartment. Mitra came to us twice a year. Although there was no improvement in their relationship, Kami was supportive and I could count on him.

Chapter 27

Strange Request

It was summer 1997. Two years had passed since we moved to Los Angeles, and Mitra made another trip to stay with us for the summer. She was now a sixteen-year-old beautiful teenager. She played basketball in a league in Stockholm and mentioned that she would like to stay with me in LA for a year to experience the high school and play basketball for the school.

I loved the idea. My biggest concern was that her father would oppose the idea. Luckily, he gave his permission with no problem. This was not typical of how Behzad handled issues if I was involved. Apparently, Mitra had promised him that her stay in the United States would be just for one year.

In no time, my world changed. I was relieved and thrilled. Kami was positive about the idea as well and helped me through the process to get her a visa and enroll her in high school.

*   *   *

However, there was still no news about my green card. My status would not change for a couple more years. Since Mitra was with me, it did not matter for me anymore. I had no reason to feel depressed or useless anymore. Life was perfect.

Mitra seemed to have a tough time adapting to the new school. Even though she never complained, I could feel her frustration. The English language was her first barrier. The other problem was that she was from a much smaller and less socially diverse country. The life style and mentality of the Swedish people were very different.

Despite those difficulties, she was strong-minded enough not to quit. On the contrary, she tried her best to assimilate by participating in all of the school activities, partying with classmates, and making some good friends. Before the semester was over, she had adapted to the changes and had some thoughts about staying for another year. She returned to Sweden to get her father's permission.

*   *   *

It was summer 1998 and Mitra was in Sweden. One day, Behzad called me with a strange request. He wanted me to consent to single custody of Mitra.

"Niki, it is a torture," he pleaded. "You can't understand; you never had to feel how painful it is. You had single custody of Mitra for a long time, but I never had any opportunity to enjoy the feeling of being the only one who had custody of my daughter. It makes me feel like a huge failure. Now it's the time that my big dream comes true."

"What do you mean? It's been ages since we had custody issues for Mitra. Why does it torture you now? I don't see any torture in it," I said with a chuckle.

"You've never understood me, Niki ...," he repeated the same old complaint.

I interrupted him, "It is a ridiculous request, and I don't see any logic in it. Good-bye." I hung up the phone.

I had a weird feeling about that very strange conversation. *Why was he suddenly thinking about custody?* I was confident that there had to be something behind this drama, but I could not figure it out. When I talked to Kami about it, he too could not find any logic in Behzad's request. He suggested that it might just be a matter of fatherly pride and that I might have overreacted.

However, Behzad didn't give up. He called practically every day, begging for the custody. While I could not trust him, I also did not want another unnecessary nasty dispute with him. One question after another filled my mind. *As long as Mitra is coming to me, why should I mess with him? How could he possibly abuse a full custody?*

He continued to call and put pressure on me every single day. It was apparent that he would retaliate by not letting Mitra to come to me, if I would not agree with him. And this concerned me most.

Behzad's calls annoyed me. So, Kami and I discussed the advantages and disadvantages in granting him full custody. Since we did not find any harm in doing so, I decided to agree to his request. I signed the form and mailed it to him.

Afterward, everything went smoothly, and Mitra returned to LA. However, she said that for letting her to come to the United States, she had to promise her father that she would be back in Sweden to celebrate her eighteenth birthday with him and Ingrid. It seemed to be an innocent request at the time.

*   *   *

In the summer of 2000, Mitra graduated from high school. The actual graduation ceremony was to be held a month later. To keep her promise to her father, she left LA for Stockholm to celebrate her eighteenth birthday with Behzad and Ingrid.

When she returned to LA she told me about her trip and mentioned that her father had asked her to sign some papers. She said that after her birthday, her father took her to a law office to sign his will. Also, she and Ingrid had signed some other related papers and two of their friends signed as witnesses.

To my question asking if she had read the papers before signing, she answered,

"No, I didn't. Baba said it was a will and he wanted make sure if something happened to him nobody could claim anything."

"You should have read it before signing. Never sign anything before reading it," I advised her.

"I know Mamman. You think I'm stupid, but it was my baba who asked me to sign, not a stranger," she said with a tone of irritation.

I said nothing further, but I felt uncomfortable and suspicious about the entire signing story. I also remembered a call I had received from Behzad a couple of years earlier. This made me think that his intention, after all, might have been to protect Mitra, in case something would happen to him. The will or other documents he had Mitra sign might have been necessary to prevent anyone making a claim to anything after his death.

I thought about a call I had received from Behzad about three years earlier and before Mitra came to the United States. He had sounded thrilled. He said he was calling from Turkey and that he had found his daughter, Kimya. Years earlier in the court, he had claimed she was killed during the war. He asked me to do him a favor. He wanted me to tell her how much he had missed her and how miserable he had been during those years away from her.

On the same day, he called again so I could talk to Kimya. I lied when I said that I had heard a lot about her. I told her that her father had talked about her and missed her a lot. Obviously, I wanted to make her feel good.

During his stay in Turkey, Behzad called me nearly every day to tell me about his grandsons and how happy he was to have found them.

Later, he brought the whole family with him to Sweden, but it was a short family reconciliation. Soon Behzad and Kimya's husband entered into a disagreement; Kimya's family left Sweden deeply disappointed with him. I never found out the reason, but whatever the reason was Kimya never talked to him again.

Now remembering Kimya and her family, I thought that Behzad might have considered that after his death they would claim the inheritance. That might have been the reason for all the signatures and the will issue.

*   *   *

Behzad and Ingrid planned to come to LA to attend Mitra's high school graduation ceremony. Ingrid came some days before the ceremony; Behzad intended to join her later. It was a good opportunity for me to become better acquainted with Ingrid. She was a nice and happy person. She seemed to be sincere, honest, and truly a Christian. It was my impression that her love for Mitra was genuine. I loved her for that.

*   *   *

Graduation day was a beautiful sunny day. Disappointingly, Behzad never made it for Mitra's important day.

Once Ingrid and I caught a glimpse of the students from a distance, each of us excitedly aimed to a point. It was as though there was a childish competition between us to be the first to find Mitra. I could feel our mutual emotions for Mitra. We finally found her in the crowd, and she came to us. She looked so beautiful and elegant in her graduation cap and gown. She gave us a quick hug and left to join the others to take a seat for the ceremony.

Kami, Ingrid, and I, watched the ceremony. When Mitra was called to receive her diploma, a sudden, swift wave of anger and disappointment toward Behzad touched my feelings. This was a big day for graduates and a moment of pride and joy for their parents, but he was not there. I felt Mitra's disappointment, but she kept her feelings private. She would never complain, but she needed her father to be there on that important day of her life. *What in the world could have been more important than his daughter?* I wondered.

I ignored the negativity and concentrated on the moments of joy.

*   *   *

Behzad came to LA some days after the graduation. On the first night after his arrival, there were some arguments and conflict between him and Mitra. He did not approve of her friends, and he believed that Mitra's attitude had changed. Consequently, despite the trips they had taken together and the times they spent with each other, the relationship was not friendly and peaceful at all. Their conflict reached its peak when Mitra announced that she would stay in the United States to go to college.

Kami and I decided not to interfere but to support her decision. Behzad, of course, tried to convince us to encourage her to leave. He asked us to tell her that she should not count on our support or staying with us. However, our position, as we told Behzad, was to respect her decision and support her.

Mitra had already made up her mind and was determined to stay. No argument changed her decision. Finally, she stayed; Behzad and Ingrid left disappointed.

*   *   *

Once again, I was suspicious of Behzad. Mitra had already told me that her father had bought a new, expensive car. In addition, prior to coming to the United States, Behzad and Ingrid had taken trips around Europe. While they were in the United States, they took a fancy trip to Hawaii. These travel expenses would exceed an ordinary Swedish family's income. Ingrid and Behzad also had purchased a public day care and established it as a private day care. Behzad took frequent trips as a Christian missionary abroad.

While some views of the picture of his life and activities seemed odd and out of place to me, I was not able to pinpoint the exact mismatch, but I felt it. I mentioned my suspicions to Kami, but nothing seemed wrong or out of the ordinary to him. I criticized myself for still being so cynical of Behzad.

*   *   *

The tension between Mitra and her father continued long after Behzad and Ingrid left. Behzad called every day to talk and argue with Mitra and me. He also had long, telephone conversations with Kami. He was trying hard to force Mitra back to Sweden.

Mitra has always been strong-minded, and she was strong enough not to give in after so much pressure. She was accepted into college and made its basketball team. She shared an apartment close to the college with two other students.

That same year Kami applied for a green card for her. It was granted and arrived in less than six months. I was still waiting for mine.

Chapter 28

Lies or Truths

In 2001, after five years of waiting, I received my green card. Now I had a work permit and was free to leave the country. I took a trip to Sweden. It was nice to visit friends and familiar places that were a part of my memories. Sweden was my second country. After all, I had lived there for more than fifteen years of my life. Sweden felt more like home than Los Angeles.

While I was in Stockholm, Behzad called me, "Niki, I have to talk to you. When are you going to leave?" he asked in a very low voice.

"Is something wrong?" I asked and ignored his question.

"I'll tell you when I see you. When are you leaving?" he asked again in the same low, mysterious voice.

"In two weeks," I answered. I was a bit puzzled.

"Which date?"

"Why is the date so important for you to know?" I asked.

"Please Niki, just tell me," he insisted.

"Okay, Okay. September 15. Do you want to know the time and exact minute too?" I mocked him.

"I'll call you later. Bye," he said and hung up.

What the heck! What was that about? Was this another game of his? I wondered and put the receiver down.

He didn't call back until the day before my flight to LA. This time, he asked me to meet him in a bakery nearby.

I was there on time and found him sitting at a table in the corner.

"What's all this cat and mouse game?" I asked him teasingly.

He stared at me for some moments, then grinned and asked, "Didn't your mamman teach you to say hello when you meet somebody?"

"She taught me not to talk to weird people like you, but I never listened to her," I replied.

We talked and teased each other for a while. Then he brought his head closer to my ear and murmured,

"Niki, this is a very serious issue I'm going to tell you! Nobody other than Ingrid and now you will know anything about it."

"Let me guess, don't tell me. You've got an incurable sickness and you're dying! Am I right?" I mocked him in a harsh way, as by the look on his face, I recognized the signs of a scam.

"That was not so nice, Niki" he said.

"Why wasn't it nice? Everybody dies. The way you talked I thought it was that serious," I said.

"Forget about it! You have never taken me seriously. I have nothing to tell you," he sounded irritated.

"Don't get upset now! Sorry! Okay, tell me," I said.

"You won't believe me anyway. Let's forget about it," he said.

"Forget about what? I want to know. Tell me. I said I'm sorry," I insisted.

He cast his look away from me to the wall and did not say a word for some moments.

"Okay, Behzad. Oh sorry, I forgot your name is Peter. Okay, Peter, what's going on?" I asked again.

"My life is in danger. This might be the last time you see me," he said.

"You said you're not dying. What do you mean?" I asked somewhat concerned.

"I mean they are after me to kill me," he said.

"Who are 'they'? Why do 'they' want to kill you?" I asked, puzzled.

"I just want you to know it. I can't tell you more," he said.

"That's it! You want me to believe that there are people who want to kill you, and you don't want to tell me why. What do you want me to say?" I grinned and asked.

"Nothing. I just wanted you to know and believe me," he answered.

"Why should I believe you since I don't know anything? Who are 'they'? Are 'they' the Iraqis?" I asked.

"No. I fooled them once, and I have nothing to do with them now," he said firmly.

"Then who are 'they'?" I asked again.

"Long ago, I had a lot of money. I've been paying them. They are like the mafia; I have to pay them. But now, I don't have money anymore, but they still want me to pay them. They are after me to kill me," he explained.

"You were rich, and I did not know about it? What a big loss! I could have killed you myself to get your money," I mocked him again.

"I knew you would never believe me," he said.

"Of course, I don't believe you! I know you well enough to understand that you have some scam agenda and are working on a new story for your game," I said.

"I'm not lying to you, Niki. Why can't you just once, just for a change, believe me? You broke my heart when you did not believe my faith in Jesus, and you are breaking my heart now," he said.

"Whether or not I'm breaking your heart, I don't believe you. Tell me something believable. At least tell me when and how you got so rich," I asked.

"The day care Ingrid and I have taken over makes us good money," he said.

"I said tell me something that I could believe. How could you get so rich by running a small day care? How could you get so rich that you could get killed for your money?" I asked him doubtfully.

"I don't have anything else to add. I'm telling you; someday you will remember our conversation. You will regret it, Niki, you'll see," he said as he took his briefcase from under his chair. He opened it and asked me to hand him my purse.

"Niki, this is what is left of my money. This is for Mitra," he said. Then he took out an envelope from his suitcase and put it into my purse.

"It's good to have a rich father," I said.

"Don't say anything to Mitra. Buy her birthday and Christmas gifts from me and Ingrid. It might cover half of her college expenses for two years," he explained.

We stood up to leave, and he hugged me passionately. Then he looked strangely into my eyes and said, "Niki, I think it's the last time I will see you."

*   *   *

The trip had positive effect on me. I felt free and energetic. I landed my first official full-time job as soon as I returned to LA. That year, I also made some trips to France to visit Shahram and Souri and their family. They had been living in France for some years.

I told Kami about the conversation I had with Behzad in Stockholm. It seemed something of a joke to both of us, but I could sense that soon or later we would get another surprise. Whatever his game, he was working hard to make it a true story.

Behzad called me a couple of times a week to express his longing for Mitra and repeat how I had split apart the nice, family life we had together. He called Mitra nearly every day to tell her that he had never been a good father to her and that he was sorry. He would cry on the phone and tell her that he might never see her again. Because the calls were so upsetting to Mitra, I asked him to either stop calling her or stop acting so foolishly and stressing Mitra.

"You've always been a good father to Mitra. Why are you acting like this and telling her this nonsense?" I asked.

"No Niki, I'm not a good father. I could have been one, but you took it away from me. Now it's too late. I'm sorry. I hurt you many times too. I still owe you my life. You gave me Mitra. She's my life and I deceived her …." He continued to talk and apologize about the past, crying at times. Once again, he asked me to believe that his life was in danger and that we would never see him again.

*   *   *

Months passed. It was the summer of 2002. Not receiving any more calls from Behzad for a while, one day, Ingrid called me. She sounded worried as she said, "Peter left some weeks ago for a two-week trip, but he's not back yet."

"Trip to where?" I asked her. After all this time, it still seemed odd to hear her refer to Behzad as Peter.

"I don't know. He usually takes trips here and there, I never ask where, but most of his trips are short. This time, he said he'd be back in two weeks, but he's not back yet," she explained. Before I could say anything, she asked, "Do you know Mrs. Amiri?"

"No, I don't. Who is she?"

"She and her family are friends of ours. She received a call from her sister who lives in Iran. Her sister asked her to tell me that Peter is fine and he'll be back soon," she explained.

"How did her sister know Behzad, uh, Peter?" I asked.

"She doesn't. Peter called her and asked her to call Mrs. Amiri to ask her to call me," she answered.

"Do you mean that he is in Iran?" I asked.

"I don't know. He did not tell her where he was."

"How is it that he had the phone number of Mrs. Amiri's sister in Iran?" I asked, suspiciously.

"I don't know," Ingrid replied.

"When had he called the sister?"

"Three weeks ago."

"Don't worry, he'll be back," I said to comfort her.

"But I am worried. He acted so strangely in the past few months before going on this trip."

"How come you don't know where he was going? Didn't you ask him?" I asked.

"He takes frequent short trips. I usually don't ask."

"Why not?" I asked again since it seemed so strange to me.

"I don't know. His trips are short and he always comes back on time. That's why I'm worried now," she said.

"At least you know that he's fine. He'll be back," I tried to ease her worry.

"I can't speak Farsi. Will you call Mrs. Amiri's sister in Iran and talk to her? Maybe she knows something else."

"If she knew anything, I'm sure she would tell you. Just wait a little longer. By the way, why don't you call Peter's family? They might know something. Call his brother Sami," I suggested.

"Peter has no contact with them, and he doesn't like me to contact them," she said.

"Why not? They are very nice people."

She ignored my question and asked me, "Do you think he's in Iran? Why didn't he call me himself?"

"I don't know, Ingrid. But I doubt that he would be in Iran. You know what? Nothing about him would surprise me," I said.

"Why do you say that?" she asked.

"Never mind!" I tried to pass over the subject.

"Do you know something?" she asked warily.

"No. How can I know anything? I'm sure he would never do anything without careful planning. Why do you think he had the number of your friend's sister in Iran with him? He had planned everything," I explained my point to her.

"Do you think so?" she asked.

"Yes, absolutely! I still don't understand why you never asked him where he was going," I repeated.

"To be honest with you, he has completely changed. I could not even talk to him. He would lose his temper and become mad for no reason," she finally explained.

During the entire time that we talked on the phone, I hoped that Ingrid could understand that the sudden disappearance of Behzad was a nasty game he played. He had tried to fool us with the story of being chased by bad people, so it would resonate with whatever he had planned to do. Obviously, there had to be something much more important behind the story.

*   *   *

Months passed with no news. Ingrid was desperate; Mitra was worried sick. We talked and speculated about her father's disappearance, but we were not able to come up with any answers.

One day Mitra called me and asked me to come to her college apartment. She said she had incredible news.

As Mitra opened the door to her apartment, she said,

"Sit down, Mamman! Take a breath! I'm sure you won't believe what I'm going to tell you," she said.

It was not easy to read her face to determine if she had bad or good news. I sat on the sofa, and she sat by my side.

"Last night, Ingrid called me. Everything is so weird Mamman. I am still in shock." Mitra paused for a moment before asking me, "Mamman, do you remember Erik?"

"Erik, my ex-boyfriend? Of course, I remember him, why?" I asked.

"Did you know that he's dead?" she asked casually.

I was shocked; this was hard to believe. "He's dead? When? Why?"

"Yes, he's dead. Ingrid said that he died four years ago," she said.

"How does Ingrid know that? Does she know Erik?" I asked.

"No, she doesn't. She asked me who Erik was and I told her." After a brief pause, Mitra continued, "I told you that it's hard to believe."

"You're confusing me. How do you know that this Erik is the same Erik? And why did Ingrid call you to tell you that?" I asked.

"Mamman, listen! He is the same Erik. Erik Michelson," she said. Then she asked me to listen to the whole story.

I sat quietly and let her to tell me what she had heard.

She explained, "Ingrid's mom is old and sick. To take care of her, Baba and Ingrid decided to move to Småland. So, one month before Baba disappeared, they sold the house and the day care. Ingrid moved to her mother's and Baba stayed in Stockholm to take care of some businesses before joining her. So when Baba disappeared, Ingrid was not in Stockholm. After some months passed with no news from Baba, Ingrid made a trip to Stockholm and went to his apartment. She found some papers and …"

I interrupted her, "What? His apartment? Didn't you say that they sold it?"

"It's not the same apartment. I will tell you, Mamman, just wait."

"Okay, sorry," I said so she could continue.

"Ingrid found some papers and a will, Erik's will. He made me his heir," she explained, still relaxed.

"You? Why you?" I asked.

"I don't know, but Ingrid said that he had stated in his will that Mitra, the little girl who one day rode on his motorcycle and bought her mom a pair of red tree sandals from the fair market, would receive all of his inheritance."

"Wow, I didn't know he loved you so much," I said.

"Listen to the rest, Mamman. Ingrid said it was about one million dollars in cash and stocks and three houses. Can you believe it?" she said.

"Oh my, God! I think I know what's going on. Continue. Tell me more," I practically shouted.

Mitra continued, "Ingrid found many other papers; all were under my name. On one of the papers, she found the phone number of Erik's girlfriend. Ingrid contacted her and learned that Erik drowned in the ocean off Thailand. He had made a trip and stayed in a hotel close to the beach."

I tried to choke back my emotions and said, "He was so happy; he used to make us laugh. Do you remember last time we saw him?" I asked.

Mitra said nothing. For some moments both of us were silent.

"Now listen to the rest," Mitra said. "Ingrid also found the phone number of Babba's lawyer and met with him to get some more information."

"You mean that Ingrid did not know anything about it?" I asked.

"She said she didn't," Mitra replied and then continued, "As Ingrid said the lawyer got so angry that his face turned red as he shouted, 'Are you telling me that Mitra has not known about it all this time? How is this possible? Peter had a letter of full authorization signed by her. That bastard has fooled me too.' Then the lawyer asked, 'What about Mitra's mom? Did she know about the inheritance?' When Ingrid said no, he became furious and called Baba names."

"Oh, my God," I shouted out. "He fooled you into signing the letter of authorization the day after your eighteenth birthday." I was shocked. But there was more to come.

"Mamman, the lawyer says that you had given Baba full custody of me. Otherwise, he would not have been able to do anything without your permission. Why did you do that Mamman?" Mitra asked.

"Because I'm a dumb donkey! Because I let him fool me again, but this time it was really big. The consequence of my stupidity made you suffer. I'm sorry," I said, as my whole body shook in anger.

"Why Mamman? How did he do that?" she asked.

I told her how he fooled me into giving him custody.

"It's not your fault, Mamman. He fooled me too, asking me to go to him for my birthday. He just wanted to get me to sign the papers, I was eighteen then; your custody letter would not be valid anymore," she said. Then in a sad voice, Mitra asked, "He is my father, Mamman. How could he do that?"

I had no answer to my daughter's question.

"Did you read the paper you signed?" I asked Mitra again even though I already knew the answer.

"No, I didn't. He said it was his will, and I signed it. Why should I suspect anything? He is my father," she sounded disappointed.

"I know; I'm sorry, Mitra jan. I really am. Now he's gone with all the money?" I said.

"It looks like it. The lawyer says that some of the inheritance was in the form of stocks that lost their value when the market crashed in 2001. Out of three houses, Baba gave one up to Erik's father and sold the two others."

"Why giving up the house? He never gives up anything at all! Why did he do that this time?" I wondered.

"The lawyer said that since Erik's father was not happy about his son giving away all of his possessions to a stranger, he intended to sue to get them back. That's why Baba gave up one of the apartments to him. The lawyer had advised Baba to let the father go to court because he would never win the case. But Baba had said no because 'Mitra wants to give something to the father, since she feels pity for Erik's father'." Mitra paused after explaining this to me.

"I think I know why your baba gave the house to him. He knew that if Erik's father sued, you would get involved. Since he wanted the whole inheritance for himself, he could not risk that you would know about it," I speculated.

"Yes, it's possible," Mitra said.

"When did Erik die?" I asked.

"In 1998, the same year I came to LA to stay with you," she answered.

Furious, I jumped up shouting, "That's why he so easily let you come to me. He wanted you to be away and not to find out about it."

"I don't know," she murmured.

It was shocking news for both of us. We talked and tried to figure out what really was going on. We didn't know if the will and Erik's death were true. I simply could not believe Erik was dead.

Mitra and I remembered him as a happy soul, full of life. The last time we saw him was some days before I moved to the United States. Mitra and I came across him as we were going to the local shopping center. I had not seen him for years, but he had not changed at all. He looked at both of us with a funny jest and expressed his surprise. Mitra was twelve at the time; he hadn't seen her since she was six years old.

"Is this the same little Mitra?" he asked.

"Yes, she is. Do you expect her to be the same little girl?" I answered.

He laughed and asked Mitra, "Do you remember telling me not to smoke or I would get sick and die?"

"Really? Did I tell you that?" Mitra laughed and asked.

"Yes, you used to tell me that each time you saw me smoking. You were not only worried about my health; you were my private hairdresser too. You would cut my hair so artistically that no hairdresser has succeeded in doing the same job you did for me," he cheerfully said.

Mitra laughed again and asked, "Did you really let me cut your hair?"

*   *   *

I could clearly remember the day Mitra rode on Erik's shoulder. She took his long hair in her small hands and in her playful childish voice protested, "Why is your hair so long? You're not a girl."

Eric put her down and handed her a pair of scissors. He asked her to cut his hair the way she wanted it to be. Mitra was excited; I could not believe he was letting her cut his hair. She started cutting his hair and kept on cutting. The floor under his chair in the kitchen was covered with his soft, light brown hair. Mitra's face, as well as Erik's, was serious as she was deep into her new assignment. I tried to hold back my laughter. When she finally got tired of cutting, I gave the mirror to Erik to look at his funny, new, hair style. As he saw his image in the mirror he could not help bursting into a guffaw. When Mitra saw us laughing hysterically, she started laughing too.

*   *   *

Erik and I had talked for couple more minutes as we stood in the middle of the crowded sidewalk. I told Erik that I was married and was leaving for the United States. Humorously, he pretended the unexpected news shocked him by putting his hand on his neck and coughing and then said, "Easy, easy girl, not so fast. Don't bomb me with too much shocking news."

When I asked what he was doing he said, "I'm not married, and I'm not going to the United States. Everything is the same."

That was the last time Mitra and I saw him. His death was a tragedy.

*   *   *

Mitra and I had been part of an unbelievable story of betrayal, hoax, and disappointment. We talked numerous times about it. She seemed to be cool and tried not to reveal any emotion, but I could feel her hidden anger and frustration. I hoped she would shout out all of her anger and cry loudly to empty the nasty feelings of betrayal by her own father. However, she stayed calm and listened to me as I expressed my frustrations.

Ours was a story with many mysterious incidents. Some are still unresolved and will remain unanswered. But other parts of the events have been proven.

Erik died in 1998 when Mitra was sixteen-years-old. A letter was sent to her to inform her about the inheritance. Behzad intercepted the letter and kept it from her and everyone else, including me and Ingrid. To keep Mitra away, so she would not suspect anything, he agreed to send her to me.

Once she was out of the way, I became the next obstacle in his plan. Cunningly, he talked me into giving him full custody of Mitra when she was seventeen. This gave him a free hand to keep the fortune for himself. A year later, when Mitra turned eighteen; he fooled her into signing a letter that authorized him to take care of her possessions in Sweden.

He made a good life for Ingrid and himself, took some expensive trips to the United States and European countries.

In 2001, he lost some of the money in the stock market crash. The last time I saw him was in a bakery in Stockholm in 2001 when he told me that his life was in danger. What happened after that remains a mystery. I have many unanswered questions and some speculations.

However, I talked to Mrs. Amiri, to look for some answers. She was the lady who had called Ingrid to let her know that Behzad was fine.

She seemed frustrated over how Behzad had fooled her to get her sister's phone number in Iran. As she said, it happened a year prior to his disappearance. This clearly indicated that he had planned this game long before.

"Peter (Behzad) helped me and my husband to get residency in Sweden. We paid him good money for his service. He was a very smart guy and knew how to challenge the system by involving the media.

"He became like a friend to my family since then; and we valued his opinion. He helped my nephew to enroll a college. In order to enroll my nephew, he wanted to talk to my sister in Iran to get her approval. It was quite odd, since my nephew's responsibility in Sweden was mine. He insisted anyway and I gave the number.

His disappearance in 2002 and the revelation that he stole our daughter's inheritance caused me to search for answers. The timing of his disappearance was a major issue that awakened a series of serious speculations for me. He had always claimed that he had tricked the Iraqis, which let us leave Iraq, but I never believed him. *Was this a wild fantasy on my part to connect his vanishing with Iraq? Was it just a coincidence that during the same period when the United States attacked Saddam Hussein, Behzad disappeared? Did the Iraqis need him and he left for some tasks? Was that the reason he was so distressed and needed to play games with me and Ingrid to make his disappearance justified? Or, more simply, did he just take Mitra's money and leave Sweden to live in another place and enjoy his life?*

*   *   *

In 2002, I made another trip to Sweden. I called Ingrid to get the phone number of Behzad's lawyer. I called the attorney's office and made an appointment with him.

Lars, a tall, middle-aged lawyer warmly shook my hand. He was as curious as I was for new information. He was upset that he too was taken in by Behzad,

"Peter fooled me and lied to me. I still am very angry. He had all the necessary documents. He always pretended that he had Mitra's approval. When Erik's father sued Mitra, do you know that he gave up one apartment to him?" he asked me.

"Yes, Ingrid told me that," I said.

"It was totally needless to do so, since there was a will and Erik's father would never get anything, and I told Peter that, but he said that it was Mitra's decision. He said that Mitra felt bad that Erik's father did not get anything and wanted to give him the apartment," Lars said and smirked sarcastically.

"I'm convinced that he was worried that if Erik's father would take the case to court Mitra would get involved too. Of course, he did not want her to know," I said.

"That's true. He could talk so convincingly and all the papers he had never made me suspicious about him. But I confess that I should have asked to meet Mitra," he said and then asked me, "There is something that I can't understand. Why did you give him custody? He could never have done anything by himself if you had joint custody."

"I know that. I admit that I was dumb," I said and told him why I had agreed to give up custody. Then I asked him to explain the inheritance to me.

He told me same story I had heard from Ingrid. Lars did not give me more information than I already had, but he confirmed that there really was an inheritance and lots of money was involved.

*   *   *

On that trip, I asked Ingrid to give me copies of the documents and papers that she had found in Behzad's apartment. She filled two big boxes with those papers. I took them with me to LA and sorted them out. I found many interesting documents.

Behzad had been living Mitra's life in Sweden. There were bills, statement, and bank accounts in Mitra's name. He had registered six different companies using her name. What he was doing through those companies was not clear. He would sell and buy stocks, transfer money from her accounts to his, and much more. I found some foreign unknown account numbers on scraps of paper. Not surprisingly, he had forged Mitra's signature on some documents.

I found also the most shocking and heartbreaking document. It was Mitra's will with "her" signature on it; all of Mitra's possessions would go to Peter and Ingrid in case of her death. It was tragic. Heat coursed through my entire body; I thought I would burst into flames. I screamed, "Bastard trash! How could you? How could you?"

This was too much and unbearable. Was he really human? How could I show this to Mitra? It would devastate her. He had already done enough damage and left her with painful, emotional scars. I cried and screamed to free myself from this enormous anger, but I still had to show the paper to Mitra. Knowing how terribly it would hurt Mitra, I hesitated.

After calming down and looking carefully at the will, I saw two signatures as witnesses. Now I had to show the paper to Mitra; it was her right to know.

Another time, when Mitra and I went through the papers together, I showed her the will and casually asked, "Is this your signature?"

She took it, looked at the signature, smiled, and said, "Yes it is. I think it's one of the papers Baba asked me to sign."

"And you just signed, crazy girl?" I teased her.

After she read the will, she turned to me with a puzzled look and asked, "What is this Mamman? Is it my will? It means that when I die Baba and Ingrid would get my money and things?"

"Aha!" I replied.

"What was Baba thinking? He wanted my money when I died? How could he think like that? I'm his daughter," she nearly whispered. She did not scream in pain and anger as I did when I first read the paper. I wished she would have done that too. Mitra merely sneered as she looked over and over the document.

"Whose signatures are here?" I pointed at the witnesses signatures on the paper and asked.

"Two of Ingrid's relatives! The day after my birthday, Baba asked them to come to be witnesses," she responded.

"Did they know what the will was for?" I asked.

"I'm sure they would not sign it before reading. I signed first and then they did." In their defense, Mitra asked, "How could they know that I did not have any idea of what I was signing?"

"I know, I know. They did not do anything wrong," I agreed.

"Do you think it's the original?" she asked as she held it in her hand.

"I don't know. It's hard to tell," I answered.

"Mamman, original or not, I want to rip it up," she said.

"Why?" I asked.

"It might be a copy and the original one might be out there somewhere. But if it's the only one, I just don't want it to exist," she replied.

"Do whatever you feel, if it makes you feel better," I told her.

*   *   *

A couple of years passed. Mitra was now twenty and a beautiful, young woman. She was energetic, positive, and social. She and Kami were comfortable with their cool relationship even though it still irritated me. However, Kami was her protector and helped her whenever she needed it.

Mitra and I maintained our very close relationship. We could talk about anything; but most of the time, we ended up talking about her father. She was an adult now. Due to the unfortunate hassle her father had put her through; she could handle any truth about him.

If Behzad had not betrayed her so harshly, I never would have told her things that would change her perception of her father. Now the circumstances were different; he had destroyed his fatherly role. Moreover, I believed it was her right to know that she had a half-brother somewhere in Iran.

I told her about my last meeting with her father in Sweden. I related the story he told me about the people who were chasing him with the intent to kill him. She listened to some other facts and events that I had witnessed through my years with him.

She too wondered about her father's real identity,

"You know, Mamman, I've never really understood what Baba's occupation was. When someone asked me what my father's job was, I didn't know what to say. He's always been so mysterious."

"I think it was part of his personality," I tried to explain. "He wanted to be mysterious. He never trusted anyone. I never knew him to have any real friends. But he was very smart. Unfortunately, he used his smartness in wrong ways. He never did anything spontaneously. He always planned carefully."

"Is it possible that his life was really in danger?" Mitra asked.

"I don't think so. I can't believe him. When I think back, I can see that he had planned this for quite long time. He closed all his accounts and credit cards, sold his home, your houses, and the day care. He also sent Ingrid to her mother, promising that he would join her later, which he never did. He took the phone number of their friend's sister in Iran with him. What does all this tell you?" I said.

"What do you think about those calls he made to me, crying and apologizing?" she asked.

"Mitra, when you ask me questions like these, I have to be honest with you. Being honest with you means that I have to say things about your baba that are my own speculations or the truth that you may not like to hear," I told her before answering her question.

"Tell me, I want to know. You won't make things worse, I promise you," she said.

"Okay, but first tell me what you think. What did those calls mean to you?" I asked.

"Maybe he had a bad conscience about fooling me," she said.

"That could be," I agreed.

"Still he could have told me! I think he did not feel well. Ingrid said that he had changed in the couple of years before he disappeared. She said he did not go to the church. He acted nervously and was angry all the time," Mitra said.

"Yes, she did tell me that too," I confirmed.

"Do you have any idea where he can be now? Is it possible that he is in Iran?" Mitra wanted to know.

"I don't think so, but I am sure that wherever in the world he is, he has changed his identity and is working on another hoax. Most likely, he is married; you may have some other brothers and sisters by now."

"You're right. Are you sure Mamman that I have just one brother and one sister? Tell me if I have some more in other places," she grinned and asked me playfully.

"Those two are the ones that I know about. My answer to the second half of your question is only speculation—it's very possible that you do," I responded.

"Did Baba ever talk about his kids? Did he miss them at all?" Mitra asked.

"To be honest with you, he never talked about them, but I asked him a couple of times. He said that they were just his biological children, but I don't know whether he really meant it or not," I replied.

"Those two were his biological kids as he said, but what about me? I grew up with him. He told me all the time that I was his whole life. How could he betray me like this?" Mitra asked.

"Regardless of what I have told you about your baba, there is no doubt that he really loves you. He was a good father to you. In my opinion, he's sick and needs to get help. He cannot stand to live a normal, honest life. He has to build a new identity and new personality as soon as he gets tired with the one he already has created. That is why he has changed name, job, places etc. so many times. He just has to be a new person all the time," I said.

"Do you think he's happy now?" Mitra asked. "Ingrid said that he was very unhappy and nervous for some months before his disappearance."

"I'm sure he's not happy now. He was like an addict. When he got his high, he was happy for a short while. He had the whole world in his hands and felt as though he could fly across the sky. But at the end of the day, he realized that he still was a miserable addict. By having his hands on your money, he may have felt some satisfaction in the beginning. But soon, he will realize that it still is not enough for him to be happy," I gave her my opinion.

"Why didn't Baba come to me and tell me about the money if that was his reason for disappearing? I don't care about the money as much as I care about him. If he had come to me and told me the truth, I certainly would have forgiven him, no matter what had happened to the money." Honestly and innocently, Mitra added, "My relationship with Baba is more important to me than the money."

"I'm sorry that he put you through this, but the money made him blind to what he was missing. So far, he has easily gotten away with all his wrongdoings. He has never had to explain or feel any remorse toward anyone. This time, I hope it will be different, but I doubt it. If he does come back, it would certainly be your right to demand a thorough explanation," I said.

"If he comes back, he definitely owes me a good explanation," Mitra agreed.

"I'm sure he will, and you may get an explanation. But I know your baba. If he comes back, he would cry and tell you a heartbreaking story. He's an expert in making up stories to manipulate people. I promise you that if he ever comes back, he would be broke after spending all of the money. He would leave a wife and one or two kids behind in some country," I speculated.

"Do you really think so?" she asked.

"It's the most probable scenario, but I have some other suspicions. I still don't know what his real business was with the Iraqis. He might have committed himself to helping them when his service was needed. I don't have any idea what kind of help or what he promised to do."

"He also took many trips to countries in central Asia, such as Tajikistan and Afghanistan, and God knows what other countries. Why would he have to take those trips? Initially, he went as a missionary. But in the recent years, according to Ingrid, he seldom went to church. By the way, the timing of his disappearance coincided with the U.S. invasion of Iraq. I don't know what to make of all of this! Maybe I have a wild imagination."

"To simplify the entire dilemma, let's assume that he was not happy with his life. When he had access to so much money, he just left to live somewhere else to start a new life." I speculated again. "Who knows?"

*   *   *

During her college life, Mitra attended a couple of universities in other states but returned to Los Angeles to finish her degree.

In 2006, at the age of twenty-five, she was about to graduate from the university. Gorgeous and tall, her delicate face and graceful manner caught everyone's attention.

Ingrid, Shahram, and his family came to LA to attend the graduation ceremony. It was a hot, summer day. The ceremony was held in the large, open area of the university. I was in high spirits, and Ingrid was cheerful and excited. We all arrived early, looking for a spot that offered a clear view of the ceremony. Kami and Homan, my nephew, had their cameras ready. Ingrid thoughtfully brought some beautiful flowers. My brother Shahram and his wife Tara joined us. Along with the other proud families, we waited for the ceremony to start.

The large group of graduates occupied the front rows on two sides of the area. It was not easy to find Mitra from a distance and in the middle of hundreds students, but we did not give up looking for her.

The ceremony began. When Mitra's name was called, she passed through the row of seats to walk up the steps and onto the stage to receive her diploma. I whispered in Ingrid's ear, "Can you believe our baby is graduating?"

"I wish Peter was here to see her," she whispered back to me.

"Forget about him. He doesn't deserve to be here. Enjoy the moment," I advised.

Dressed in the graduation cap and gown, Mitra looked so beautiful. Watching her receive a diploma added another unforgettable, cherished moment to my life. The first such moment was the day twenty-five years earlier when I looked at her tiny little face in the delivery room at 7:09 AM.

After the ceremony, we somehow found her in the middle of the crowd. Ingrid gave her the flowers. That particular moment, when we all encircled her, I thought, *God truly loves Mitra to bless her with so many nice and accountable people around her. She even has two moms who truly love her. Who cares about a dishonest runaway father?*

*   *   *

Ingrid stayed in LA and we spent some time together. Of course, she talked about Peter. This gave me an opportunity to get closer to her and understand her mind-set.

I found her to be an honest and sincere person. I liked her. She was very religious, and to some degree, very naive. Her husband's disappearance almost four years earlier had crushed her. Yet she tried to keep her spirit high by praying to Jesus. She believed that her strength was being tested by God. She searched for signs from Jesus to show her how to handle the situation and lead her through it. She stayed up at nights to watch Christian TV programs to pray and cry with the preacher. Despite all those attempts she still was miserable.

She admitted that some years before Peter had abandoned her, he had changed dramatically. Their married life was in jeopardy because of his temper. She also discovered that he had been involved in some fraud deals while they lived together. Her greatest frustration was that he quit attending the church regularly and put distance between himself and Jesus.

Regarding money, she confided that in recent years he spent money in a quite unusual way. Although the spending surprised her, she trusted him at the time and never confronted him regarding the source of the money. The only time she reacted, she said, was when he bought an expensive, new car for cash.

I told her what I knew about Behzad and revealed his past deceitful life. Strangely enough, nothing changed how she thought of him. She strongly believed that he was a true Christian. She admitted that he had gone astray but was certain he would find his way back to Jesus. She believed that once he put his faith in Jesus, he would be guided by him forever.

* * *

Mitra was very concerned about Ingrid and wished she would get on with her life. She did not want Ingrid to suffer and torture herself by waiting for Behzad's return. Mitra, Kami, and I had long talks with her to encourage her to think about herself and not let Behzad destroy her and her life any longer.

Finally, the day that she left us, to return to Sweden, she announced that she had made up her mind. She would no longer wait for her husband's return. She sounded very resolute, which made Mitra, in particular, happy and relieved.

Chapter 29

⌒∿⌒

Betrayal

In 2007, I made a trip to Iran. Memories of my past experiences flooded me. That trip gave me the idea to write about my life. Despite the fact that I was not proficient in the English language, I decided to challenge myself to write my story in English.

*   *   *

I had a happy life with Kami. Mitra got a good job, moved to a bigger apartment, and made a good life for herself. We still had no news about her father. Upon Ingrid's return to Sweden, she remained undecided regarding her life. Despite promises to change, she still waited for Behzad—I never could call him Peter—to show up one day.

*   *   *

During that summer, I received a call from Ingrid. Her voice sounded excited. Behzad had called her. He had not explained anything, but he was coming home. She said that upon hearing his voice after four years, she froze and could not believe it was really him. She was overjoyed. It seemed his extended absence did not matter to her anymore.

I called Mitra after hearing the news. She was happy to learn that her father was still alive, but she seriously emphasized that he owed her an explanation. I doubted that she would get any.

Some days later, Ingrid called again and was very upset. Behzad had called her again. However, this time, she complained about his long disappearance.

Angry, he told her, "If you think I'm a bad person, I won't call anymore." Then he hung up the phone on her.

"Ingrid, what did you expect from him? He's back now because he needs you for some reason. He'll call you again, I promise," I said. Then, because I was so curious to know, I asked her, "Can you take him back after so many years?"

"I had almost made up my mind to divorce him, but God has sent him back for some reason. I don't know what I have to do now," she responded.

"Don't forget what he has done and how miserable you've been all these years.

262

He's smart, don't let him get away with all the nasty things he's done to you and Mitra," I reminded her.

"I won't. He has to give me a true explanation," she said determinedly.

"I can assure you that he will not be truthful. He certainly will have a sad story for you. Just don't let him fool you," I said.

After that conversation and many others, she stopped calling me but kept in contact with Mitra.

*   *   *

"Mamman, why is it that Baba doesn't call me?" Mitra asked me once we were talking about her father and Ingrid.

"He knows what he's doing. Do you remember how he reacted when Ingrid asked him to give her an explanation? He hung up on her and did not call for awhile. Do you know why? Because he has no genuine explanation for his actions, but he knows how weak and naive Ingrid is. He made Ingrid wait to hear from him again after the first phone call. He was confident that she would be frightened over losing him again and would not demand an explanation again."

I let that sink in for a minute before I continued. Looking directly into Mitra's eyes, I said, "But you are not Ingrid. He fooled you, betrayed you, took your money, and ran away. He has to give you an explanation; he has to give you your money back. He is playing a game with you. Now, that you know he is back, he expects you to call him."

"Do you really think that he's waiting for me to call?" Mitra asked.

"I am positive. I'm sure he has some phony story to tell you. He'll tell you how your money put his life in danger and how he sacrificed all those years for you. I promise he would tell you that, just because of you, he had a miserable life during those years." I responded.

"Why because of me?" she asked.

"Have you forgotten that he told me that people were after him to kill him? He'll tell you that he never told you about the money in order to protect you. He will claim that he put his own life in danger." I tried to explain how her father deftly wove stories of intrigue.

"What a crazy fantasy you have Mamman," she laughed and said.

"Just wait, you'll see. He'll tell you a story. At the end of his tale, you will feel guilty instead of him. He is so good at this, you may end up apologizing to him," I speculated.

Mitra chuckled and changed the subject to Ingrid. "It's crazy! I can't believe how Ingrid could take him back after all of this."

"She thinks that her prayers were answered by God. She's a needy, naive woman. She has hidden herself behind God and Jesus. Your baba and Ingrid deserve each other," I said.

"I feel that she has betrayed me too. She used to call me talking and crying for hours. I listened to her and tried to console her, but now she has chosen Baba over me. If he had given her any explanation, it would not hurt me as much."

"How do you know that he hasn't given her a good excuse?" I asked.

"He has not. Ingrid told me that she has already forgiven him and that he does not need to give her any explanation," Mitra responded.

"Well, good for her," I stated.

"The last time I called her house, she said that they were living together. I told her that I would never call her at home, but she could call me."

"Mitra jan, she needs him. She knows who she's dealing with. She fools herself," I said.

"She betrayed me more than Baba did; at least it feels like it," Mitra said.

"I know, but she's sick too. Both of them need counseling," I said, trying to justify Ingrid's deed.

"Do you think any of my money is left?"

"Four years is long time, but it was lot of money too. I think he probably has some left, but not in Sweden. He'd keep the money in some bank account in some other country to protect it and himself. I just wish I knew why he's back and how long he plans to stay. Maybe he's running away from something he's done in other countries. Maybe he has some business to do here. But in either case, he will leave again sooner or later." I paused before I asked, "What do you think of going after him to get your money back?"

"How?" she asked.

"We'll hire an attorney. We have enough evidence to go after him. And how do we know that he's not still using the power of attorney you signed for him? He may still be using it for his own gain," I replied.

"You're right. But I don't want him to end up in jail," Mitra said.

"I know. Unfortunately, he is your father. We'll go as far with this as you feel comfortable. Personally, I would love to see him behind bars," I said.

"I don't know, let me think about it," Mitra said.

"Okay, meanwhile I will find a lawyer to get some advice."

*   *   *

I needed an American-Swedish lawyer who should be familiar with the legal systems in both counties and have connections in Sweden to lead the case there.

After an online search, I found a Swedish-American attorney with an office in Maine. I made a phone call to consult with him.

After hearing the case, he positively assured me that it would be a case to win. He suggested that we sue Behzad. Not only could we get the money back, but he would be sent to jail for forgery and fraud.

Mitra agreed to sue him for getting her money back, when I told her what Mats, the lawyer, suggested. However, she did not want to pursue the case beyond that to put her father in jail.

I called Mats again, and we agreed that he should first search for any banks in Mitra's name in Sweden and then go after Behzad. Mats, whom Mitra and I were in contact with on a daily basis in order to exchange information, seemed to be a very trustworthy attorney. He showed particular enthusiasm regarding this case. Therefore, he agreed to take the case for a much lower legal fee.

He searched and found a very small amount of money in some accounts in Mitra's name in different Swedish banks. He withdrew the money and sent it to Mitra. He also sent a letter of cancellation to the authorities announcing that the power of attorney to Behzad, which was signed by Mitra years earlier, was no longer valid.

The second step was to sue Behzad. Mats had colleagues and friends in Stockholm, who would help him locally with this case.

As soon as the process started and Behzad received notice about the lawsuit, Mitra received an e-mail from Ingrid begging her to stop the legal action against her own father. She claimed that it would make them miserable.

Mitra never responded to the e-mail.

Not receiving any response from Mitra, Behzad finally called her.

Mitra called me after their conversation. She sounded upset and disappointed,

"He's weird Mamman. I can't believe it," she said as soon as I answered her call.

"Who is weird? Who're you talking about?" I asked.

"Baba! He called me after so many years, acting like nothing has ever happened," she said, sounding very upset.

"He did? Finally!" I said.

"When I first heard his voice, I froze. I didn't know what to say. Then he began telling me how much he loved me and asking me how I was doing. Mamman, he just kept on talking as though we had talked yesterday. Can you believe it?" she said.

"What did he want?" I asked.

"He said we were family and he missed me, and we should act like a family. I told him that he could not just call me and pretend nothing had happened. I demanded an explanation about everything. He listened to me, but then he began talking nonsense over and over. When I say nonsense, I really mean nonsense! He repeated that he loved me and was my father. I finally told him that I did not need a father like him. He started crying.

"After that, he finally mentioned the real reason he called. According to him, if I pursued this legal action, he would go to jail for the rest of his life and die in jail. He was annoying, and I could not tolerate it, so I hung up on him," she said.

"I'm sorry darling, and I don't know what to say. You did the right thing. He's shameless! He thinks he can get away again by talking and manipulating.

He is so arrogant! Just because he finally called you, he thinks you should be so happy and forget about what he did," I said.

Behzad's call totally disappointed Mitra. Her last hope for any kind of reconciliation with her father evaporated.

*   *   *

However, with help of Mats and Fredrik, the new attorney in Sweden, the legal process began. It took approximately two years before the case went to court. It had been delayed because Behzad had gone into hiding to avoid being served a subpoena.

Finally, in 2009, the court appointed a defense attorney for him in order to proceed with the case in his absence.

In 2010, the court reached its decision. Fredrik, the attorney in Sweden, called to inform us about the ruling. Behzad was found guilty and adjudged to pay Mitra her money.

After the verdict, Mitra received calls from some Swedish newspapers, which had followed the case, for an interview. (Appendix H and I)

This lawsuit against Behzad and the court's ruling did not bring any satisfactory explanation to Mitra from her father which she was entitled to and expected to receive.

The verdict, however, may bring no money back to Mitra, since both Behzad and Ingrid are nowhere to be found. Whether they are still in Sweden or abroad, nobody knows. It might have justified her conviction to reject any relationship to her father if she still had any doubt or a guilty conscience.

Chapter 30

Wonderful Journey

This excursion to the various chapters of my life was a wonderful journey. I enjoyed the ride even though the road was not paved.

Reliving these memories enabled me to realize that those experiences—whether good or bad, painful or joyful—have defined the person I am today. Each of the events in my life, and every single person in my life, left a momentous influence on me. No matter if the impact was positive or negative; all the experiences resulted in a valuable adventure. I exercised those assets to build a meaningful life for myself.

The difficulties and uneasiness of a long period of my life is over and no longer hurts me. The love and kindness of the people who were part of my life still keeps my heart warm.

After all that has happened, I cannot consider Behzad's presence in my life as a misfortune or tragedy even though I seldom understood him. He gave me the opportunity to see and experience the other side of the world and people.

Mitra is the most precious and the sweetest fruit of that particular period of my life; I will always be grateful for her.

My mother and Shahram have given me the marvelous feeling of security and comfort. They never left my side. Their unconditional love gave me the courage and strength to face the difficult times in life.

Kami granted me the joy of peace and harmony after years of living an apprehensive life. He opened my heart to love and passion.

God's presence in every aspect of my life has been so apparent. He came to me during those difficult times when I needed him the most.

I don't believe in providence or destiny. But I do believe all of us have been entrusted with a path of life, and we must decide how to pass that life. For my path of life, I was free to choose as well. Some of my decisions were not wise, but it was my path and it was worth it.

On my way, I found Kami, who opened my heart to true love and honesty. He has changed my and Mitra's faith for a better and flourishing one. Kami and I continue to have a harmonic, loving, and friendly life together.

At twenty-eight, Mitra is a decent, honest, kindhearted, happy, and beautiful person. She has a rich social life and good career. We have a close mother-daughter relationship. Sadly, she still feels put upon by her father and has to deal with this ugly feeling.

Neither Mitra nor I have any idea where her father and Ingrid are and how they are doing. Time, as it says, heals all wounds. It worked for us and there is no hard feeling or revenge toward Behzad anymore, even if we are still hoping for some explanation in order to have closure.

*   *   *

This is a true story, but since reality is far from fiction, my story has no ending. I leave it to the reader to find an ending through his or her imagination.

Appendix

A- Revolution Causes (Source Wikipedia)

The revolution was populist, nationalist and later Shi'a Islamic. It was in part a conservative backlash against the Westernizing and secularizing efforts of the Western-backed Shah, and a liberal backlash to social injustice and other shortcomings of the ancient régime. The Shah was perceived by many as beholden to—if not a puppet of—a non-Muslim Western power (the United States) whose culture was impacting that of Iran. The Shah's regime was seen as oppressive, brutal, corrupt, and extravagant; it also suffered from basic functional failures—an over-ambitious economic program that brought economic bottlenecks, shortages, and inflation.

B- Ghatlhaie Zangirehee

This term means Chain Murders. There was or maybe still is an organized gang, whose duty was to slay the Islamic regime's critics, as well as those whose activities were not within the law of Islam. The gang performed a number of assassinations of opposition in very brutal ways.

C- The Baha'i Faith

Islam recognizes only those religions that were established before Islam and have their own Holy Books. To Muslims, Islam is considered as the most complete religion and the Holy Quran is the final script. They also believe that the Prophet Muhammad is the last messenger of God. The Baha'i faith was established in Iran in 1844, about twelve centuries after Islam, by Mohammed Baab. In most Islamic countries, Baha'i believers were never recognized as a religious minority and have been acknowledged as infidels or kafar. In most Islamic countries, they still have no social and human rights; if found, they are imprisoned or executed.

D- Shahpour Bakhtiar

Shahpour Bakhtiar was the last Prime Minister of the Pahlavi regime. He was deputy Minister of Labor in Dr. Mohammad Mossadegh's cabinet in 1951.

He was a competent politician, who could predict the devastating consequences of "Mullahs"—Muslim Clerics— taking over. His goal was to restore democracy and freedom within the then constitiution. In 1979, he escaped to exile in France. He was assassinated in his heavily guarded home in Paris in 1991.

E- **Iranian Kurdistan**
The Iranian Kurdistan, inhabited by Kurds, is located in northwestern Iran and borders Iraq and Turkey. The Kurds always fought for an indepdent Kurdistan. The central governments of involved countries refuse to permit the Kurds to have local autonomy. After the revolution, the situation for the Iranian Kurds did not improve. Consequently, the Kurdish activists launched a fight against the Islamic regime. In August 1979, Ayatollah Khomeini declared a Jihad (holy war) against the Kurdish fighters. Thousands of Kurdish rebels were killed; numerous cities and villages were ruined. Many Kurdish leaders were executed in 1983. The government finally succeeded in maintaining control over Kurdistan, but occasional fights still take place.

F- **Mujahedeen Khalqe Iran**
Mujahedeen Khalqe Iran is an armed resistance movement. The organization used to fight against the Pahlavi regime. At the beginning of the revolution, the organization collaborated with the central revolutionary government. However, due to differences in political views with the Islamic regime, the Mujahedeen became the Islamic regime's worst enemy. They carried out a number of terrorist actions by assassinating some key figures in the regime. The Islamic regime, in response, persecuted members of the movement as well as the sympathizers.

The leadership of the organization escaped to Iraq and its sympathizers were executed.

During the Iran-Iraq war the organization collaborated with Iraqis and lost their popularity among Iranians.

G- **The Iran-Iraq War**
The war initiated by Saddam Hussein on September 22, 1980. He invaded Iran under the assumption that Iranian army was weak and disbanded.

At the time, Iran was under economic sanction by the United States and some European countries. The U.S. government supported Iraq.

The war made Iranian people united against an external enemy and consequently the legitimacy of the Islamic regime was established. The war ended in 1988 with no winner.

The majority of the people believed that if the war had not happened, this regime would have not survived.

H- **The Original Article in Swedish**
Dotter blev av med miljonarv

NYBRO 2010-03-10 | Uppdaterad 2010-03-10

En dotter har stämt sin pappa för att ha undanhållit eller förbrukat ett arv värt sex miljoner kronor.

Den idag 28-åriga kvinnan bor sedan i mitten av 90-talet i USA, dit hon flyttade tillsammans med sin mamma. Hennes pappa är bosatt i Nybro och är den person som förvaltat kvinnans arv.

Kvinnans mamma hade tidigare ett förhållande med en annan man som avled 1997. 28-åringen ärvde mannens tillgångar och dödsboet skiftades den 1 januari 1999. Vid den tidpunkten var kvinnan omyndig och arvsskiftet företräddes av hennes pappa.

Vid tiden för mannens bortgång kände den 28-åriga kvinnan inte till att hon ärvt honom. När hon skrev fullmakten till sin pappa att handha hennes ekonomiska angelägenheter i Sverige var ovetande om att hon var ägare till 6 miljoner kronor. I fullmakten har hon inte gett tillåtelse för pappan att använda hennes pengar för egen del. Hon menar i tredskodomen från Kalmar tingsrätt att pappan medvetet utnyttjat hennes ovetskap när han övertygade henne att utfärda en generalfullmakt för honom.

Tingsrätten anser att pappan har använt fullmakten till att tillskansa sig tillgångarna utan att redovisa dem. Kvinnan har flera gånger begärt att pappan ska redovisa var tillgångarna är och att återbetala dem till henne utan att lyckas.

Kvinnan har inga invändningar mot att tillgångarna kan ha minskat i värde så länge de placerats på ett riktigt sätt. I arvet ingick kontanter, en bostadsrätt i Stockholmsregionen, flera aktieposter i bland annat Ericsson, Nokia, Astra och Lap Power plus premieobligationer. Kontanterna och aktierna placerades hos olika fondkommissionärer i kvinnans namn. Efter viss efterforskning har det visat sig att pappan avslutat kontona och det finns inte längre några aktier och fonder i kvinnans namn. Rätten tror också att bostadsrätten är såld sedan länge. Pappan måste nu utge de tillgångar från arvet till dotter. Skulle pengarna vara förbrukade ska han betala ett skadestånd på 6 miljoner kronor till dottern. Tingsrätten bad pappan att yttra sig men han har inte hört av sig.

Bjorn Bood
bjorn.boode @ barometern.se

The link below refers to the original article published in Swedish newspaper "Barometern" dated 03-10-2010.
http://www.barometern.se/nyheter/nybro/dotter-blev-av-med-miljonarv(1816832).gm

I: **The Swedish Article Translated in English**

Daughter Lost Millions in Inheritance

NYBRO 2010-03-10 | Uppdaterad 2010-03-10

A daughter has filed a lawsuit againstt her father for withholding or spending an inheritance worth six million SEK.

The now 28-year-old woman has been living in the United State since the mid 90s, where she moved with her mother. Her father lives in Nybro and is the person who has administered the woman's inheritance.

The woman's mother had a relationship in the past with the man who died in 1997. The 28-year-old inherited the man's assets; and the estate was shifted on January 1, 1999. At that time, the woman was under age; and the estate distribution was represented by her father.

At the time of the man's death, the 28-year-old woman did not know she had inherited from him. When she signed the power of attorney, which allowed her father handle her financial affairs in Sweden, she was unaware that she owned six million SEK. In the power of attorney, she did not grant her father permission to use the money in behalf of his own. Her position in the default judgment by the Kalmar district court is that her father deliberately used her unawareness when he convinced her to issue a power of attorney to him.

The district court considers that the father used the power of attorney to seize the assets without accounting for them. The woman has repeatedly requested that the father should present where the assets are and to repay her, but without any success.

The woman has no objection regarding the fact that the assets might have lost value, as long as they have been placed properly. The estate included cash, a condominium in the Stockholm area, stocks (shares) in companies like Ericsson, Nokia, Astra and Lap Power plus premium bonds. The cash and stocks were invested with different brokers in the woman's name. After some investigations, it appears the father has closed all the accounts, with no stocks or funds left in the woman's name. The court also believes the condominium was sold long ago.

The father must now pay the assets from the estate to his daughter. If the money has been spent, he must pay six million SEK in punitive damages to the daughter. The district court has asked the father to speak up but the court has not heard from him yet.

Bjorn Bood
bjorn.boode @ barometern.se